PERGAMON INSTITUTE OF ENGLISH

English in the International Context

The Alchemy of English

*The Spread, Functions and Models
of Non-native Englishes*

ENGLISH IN THE INTERNATIONAL CONTEXT

Series Editor: BRAJ B. KACHRU

Other titles in this series

Sidney Greenbaum (ed.), *The English Language Today*
Larry E. Smith (ed.), *Discourse Across Cultures: Strategies in World Englishes*

See also:

Braj B. Kachru (ed.),
The Other Tongue: English Across Cultures

Larry E. Smith (ed.),
Readings in English as an International Language

Christopher Brumfit (ed.),
English for International Communication

Peter Strevens,
Teaching English as an International Language

and the journal

World Englishes: *a journal of English as an international and intranational language,* edited by Braj B. Kachru and Larry E. Smith

The Alchemy of English

The Spread, Functions and Models of Non-native Englishes

BRAJ B. KACHRU

University of Illinois

PERGAMON INSTITUTE OF ENGLISH

a member of the Pergamon Group

Oxford · New York · Toronto · Sydney · Frankfurt

U.K.	Pergamon Press Ltd., Headington Hill Hall, Oxford OX3 0BW, England
U.S.A.	Pergamon Press Inc., Maxwell House, Fairview Park, Elmsford, New York 10523, U.S.A.
CANADA	Pergamon Press Canada Ltd., Suite 104, 150 Consumers Road, Willowdale, Ontario M2J 1P9, Canada
AUSTRALIA	Pergamon Press (Aust.) Pty. Ltd., P.O. Box 544, Potts Point, N.S.W. 2011, Australia
FEDERAL REPUBLIC OF GERMANY	Pergamon Press GmbH, Hammerweg 6, D-6242 Kronberg, Federal Republic of Germany
JAPAN	Pergamon Press Ltd., 8th Floor, Matsuoka Central Building, 1-7-1 Nishishinjuku, Shinjuku-ku, Tokyo 160, Japan
BRAZIL	Pergamon Editora Ltda., Rue Eca de Queiros, 346, CEP 04011, São Paulo, Brazil
PEOPLE'S REPUBLIC OF CHINA	Pergamon Press, Qianmen Hotel, Beijing, People's Republic of China

First edition 1986

Library of Congress Cataloging in Publication Data

Kachru, Braj B.
The alchemy of English.
(English in the international context)
Bibliography: p.
Includes index.
1. English language—Foreign countries.
2. English language—Variation. 3. Intercultural
communication.
4. Languages in contact.
I. Title. II. Series.
PE2751.K3 1985   420'.9   85-3561

British Library Cataloguing in Publication Data

Kachru, Braj B.
The alchemy of English: the spread, functions
and models of non-native Englishes.—(English
in the international context)
1. English language—Foreign countries
2. English language—Variation
I. Title II. Series
427'.9   PE2751

ISBN 0-08-031079-6

·Printed in Great Britain by A. Wheaton & Co. Ltd., Exeter

For

Raja Rao

vāktattvamunmiṣati kasyacideva puṃsaḥ

Preface

This volume includes ten studies on the issues currently articulated with increased concern by professionals involved in research on and teaching of English. These issues have interested me, both as a researcher and as a teacher, since the early 1960s. In a sense, then, this volume is a continuation of my earlier research. However, in *The Alchemy of English* I have elaborated on several previously discussed topics, provided fresh data from varieties of English in addition to those of South Asia, and included some new aspects of non-native Englishes.

The volume is organized in four parts. The introduction discusses the transmutation associated with the learning of English. That is, the power of change attributed to English in materialistic, social, and technological senses has contributed to the continued phenomenal spread of this language on practically every continent, and its retention in the former colonies of Asia and Africa. It is, therefore, understandable that the colonial associations of English, and its Western cultural values, are now underemphasized. Instead, what seems to be stressed is the power of English as an instrument of individual and societal transformation. Whether these attributes are real or imagined is not important; what is vital is the public attitude toward English, the love–hate relationship with the language, and the acceptance of the functional power of English in all parts of the world. This power is now recognized, though grudgingly, even by those who would like to see English replaced by regional or national languages in Africa or Asia.

Part I ("Varieties and Functions") consists of three chapters, primarily focusing on the institutionalized second-language varieties used in the regions that were primarily under the political control of the United Kingdom or the United States of America. The South Asian case study included here characterizes the processes of nativization that English has undergone in this region. However, this case study has wider diachronic and synchronic implications. It shows several striking shared formal and functional characteristics with other institutionalized non-native varieties of English, and in that sense it provides insights regarding many processes related to non-native Englishes. The chapter that follows discusses the concept of "verbal repertoire" in bilingual and multilingual societies, and the types of code alteration in which English or "mixed" varieties of English are used with clear pragmatic goals in mind.

The three chapters in Part II ("Models, Norms, and Attitudes") address often debated and nagging educational and methodological questions: What are the international and localized models and norms for English? What are the attitudes toward such norms and toward learning English?

These controversial issues are continuously discussed in professional journals and other public forums by policy makers and by concerned students and teachers. This debate is heard both in countries where English is the first language and in countries such as India, Singapore, Sri Lanka, and Zambia, where English is an important additional language. My concern is with the latter countries. The non-Western viewpoints and the pragmatic contexts of the use of English bring to such deliberations a complex and challenging perspective. One also sees in this a new awareness about English, which is now seen less and less as a European language and an exclusive exponent of the Judeo-Christian tradition, and is instead viewed more as a language with multiple cultural identities and traditions.

Part III ("Impact and Change") presents an aspect of English which, unfortunately, has not attracted the serious attention of sociolinguists and literary scholars. The impact of English on other major languages and literatures of the world, and the resultant language change, provides insights into several related disciplines and opens fresh research possibilities for cross-cultural linguistic studies and comparative literary studies. The brief discussion of Englishization is, again, related to the South Asian context. However, as several preliminary studies have shown, what is true of South Asia is also true of Southeast Asia, the Philippines, and the English-using parts of Africa, to name just three other regions. A number of such studies are listed in the bibliography.

Part IV ("Contact, Creativity, and Discourse Strategies") takes us to interesting areas such as the bilingual's creativity and the "contact literatures" in English. The questions raised here are a natural consequence of the use of English for creative expression in, for example, novels and short stories in nations where English has become an important medium for creativity, even though it is essentially a second language. Especially since the 1950s, such literatures have developed in India, Singapore, Malaysia, Nigeria, Kenya, Sri Lanka, and the Philippines. The history of such writing, however, dates back to the turn of the century.

The chapters included here were originally written as invited papers for books and journals between 1981 and 1985, except Chapters 6, 7, and 9 which appeared in 1976, 1977, and 1979, respectively. This has naturally resulted in unavoidable repetitions which, in a few cases, I have retained in order to make each chapter more or less self-contained. However, every chapter has been revised and updated, and repetitions have been minimized by cross-referencing. A selected bibliography has been included, in the hope that it will prove a useful resource for readers interested in the fast-growing body of linguistic, literary, and methodological literature on the world varieties of English.

I would like to express my special thanks to the group of unusually enthusiastic research students who completed their dissertations with me during 1983–5 on topics related to non-native Englishes. They include Maurice Chishimba, Pornpimol Chutisilp, Benjamin Magura, Cecil Nelson, and Peter H. Lowenberg. Discussions with them helped me to deepen my understanding of the uses of English in parts of Africa and Southeast Asia.

I am grateful to Yamuna Kachru and S. N. Sridhar, who, as always, patiently acted as sounding boards for many of the ideas presented in this book. Their constructive and often provocative criticism helped to clarify several points and certainly reduced my inadequacies and errors of judgment. I thank Henry Kahane, Peter Strevens, and Ladislav Zgusta for exchange of ideas and numerous suggestions; Tej K. Bhatia, Eyamba G. Bokamba, Rajeshwari Pandharipande, R. Parthasarathy, and Kamal K. Sridhar for ungrudgingly sharing their research findings on varieties of English and other related areas; and Jean D'souza and Tamara M. Valentine for their valuable research assistance.

I also benefited from interaction with the students and faculty at the National University of Singapore, where I taught for a semester during 1984, and from extensive discussions with Larry E. Smith and Wimal Dissanayake at the East–West Center, Honolulu, Hawaii, where I was a Fellow for parts of 1984 and 1985.

The research on this book was facilitated by the support of the Research Board of the Graduate College of the University of Illinois at Urbana-Champaign and by the American Institute of Indian Studies. My thanks to both the agencies, and particularly to Pradeep Mehendiratta, Director of the Institute in India.

An unexpected summer 1982 meeting in New Delhi with the philosopher and creative writer Raja Rao resulted in numerous subsequent meetings and telephone conversations with him in Delhi, Austin, Urbana, and Honolulu. In his own unique way he provided much needed stimulus, encouragement, and a new perspective for my understanding of language and literature. For that, and much more, I am indebted to him.

Honolulu, Hawaii   Braj B. Kachru
15 August 1985

Contents

Chapter 1

Introduction: The Alchemy of English

WHAT IS THE APPROPRIATENESS of the term "alchemy" to the functions of the English language today? In a metaphorical sense, this term captures the attitudinal reactions to the status and functions of English across cultures during our times. Competence in English and the use of this language signify a transmutation: an added potential for material and social gain and advantage. One sees this attitude in what the symbol stands for; English is considered a symbol of modernization, a key to expanded functional roles, and an extra arm for success and mobility in culturally and linguistically complex and pluralistic societies. As if all this were not enough, it is also believed that English contributes to yet another type of transmutation: It internationalizes one's outlook. In comparison with other languages of wider communication, knowing English is like possessing the fabled Aladdin's lamp, which permits one to open, as it were, the linguistic gates to international business, technology, science, and travel. In short, English provides linguistic power.

One might, then, say that acquiring English is like going through a linguistic reincarnation. And from the perspectives of the Indian subcontinent, which is the main focus of this chapter, English initiates one into the caste that has power and, more important, that controls vital knowledge about the miracles of science and technology. Thus, as Cooper 1985 mentions specifically in the case of Israel, there is at present a "hunger" and an "indecent passion" for acquiring English. What is true of Israel applies to practically all other parts of the world as well.

This power of alchemy or transmutation was not always associated with English. The sociolinguistic context of the English language has been changing constantly from the sixteenth century to the present era (see, e.g., Baugh 1935). However, this change has accelerated—and has been rather unexpected in some ways—during the post-Colonial period. (Various reasons for this change are discussed in Kachru, ed. 1982).

The legacy of colonial Englishes has resulted in the existence of several transplanted varieties of English having distinct linguistic ecologies—their own contexts of function and usage. These non-native varieties have, in turn, brought about changes in the native varieties of English and have also resulted in numerous sociolinguistic, linguistic, and literary questions being posed which have rarely been asked about English before. In recent years such questions have been discussed in several conferences and colloquia, in various types of publications, and in specialized journals devoted to English in the world context (Bailey and Görlach, 1982;

1

Greenbaum, ed. 1985; King, 1980; Strevens, 1980; Smith, ed. 1981; Kachru, ed. 1982).

I am concerned here with a small slice of this total time-span: the post-Colonial period since the 1940s and, in particular, three aspects of the colonial Englishes on the Indian subcontinent. First, I shall deal with the sociolinguistic consequences of the use of a Western language as a restricted code of communication that has rapidly become a symbol of power, authority, and elitism in the non-Western world. In such non-native contexts, English has become a vehicle of values not always in harmony with local traditions and beliefs. Second, I shall consider English as an "in-group" language, uniting elite speakers across ethnic, religious, and linguistic boundaries used for political change. Third, I shall examine the linguistic and cultural adaptation English has undergone in the process of maintaining various patterns of administrative, legal, educational, and professional power.

Language as Power, Language and Power

What does one mean by associating power with language? The term "power" is used here in an abstract sense, to refer to the control of know-ledge and to the prestige a language acquires as a result of its use in certain important domains. The more important a domain is, the more "powerful" a language becomes. This, then, is reflected in the attitude of native or non-native users toward a language or a specific variety of a language. In many societies language has traditionally been viewed as possessing intrin-sically a mystic or superhuman power; one sees it in the word *śakhti* when attributed to *dev-vānī* (god's-language) referring to Sanskrit. (Ferguson (1982b) and Samarin (1976) discuss language in the religious context.)

The mystic power attributed to a language, or the *mantra*[1] (verses or phrases believed to possess magical or religious efficacy) is as old as, for example, the Hindu tradition. In the case of Sanskrit, the relationship of language and power was subtly exploited for standardizing language and for maintaining its *śudda* (pure) form. In the *Aṣṭādhyāyī* (Eight Chapters), compiled by Pāṇini (fourth century B.C.), a prescriptive norm was estab-lished for Sanskrit. At that time Sanskrit was developing regional variations, which would eventually endanger intelligibility between speakers of its different varieties. A description of the language had to be made available that would provide a model for the learner and thus pre-serve, in an oral tradition, the sacred Hindu hymns. This prescriptive (and applied) motivation of the Indian grammarians, Pāṇini included, led to major theoretical and analytical breakthroughs in linguistics (Varma, 1929; Allen, 1953; Staal, 1975).

Of course at that time there were no organized academies to oversee the codification of language; therefore, divine wrath was threatened in various *sūtras*[2] (religious aphorisms), warning the reciter of the hymns of the con-sequences (psychologically severe and physically damaging) of any careless pronunciation or deviation from the prescribed text. The *sūtras* (Fremantle, 1974:18–30) warned that

[When a *mantra* is] deficient in a syllable it tends to diminish life, and [when it is] lacking in proper accent it makes the reciter troubled with illness, and the syllable (wrongly treated) will strike one at the head as a thunderbolt.

A *mantra* [hymn] recited with incorrect intonation and "careless" arrangement of *varṇa* (letters) [reacts] like a thunderbolt and gets the reciter destroyed by God Indra [the chief vedic god, also the god of rain and thunder].

The enunciation of *varṇa* should be perfect. The letters should be handled with the same care with which a tigress carries her cubs with her teeth. She is so careful that no cub is hurt, destroyed, or pained.

Pāṇini, the ancient Hindu grammarian, was seen as part of the divine scheme for codifying Sanskrit, and homage was paid to him "who having received the traditional lore of speech-sounds (*varṇa-samāmnāya*) from Siva [Hindu god of creation and destruction] has told us the entire grammar" (Fremantle, 1974:30).

In such ancient texts, the power of the word is recognized as supreme. The first attempts toward prescriptivism in language (the supporting of a preferential model) were thus motivated by religion. Much later, the same purpose was served by the language academies (established, for example, in Italy in 1582, and France in 1635). The relationship of language *and* power (not in a superhuman sense) has also been well documented in the literature (Kramarae, 1981). But the language policies that the prolonged colonizers (e.g., British, French, American) or short-term colonizers (e.g., Japanese in Korea, Malaysia and Indonesia), developed for control and stability has yet to be distinguished from linguistic, educational, and political perspectives.

The spread of English did not always entail the teaching and learning of a standard (or codified) variety prescribed by an authority such as an academy or by the sanctity of religion (Kachru, 1982c). In liturgical use, or as a symbol of Christianity, English was a minor linguistic tool, at best. The Christian missionaries and colonial administrators were not of one opinion about the role of English in proselytization. The controversy between the Orientalists and Anglicists (Occidentalists) is insightful concerning the role of English in the Indian subcontinent (Kachru, 1983: 68–69; for Africa see Chishimba, 1983 and Magura, 1984). This contrasts with the association of Arabic with Islam, and Sanskrit with Hinduism. Ferguson (1982b:104) rightly observes that

all Brahmin priests, no matter what their sect or mother tongue, can make use of *some* sanskrit if they meet together in Benaras, and all Muslim pilgrims to Mecca make some use of Arabic, but there is no common language for Buddhists or Christian clergy to recite the Three Treasures or Our Father.

English as a Language of Power

The monarchy of Britain may have at one time claimed "divine rights," but those rights were never extended to the language of the monarchs. The power of English is, therefore, of a more wordly nature—in what Quirk *et al.* (1972:2) have termed the "vehicular load" of a language, which English carries as the "primary medium for twentieth-century science and techno-logy." The other, equally important, markers of that power of English are its demographic distribution, its native and non-native users across cultures, its use in important world forums, and its rich literary tradition.

The power of English, then, resides in the domains of its use, the roles its users can play, and—attitudinally—above all, how others view its impor-tance. On all these counts, English excels other world languages. One would not have foreseen this situation easily in the sixteenth century, though even in 1599 Samuel Daniel, a minor poet, fantasized about the "treasures of our language" going to "the strange shores." The questions Daniel asked (in his poem *Musophilus*) then have been fully answered and realized in the succeeding four centuries:

> And who, in time, knows wither we may vent
> The treasures of our tongue, to what strange shores
> This gain of our best glory shall be sent,
> To enrich unknowing nations with our stores?
> What worlds in the yet unformed Occident
> May come refined with the accents that are ours?
> Or who can tell for what great work in hand
> The greatness of our style is now ordained?
> What powers it shall bring in, what spirits command,
> What thoughts let out, what humours keep restrained,
> What mischief it may powerfully withstand,
> And what fair ends may thereby be attained?

Perhaps one could not take these rhetorical questions too seriously before the full impact of William Shakespeare, Ben Johnson, and others who make the Elizabethan period the glory of the English language. The exploits of the Raj had not yet unfolded; the "alien shores" were still not part of the Empire. As John Dryden lamented in 1693, the English language possessed "no prosodia, not so much as a tolerable dictionary or a grammar, so that our language is in a manner barbarous" (quoted in Baugh and Cable, 1978:255). The picture had changed little for almost a century from 1582 when, in the words of Richard Mulcaster, English was "of small reach," extending "no further than this Island of ours, nay not there over all" (quoted in Kachru and Quirk, 1981:xiv). But that cynicism was short-lived, as the following centuries were to prove.

Today the linguistic vision of Samuel Daniel has been realized, the English language is a tool of power, domination, and elitist identity, and of communication across continents. Although the era of the "White man's burden" has practically ended in a political sense, and the Raj has retreated to native shores, the linguistic and cultural consequences of imperialism have changed the global scene. The linguistic ecology of, for example, Africa and Asia is not the same. English has become an integral part of this new complex sociolinguistic setting. The colonial Englishes were essentially acquired and used as non-native second languages, and after more than two centuries, they continue to have the same status. The *non-nativeness* of such varieties is not only an attitudinally significant term, but it also has linguistic and sociolinguistic significance (see Kachru, 1984a).

English as a Colonial Language

The political power of the British (and Americans in the Philippines or Puerto Rico) gave to them as colonists a lot of political stature, requiring them to adopt a pose fitting their status. The white man's language became a *marker* of his power. Englishmen became different persons while functioning in Asia and Africa. The sahibs in the colonies underwent a change facilitated by the new-found prestige of their native language. What was true of the Indian scene was also true in other parts of the world, and E. M. Forster (1952 [1924]) captured it well in *A Passage to India*. Referring to the Englishmen in India, two of the novel's characters say,

India likes gods.
And Englishmen like posing as gods.

The English language was part of the pose and the power. Indians, Africans, and others realized it and accepted it. Therefore, it is not surprising that when a native tried to adopt the same pose—that is, to speak the same language, particularly with the sahib's accent—it made the sahib uncomfortable.

The term "non-native" Englishes is used here, following my earlier use of the term (Kachru, 1965, and later) for those transplanted varieties of English that are acquired primarily as second languages. In such a context, whatever other motivations there may be, English is used as a tool of power to cultivate a group of people who will identify with the cultural and other norms of the political elite. In India, T. B. Macaulay, in his often-quoted *Minute*, dreamt of developing a culturally distinct group who would form "a class who may be interpreters between us and those whom we govern, a class of persons, Indians in blood and colour, English in taste, in opinion, in morals and in intellect" (cited in Sharp, 1920–1922:I, 116).

Almost at the same time, another English-speaking nation, the United States, "set out to Americanize Puerto Rico with a vengence during the first fifty years of its occupation" (Zentella, 1981:219). The U.S. government's view, as Zentella observes, was presented by Victor Clark, the Commissioner of Education:

if the schools became American and the teachers and students were guided by the American spirit, then the island would be essentially American in sympathies, opinions, and attitudes toward government.

The year 1898 saw American power extend in another direction as well—to the Philippines, where "the mock battle of Manila Bay marked the end of 300 years of Spanish and the beginning of American colonial domination." The U.S. attitude toward this colony was no different from the one toward Puerto Rico. President McKinley (1843–1901) is reported to have said the American duty toward the newly acquired colony should be "to educate the Filipinos and uplift and civilize and Christianize them to fit the people for the duties of citizenship" (quoted in Beebe and Beebe 1981: 322).

Such views had been expressed a little earlier in South Asia by colonizers from the other side of the Atlantic. Charles Grant believed that

> the true curse of darkness is the introduction of light. The Hindoos err, because they are ignorant and their errors have never fairly been laid before them. The communication of our light and knowledge to them, would prove the best remedy for their disorders. [Grant, 1831–1832:60–61].

In what was then known as Ceylon (now renamed Sri Lanka) the same pattern was repeated. In 1827 Sir Edward Barnes (the governor of Sri Lanka from 1824–1831) laid the foundation of a "Christian Institution":

> to give a superior education to a number of young persons who from their ability, piety, and good conduct were likely to prove fit persons in communicating a knowledge of Christianity to their countrymen [Barnes, 1932:43].

In imparting such education, the governor, as Ruberu says (1962:158–159), did not desire any association with or support from the American missionaries who were then present in Sri Lanka. Therefore, a letter was sent to the American missionaries on the island saying that "the means we possess in our own country for the conversion of our heathen subjects to Christianity are in the Lieutenant Governor's opinion fully adequate to all purposes" (quoted by Ruberu, 1962:158). This was said much before Rudyard Kipling's (1865–1936) call to

> Take up the White man's burden—
>   Send forth the best ye breed—
> Go bind your sons to exile
>   To serve your captives' need.

In these statements English is associated with a power more subtle than mere wordly success: it is considered to be a tool of "civilization" and "light". Provision of that tool is perceived as a colonizer's contribution—and duty—to the well-being of the inhabitants of newly acquired colonies. According to this view, then, language can open the gates for the emancipation of souls. And here we find a subtle parallel to the power attributed to the Sanskrit texts.

Along with its "other-worldly" reward, English also provided an earthy bonus as a medium for understanding technology and scientific development. For more pensive minds, it made available the literary treasures of the European languages. To newly "awakened" Asian and African minds, that literature in itself was a revelation. Macaulay had already warned the insecure among them that

I have no knowledge of either Sanskrit or Arabic. But I have done what I could to form a correct estimate of their value. . . . I am quite ready to take the Oriental learning at the valuation of the Orientalists themselves. I have never found one amongst them who could deny that a single shelf of a good European library was worth the whole native literature of India and Arabia. [Sharp, 1920–1922].

The Industrial Revolution's technological impact and the cultural dimensions of the Renaissance clearly brought before non-Western intellectuals the accomplishments of the West. The ambitious among the colonized viewed English as their main tool with which to emulate such accomplishments.

Slowly the new political reality bestowed the socially and administratively dominant roles on the newly installed language. Ultimately the legal system, the national media, and important professions were conducted in English. The medium was associated with the message of medical miracles and of technology. There already existed an ambitious (albeit small) group who wanted to acquire English for "mathematics, natural philosophy, chemistry, anatomy, and other useful sciences, which the natives of Europe have carried to a degree of perfection" (Raja Rammohan Roy (quoted in Kachru, 1969, 1978b:482)). For this purpose Roy was pleading that the "European gentlemen of talent and education" be appointed "to instruct the natives of India."

Eventually the small number of Indians, Africans, or Filipinos who became skilled in such professional roles became the symbols of what was termed "Westernization" (or, to use a neutral term, "modernization"). The "brown sahibs" seemed to feel solidarity, at least attitudinally, with the "white sahibs." Whether or not this feeling was reciprocated or exploited, the fact remains that a linguistic tool of power was steadily being shared. The domains of language use defined the power and prestige of language. English acquired a strong non-native base, and the local languages slowly lost the battle for prestige and power.

The elite language was eventually used against the Englishmen, against their roles and their intentions; it became the language of resurgence of nationalism, and political awakening at one level. And now the colonized, like Caliban (Shakespeare, *The Tempest*), were sometimes heard to say,

You taught me language and my profit on't
Is, I know how to curse! The red plague rid you
For learning me your language.

There are some who consider it a "grotesque perversion of the truth" that English "was imposed on a subject people by a set of foreign rulers for the sake of carrying on their alien government" (Chaudhuri, 1976:89). The word "imposed" is tricky here, for what was attitudinally prestigious and pragmatically desirable and rewarding did not need imposition: Power seems to have a way of creating its linguistic base.

The linguistic and cultural pluralism in Africa and South Asia contributed to the spread of English, and helped foster its retention even after the colonial period ended. The nationalist awakening needed a pan-national medium for a resurgence; the medium chosen was, ironically, the "alien" language. And there were reasons, both cultural and linguistic, for that choice.

True, Indian leaders like Mohandas K. Gandhi (1869–1948) were struggling to create consensus for a mutually acceptable native variety as the national language (Desai, 1964), but their message to the elite was expressed in English. By the 1920s, English had become the language of political discourse, intranational administration, and law, and it was associated with liberal thinking. These roles, and such an attitude toward English, maintained its power over local languages even after the colonial period ended.

Acquiring Domains of Power

Ease in acquiring domains of power is not necessarily related to the number of a language's users. The number of bilinguals able to use English in non-native contexts has always been limited: in South Asia for example, it has not exceeded 3 percent of the literate population.[3] However, that small segment of the population controls domains that have professional prestige; therefore, these people are considered worthy of emulation. One might say that they control certain types of knowledge that ambitious parents would like their children to possess. And whose parents are not ambitious?

In India, only Sanskrit, English, Hindi, and to some extent Persian have acquired pan-Indian intranational functions. The domains of Sanskrit are restricted, and the proficiency in it limited, except in the case of some professional pandits. The cause of Hindi was not helped by the controversy between Hindi, Urdu, and Hindustani. Support for Hindustani almost ended with independence; after the death of its ardent and influential supporter, Gandhi, very little was heard about it. The enthusiasm and near euphoria of the supporters of Hindi were not channeled in a constructive (and realistic) direction, especially after the 1940s. The result is that English continues to be a language both of power and of prestige (Kachru, 1976b; K. Sridhar, 1982).

For governments, English thus serves at least two purposes. First, it continues to provide a linguistic tool for the administrative cohesiveness of a country (as in South Asia and parts of Africa). Second, at another level, it provides a language of wider communication (national and international). The enthusiasm for English is not unanimous, or even widespread. The disadvantages of using it are obvious: Cultural and social implications accompany the use of an external language. But the native languages are losing in this competition (see, e.g. Apte 1976; Das Gupta 1969, 1970).

English does have one clear advantage, attitudinally and linguistically: it has acquired a *neutrality* in a linguistic context where native languages, dialects, and styles sometimes have acquired undesirable connotations. Whereas native codes are functionally marked in terms of caste, religion, region, and so forth, English has no such "markers," at least in the non-native context. It was originally the foreign (alien) ruler's language, but that drawback is often overshadowed by what it can do for its users. True, English is associated with a small and elite group; but it is in their role that the *neutrality* of a language becomes vital (e.g., for Tamil speakers in Tamil Nadu, or Bengali speakers in the West Bengal). In India the most widely used language is Hindi (46 percent) and its different varieties (e.g., Hindustani, Urdu), have traditionally been associated with various factions: Hindi with the Hindus; Urdu with the Muslims; and Hindustani with the maneuvering political pandits who could not create a constituency for it. While these attitudinal allocations are not necessarily valid, this is how the varieties have been perceived and presented. English, on the other hand, is not associated with any religious or ethnic faction.

Whatever the limitations of English, it has been perceived as the language of power and opportunity, free of the limitations that the ambitious attribute to the native languages.

Attitudinal Neutrality and Power

In several earlier studies it has been shown (Kachru, 1978a and 1982a) that in *code-mixing*, for example, English is being used to *neutralize* identities one is reluctant to express by the use of native languages or dialects. "Code-mixing" refers to the use of lexical items or phrases from one code in the stream of discourse of another. Neutralization thus is a linguistic strategy used to "unload" a linguistic item from its traditional, cultural, and emotional connotations by avoiding its use and choosing an item from another code. The borrowed item has referential meaning, but no cultural connotations in the context of the specific culture (Kachru, 1982a). This is not borrowing in the sense of filling a lexical gap, as I have discussed in Kachru, 1982a and 1983a (p. 195–197). Let me repeat some of those examples here:

In Kashmiri the native word *mɔnḍ* ("widow") invokes the traditional connotations associated with widowhood. Its use is restricted to abuses and curses, not occurring in "polished" conversation. *vedvā* (Hindi *vidhwā*) or English *widow* is preferred by the Hindus. In Tamil, as shown by Annamalai (1978) *maccaan* and *attimbeer* reveal the caste identity of the speaker—not desirable in certain situations. Therefore, one uses English *brother-in-law*, instead. English *rice* is neutral compared with *saadam* or *soru* (purist) in Tamil. A lexical item may be associated with a specific style in the native language as are *manaivi* (formal) and *penḍīṭṭi* (colloquial) in Tamil, but the English equivalent *wife* has no style restrictions.

In such contexts, then, the power of neutralization is associated with English in two ways. First, English provides—with or without "mixing"—an additional code that has referential meaning but no cultural overtones or connotations. Thus the types of linguistic features (especially lexicalization) that mark *granthika* (classical) versus *vyāvahārika* (colloquial) in Telugu, *sādhubhaṣa* (literary) versus *cɔlitbhasa* (colloquial) in Bengali, and

Hindu versus Muslim Kashmiri, are obscured by using English or by lexi-calization from English. English neutralizes discourse in terms of "identity," providing another identity. The bilingual (or multilingual) speaker can use codes for an identity shift: to obscure one identity and bring into the foreground another. Second, such use of English develops new code-mixed varieties of languages (Kachru, 1978). Lexicalization from English is particularly preferred in the contexts of kinship, taboo items, science and technology, or in discussing sex organs and death. What Moag (1982:276) terms the "social neutrality" of English in the case of Fiji is applicable in almost all the countries where English is used as a non-native language. In the Fijian context, Tongans and Fijians,

> find English the only safe medium in which to address those of higher status. English not only hides their inability in the specialized vernacular registers, but also allows them to meet traditional superiors on a more or less equal footing.

Varieties and Styles: Their Functional Power

The colonial Englishes, like any other variety of English, are not homo-geneous. There is variation within each variety (see e.g. Smith, ed. 1981). As the range and depth of functions increase, so does the variation of any language. The competence of speakers varies from the educated to the pidginized varieties. For example, in Nigeria, four varieties of English have been identified by their linguistic characteristics (Bamgbose, 1982). In Singapore, Malaysia (Platt and Weber, 1980; Wong, 1981; Tay and Gupta, 1983) and India (Kachru, 1965, and later) one notices the same cline of bilingualism. (See Kachru (1983a:4–5) for a discussion of variation and cline of bilingualism.)

The varieties are also distinguished on the basis of settings—formal or informal.

> In Singapore English, a final sentence particle *la*, probably of Hokkien origin, is extensively used when English is employed in informal settings and where the speech event calls for solidarity, rapport, etc. (Richards, 1982).

In Malaysian English the situation is identical. Consider the following examples given by Wong (1983:142).

> Better you speak to him yourself *lah*.
> He just sitting there and doing nothing *lah*.
> I don't know *lah*.
> I cannot move it *lah*.
> Don't be stubborn *lah*.

It is, however, in the nativized communicative acts, and situationally dependent (non-Western) rhetorical styles, that one finds the subtle use of English. I shall not elaborate on this aspect, since it would take us into a detailed discussion of stylistic devices used in contact literatures in English (see Kachru (1983b) for discussion and illustrations). I will only mention that a non-native writer of English faces a dilemma. On the one hand, Naipaul (1973:12) is right when he says,

> It is an odd, suspicious situation: an Indian writer writing in English for an English audience about non-English characters who talk their own sort of English. . . . I cannot help feeling that it might have been more profitable for me to appear in translation.

On the other hand, several non-native writers in English have taken quite the opposite view (for example, poets A. K. Ramanujan and R. Parathasarthy, and fiction writers Mulk Raj Anand, R. K. Narayan, and Raja Rao). Narayan is "particularly fond of the language (English) . . . it is . . . very adaptable . . . and it's so transparent it can take on the tint of any country" (Walsh, 1971: 7: quoted in Weir, 1982). This view is almost identical to the view of the African creative writer Achebe (1965:222) when he asks, "Can an African ever learn English well enough to be able to use it effectively in creative writing?" And he answers affirmatively, but qualifies his answer;

> If on the other hand you ask: "Can he ever learn to use it like a native speaker?" I should say, "I hope not. It is neither necessary, nor desirable for him to be able to do so. . . . I feel that the English language will be able to carry the weight of my African experience. But it will have to be a new English, still in communion with its ancestral home but altered to suit its new African surroundings.

Contact Literatures in English: Creativity in the Other Tongue

The contact literatures in English have several characteristics, of which two may be mentioned here. In South Asia, to take one example, there are three more or less pan-South Asian literatures: Sanskrit, Persian, and Hindi. In terms of both style and content, Sanskrit has been associated with the native Hindu tradition. Persian (in its Indian form) and Urdu have maintained the Perso-Arabic stylistic devices, metaphors, and symbolism. It is this aspect of Urdu that alienated it from the traditionalist Hindus, who believe that in its formal experimentation, thematic range, and metaphor, it has maintained and "un-Indian" (Islamic) tradition, and continues to seek inspiration from such non-native traditions. This attitude toward Urdu tells only part of the story, and negates the contribution that the Hindus have made to the Urdu language, and the way it was used as the language of national revival. Indian English literature cuts across these attitudes. It has united certain pan-South Asian nationalists, intellectuals, and creative writers. It has provided a new perspective in India through an "alien" language.

In Indian English fiction (see, e.g. Mukherjee, 1971; Parameswaran, 1976) R. K. Narayan, Mulk Raj Anand, and Raja Rao (e.g., his *Kantha-pura*) have brought another dimension to the understanding of the regional, social and political contexts. In the process, linguistically speaking, the process of the Indianization of English has acquired an institutionalized status (Kachru, 1983a).

In a sociological sense, then, English has provided a linguistic tool and a sociopolitical dimension very different from those available through native linguistic tools and traditions. A non-native writer in English functions in two traditions. In psychological terms, such a multilingual role calls for adjustment. In attitudinal terms, it is controversial; in linguistic terms, it is challenging, for it means molding the language for new contexts. Such a writer is suspect as fostering new beliefs, new value systems, and even new linguistic loyalties and innovations.

This, then, leads us to the other side of this controversy. For example, what have been the implications of such a change—attitudinally and socio-logically—for the Indian languages (and for African languages) and for those speakers whose linguistic repertoires do not include English? Additionally, we need to ask what are its implications for the creative writers whose media are "major" or "minor" Indian languages. (For further discussion, see Ansre (1979) for Africa, and Kachru (1982b) for South Asia).

Post-Colonial Period

Since independence, the controversy about English has taken new forms. Its "alien" power base is less an issue; so is its Englishness or American-ness in a cultural sense. The English language is not perceived as necessarily imparting only Western traditions. The medium is non-native, but the message is not. In several Asian and African countries, English now has national and international functions that are both distinct and complementary. English has thus acquired a new power base and a new elitism. The domains of English have been restructured. The result is that one more frequently, and very eloquently, hears people ask, Is English really a non-native ("alien") language for India, for Africa, and for South-east Asia?[4]

In the case of India one wonders: has India played the age-old trick on English, too, of nativizing it and acculturating it—in other words, Indian-izing it? The Indian writer and philosopher Raja Rao (1978:421) associates power with English which, in his mind is equal to if not greater than Sanskrit, when he says,

> Truth, said a great Indian sage, is not the monopoly of the Sanskrit language. Truth can use any language, and the more universal, the better it is. If metaphysics is India's primary contribution to world civilization, as we believe it is, then must she use the most universal language for her to be universal.... And as long as the English language is universal, it will always remain Indian.... It would then be correct to say as long as we are Indian—that is, not nationalists, but truly Indians of the Indian psyche—we shall have the English language with us and amongst us, and not as a guest or friend, but as one of our own, of our caste, our creed, our sect and our tradition.

These new power bases in Africa or in Asia have called into question the traditionally accepted, externally normative standards for the institu-tionalized varieties. The new varieties have their own linguistic and cultural ecologies or sociocultural contexts. The adaptation to these new ecologies have given non-native Englishes new identities. That the recognition of such an identity has implications for the local languages was pointed out by Halliday *et al.* (1964). In the case of India, for example, they felt that those who favor English as a model "should realize that in doing so they may be helping to prop up the fiction that English is the language of Indian culture and thus be perpetuating the diminished status of the Indian languages." The warning was too late. By 1964, English had already become a vital part of the Indian linguistic repertoire. What was "fiction" in the 1960s has now become a reality in the 1980s.

The wider implications of this change in the ecology of world Englishes are significant: The new nativized (non-native) varieties have acquired an ontological status and developed localized norms and standards. Purists find that the situation is getting out of hand (see, e.g. Prator, 1968); they are uncomfortable that the native speakers' norms are not universally accepted. There are others who feel that a pragmatic approach is war-ranted and that a "monomodel" approach for English in the world context is neither applicable nor realistic. (Kachru, 1982c and 1984a provide a detailed discussion of this topic.)

The extended non-native uses of English also raise serious theoretical issues, both in sociolinguistic and linguistic research. These are not neces-sarily related to the questions of "power," but to language analysis and description. It seems that linguists' traditional preoccupation with the monolingual "native speaker" is now being questioned—and rightly so. Does one need a new perspective and a new theoretical and descriptive technique for writing bilinguals' or multilinguals' grammars? Such probing questions are the result of the spread of English, and of the alchemy that English uses for changing itself, and for "Englishizing" the non-Western languages with which it has prolonged contact (discussed by Ferguson, 1978, 1982a; Kachru, 1984a). What we see here is that the "power" of English has deeper implications, going beyond what we see on the surface.

One might say that contemporary English does not have just one defin-ing context but many—across cultures and languages. This is also true of the growing new literatures in English. The concepts of "British literature" or "American literature" represent only a part of the spectrum. The new traditions—really not so new—must be incorporated into the tradition of "literature in English" (Narasimhaiah, ed. 1978).

The power bases for English today exist on almost all continents. This unprecedented linguistic situation, therefore, needs new understanding and pragmatics. In each context the English language is manipulated dif-ferently, as a medium of power, control, authority, and cohesion. English has therefore acquired intranationally and internationally most important roles. In each English-using country, these roles are in the hands of a small portion of the total population. If this linguistic power is wielded without sensitivity, without understanding, English becomes a language for oppres-sion (Ansre, 1979).

The alchemy of English (present and future), then does not only provide social status, it also gives access to attitudinally and materially desirable domains of power and knowledge. It provides a powerful linguistic tool for manipulation and control. In addition, this alchemy of English has left a deep mark on the languages and literature of the non-Western world. English has thus caused transmutation of languages, equipping them in the process for new societal, scientific, and technological demands. The process of Englishization has initiated stylistic and thematic innovations, and has "modernized" registers. The power of English is so dominant that a new caste of English-using speech fellowships has developed across cultures and languages. It may be relatively small, but it is powerful, and its values and perspectives are not necessarily in harmony with the traditional values of these societies. In the past, the control and manipulation of international power have never been in the hands of users of one language group. Now we see a shift of power from the traditional caste structure; in the process, a new caste has developed. In this sense, English has been instrumental in a vital social change, and not only in that of language and literatures.

One might ask, does one see signs of change in the international power of English? We have seen legislation or educational planning in, for example, Africa or Asia, has failed to accomplish this change fully. One reason for failure is that such a change entails changing attitudes toward a language and initiating effective policies to provide a power base for other languages. This has not happened, and the consequences are that in many respects the roots of English are deeper now than they were during the period of political colonization. English continues to be used as an alchemy for language modernization and social change. It continues to provide unprecedented power for mobility and advancement to those native and non-native users who possess it as a linguistic tool.

But there are murmurs that cannot be ignored: These are not necessarily heard from the purists or from traditional anti-English groups. An appropriate question is often heard now: How does one "domesticate modernization"? Perhaps one answer is that there is a need for "a circumscription of domestic use of English" (Jernudd, 1981:50). Such an approach, Jernudd believes, will "liberate English for use as a truly international language, a role that today is tarnished by the misuse of English to prevent the economic, sociopolitical, and cultural advancement of those who do not possess it."

In more and more countries, as in India, English is also perceived by some as the language of oppression, as yet another way to exclude large populations from participation in vital national decision-making processes, and from various educational, political, and scientific domains. In other words, the argument goes, English has introduced a "language bar" in regions that are still fighting against the traditional "caste bar" or "tribal bar." This reaction to English is particularly reflected in the non-English-language press, political pamphleteering, party manifests, and in uncontrollable language riots that take place in different parts of the world.

In India, as elsewhere, politicians of different hues exploit the language issues and invariably paralyze the educational and administrative systems.

However, the more pragmatic among them see to it that their own children, and other loved ones, are able to get an English education. Is this, then, a case of linguistic schizophrenia? The answer is: Yes. Thus, in anti-English circles, there is one policy for the home and another for outside; the language policy is designed for specific consumers. (For further discussion on related issues and references see Apte, 1976, Brass, 1974, and Das Gupta, 1970).

However, for the present this fact remains: As Quirk *et al.* (1972) observe, the real power of English is in its "vehicular load," in the attitude toward the language, and in the deep and increasing belief in its power of alchemy linguistically to transmute an individual and a speech community.

Notes

This chapter is a revised version of "The Alchemy of English: Social and Functional Power of Non-Native Varieties" in *Language and Power*, edited by Cheris Kramarae, Muriel Schulz and William O'Barr. Beverley Hills, CA: Sage Publications, Inc., 1984, pp. 176–193.

1. *Mantra* means "an instrument of thought." In literature it is also used as a general term for a sacred text, syllable, word, or verse, which if repeated, has a spiritual or a temporal effect.
2. Aphorisms compiled mainly between the sixth and second centuries B.C.; *sūtras* provide instruction concerning human conduct, domestic ritual, and scriptual interpretation.
3. This percentage is misleading, since in actual numbers it includes over 28 million people—indeed, a large segment of the world's population. The number of English speakers in South Asia is greater than the English speaking population of three English speaking countries: Australia, Canada, and New Zealand.
4. For a detailed discussion of each area and for bibliographical references see, e.g. for South Asia, Lal, 1969; R. Rao, 1978a; Kandiah, 1981; Kachru, 1983a; for Africa see relevant chapters in Kachru, ed. 1982 and Chishimba, 1983; Magura, 1984; for Southeast Asia, see Llamzon, 1969 and 1983; Marasigan, 1981; Platt and Weber, 1980; Tay and Gupta, 1983; Wong, 1981 and 1983; Richard, 1982 and Chutisilp, 1984; for a discussion of American English and other Englishes see Kachru, 1981a.

PART I
Varieties and Functions

Chapter 2

Institutionalized Varieties

WHATEVER vagueness one at first associates with the term *second*-language varieties of English as opposed to *foreign*-language varieties slowly diminishes when one assesses the international uses of English in geographical historical, attitudinal, linguistic, and sociolinguistic contexts. The term *second*-language varieties acquires more meaning once the world varieties of English are further seen in terms of their functional distribution and localized formal characteristics. Who are the second-language users of English? Internationally, the users of English are viewed from three perspectives: that of a native user for whom English is the first language in almost all functions; that of a non-native user who considers English as a foreign language and uses it in highly restricted domains; and that of a non-native user who uses an institutionalized second-language variety of English. I am concerned here with the last group, which must ideally be separated from those who use English as a foreign language. The two non-native groups differ in their acquisitional settings, in their motivations for learning English, and in their reasons for nativizing it.[1]

These non-native varieties of English have alternatively been labeled "interference" varieties since in such second- or foreign-language varieties there is a clear linguistic and cultural interference from what may be termed the first language(s) and culture(s) of the user. The term "institutionalized" varieties generally refers to the varieties used by second-language users to distinguish them from the "performance" varieties of English, used essentially as foreign languages. This distinction is useful in understanding the context for the use of English in a particular region, and for planning the strategies for teaching. The terms are not vital, but understanding the underlying shared and non-shared characteristics of these two types of varieties is important. (See, for example, Kachru and Quirk, 1981, and Kachru, ed. 1982, 1983a.) The institutionalized second-language varieties have a long history of acculturation in new cultural and geographical contexts; they have a large range of functions in the local educational, administrative, and legal systems. The result of such uses is that such varieties have developed nativized discourse and style types and functionally determined sublanguages (registers), and are used as a linguistic vehicle for creative writing in various genres.[2] We find such uses of English on almost every continent, for example, in Nigeria, Kenya, the Republic of South Africa, and Ghana in Africa; Bangladesh, India, Pakistan, and Sri Lanka in South Asia; and the Philippines, Singapore, and Malaysia in Southeast Asia.

The number of foreign-language and second-language users together adds up to 300 to 400 million, depending on whose figures one accepts.[3] Whatever the exact figures, this is a historically unprecedented phenomenon of language spread. When we add to this figure almost 300 million native speakers, we get 700 million users of English around the world. This figure puts English numerically among the most widely used world languages: Chinese, Hindi-Urdu, Russian, and Spanish.

Moreover these figures are not mere numerical indicators. They also convey the message that the non-native users of English have given a wide geographical distribution to this language. English has acquired a variety of intranational and international functions across cultures and languages, and has gained the unprecedented status of a universal language. What was until recently a "colonial alien language" is now being used and spread by the former colonial subjects. The roles which linguistic visionaries foresaw for an artificial international language have slowly been assumed by English. As the statistics show, those who use English as their second or foreign (or "additional") language now outnumber the users of Australian (15.8 million), Canadian (25.4 million), British (56.4 million), American (238.9 million), and New Zealand (3.3 million) varieties. By their geographical distribution, numerical strength, and varied users of English, the non-native users have made English, as it were, a window on the world.

But the spread of English in its various incarnations has not been an unmixed blessing—at least in the opinion of some. The more localized "unEnglish" uses English acquires, the more varieties of new (non-native) English come into existence. Cynics and purists see a sign of disintegration in the modification of English by alien users of the language: they seem to foresee the same fate for English which, for example, Latin met in Europe.

Is this attitude linguistically and pragmatically sound? Has the English language really fallen on hard times, especially on foreign shores in the speech and writing of those who use it as their second language? We might gain some insights into the sociolinguistic issues by exploring two perspectives on second-language varieties. First, there is the attitude that second-language users manifest toward English in its various native and non-native models, and toward the innovations which are deviant from British or American English. Second, there is the attitude of native speakers of English toward these varieties.

The term *linguistic attitude* is used here in a broad sense. One might reveal such an attitude by using what may be termed *attitude-marking modifiers* for a variety of English (e.g. *Babu* English, *Indian* English, *cheechee* English, *Singapore* English, *Nigerian* English), or toward a variety within a variety, or toward non-native innovations in pronunciation, vocabulary, usage, discourse, and style types.

As is well documented, there are no authoritative codifying agencies such as language academies with the power to prescribe norms for using English as a second language. The codification is more in the sense of a preferred model, the preference being determined by such considerations as historical accident of exposure to a particular model, political colonization, geographical proximity, and attitude toward a variety. Who are the regulators of the norm? In the case of English, such regulators have been indirect and very subtle: dictionaries, pedagogical manuals, preferred models on television, radio, and in other media, and expressed social attitudes toward a particular manner of language use.

In earlier periods, both in Britain and in the U.S.A., organized efforts for codification have invariably failed.[4] But that failure has not deterred the messengers of linguistic doom from foretelling linguistic disintegration. In every generation such Cassandras arise who express concern about the decay of English among the native or non-native users, recent examples being Edwin Newman, and (for teaching English internationally) Clifford Prator,[5] and several other zealous practitioners of teaching English internationally.

For English it is possible to choose between an idealized exo-normative model and an institutionalized endo-normative model. An exo-normative model refers to a native model (e.g. American or British) for emulation and teaching. On the other hand, an endo-normative model provides a local educated variety as the model for teaching and learning (e.g. by and large in India and Nigeria). The division is not always clear-cut: one finds coexistence of the two, and a wide range of variation between the accepted norm and the actual linguistic behavior.

In the history of attitudes towards second-language varieties we find several overlapping stages (see Kachru ed. 1982, chapter 3). These stages are discussed in chapter 7. However, I will summarize these here for reader's convenience. One first notices non-recognition of the localized variety, in the period of an "imitation model." This is followed by an extensive diffusion of local varieties of English, with varying degrees of success in teaching an exo-normative model. The third stage shows less discrepancy between the norm and the behavior: The localized (educated) norm is recognized by contextualizing the teaching materials to fit the local sociocultural situations, by recognizing the intranational uses of English, and by accepting local creative writing in English as part of national writing, as is certainly happening, for example, in Nigeria, Kenya, India, Singapore, and Malaysia.

I shall term these stages as *internal* within the speech fellowship that uses English as a second language. Attitudinally, however, a second-language user seems to stand between a rock and hard place; the internal attitude is only one aspect of the picture. It is equally vital to investigate the attitude of native speakers toward the users of second-language varieties, or toward a particular second-language variety. Such attitudes provide fascinating sociolinguistic data.

Native speakers have traditionally viewed non-native innovations in (and nativizations of) English with ambivalence. Nativization has essentially been seen as *deficiency*, not as *difference*, as has been discussed with illustrations in several studies (for example, Kachru, ed. 1982; especially chapters 3 and 20). Nativization must be seen as the result of those productive linguistic innovations which are determined by the localized functions of a second language variety, the "culture of conversation" and communicative strategies in new situations, and the "transfer" from local languages.

There may also be other reasons for such innovations—for example, acquisitional limitations, inadequate teaching, and the lack of a consistent model for practice. There has been, furthermore, a subtle political reason: the desire to establish and maintain "language distance." The colonizers insisted on not teaching their language too well to "non-ingroup" Asians or Africans, the underlying idea being that the colonizers' code, if shared equally with the colonized, would reduce the distance between the rulers and the ruled. At the same time, the inevitable nativization of English by the brown and black sahibs (as the English-knowing natives were called) did not go unnoticed by the colonizers and provided a storehouse of hilarious linguistic anecdotes to be related in the "white only" clubs. In South Asia, the mythical "Babuji" became the source of such linguistic entertainment. The second-language user never seemed to win in this see-saw of attitudes. If he gained "native-like" linguistic competence he was suspect; if he did not gain it he was an object of linguistic ridicule.

The above discussion gives us some idea about the complexity of the issues. I shall now discuss manifestations of the attitude of second-language users toward models of English, toward functions of English, and toward linguistic innovations.

Traditionally, the main acquisitional models for English have been the educated British and American varieties. In order to illustrate this point, let me take the specific example of India. India has a long tradition of teaching English as a second language, and the Indian variety of English is used in a number of domains of language function. In a 1976 survey two types of reactions concerning the preferred model have been reported (Kachru, 1976, especially pp. 229–234). One is the ranking of faculty preference for a model; a second is graduate students' attitudes toward various models of English, and their ranking on a scale of preference (see Tables 1 and 2 below). The survey was based on written questionnaires administered to 700 Indian students enrolled in Bachelor's and Master's degree courses in selected urban and rural universities and colleges, 196 teachers of English in selected universities and colleges, almost all holding graduate degrees in English, and 29 heads of departments of English. In Tables 1 and 2 the "scale of preference" or "preference rating" indicates

TABLE 1. *Faculty Preference for Models of English Instruction*

Model	Preference		
	I	II	III
American English	3.07	14.35	25.64
British English	66.66	13.33	1.53
Indian English	26.66	25.64	11.79
I don't know		5.12	

TABLE 2. *Indian Graduate Students' Attitude Toward Various Models of English and Ranking of Models According to Preference*

Model	Preference		
	I	II	III
American English	5.17	13.19	21.08
British English	67.6	9.65	1.08
Indian English	22.72	17.82	10.74
I don't know		5.03	
"Good" English		1.08	

the preference in terms of choosing a particular model out of three possible models (i.e. American, British, and Indian).

Perhaps more revealing (than Tables 1 and 2) is the graduate student's "self-labeling" of their own English (see Table 3) which provides an important indication about the attitudes of users of this variety toward other varieties. It is generally believed that only a generation ago the gap between linguistic behavior and perceived norm, was much wider. At that time, one would have hesitated to label one's own English "Indian," but by 1976 the picture was different, and it is still changing.

A study by Shaw[6] includes the preference of Singaporeans, Indians, and Thais for the variety of English they should learn to speak (see Tables 4 and 5).

TABLE 3. *Indian Graduate Students, "Self labelling" of the Variety of Their English*

Identity-marker	%
American English	2.58
British English	29.11
Indian English	55.64
"Mixture" of all three	2.99
I don't know	8.97
"Good" English	.27

TABLE 4.

	Preference for models of English		
	Singaporeans	Indians	Thais
British	38.3	28.5	49.1
American	14.4	12.0	31.6
Australian	.6	.3	.3
Own way	38.9	47.4	3.5
Others	7.8	11.8	15.5

TABLE 5. *Comparisons of Percentage choosing Native and Non-native Standards*

	Present			Future		
	Singaporeans	Indians	Thais	Singaporeans	Indians	Thais
Native	47.0	30.6	34.5	53.3	40.9	80.9
Non-native	53.0	69.4	65.5	46.7	59.1	19.1

But before drawing any far-reaching conclusions, one must note that the attitude toward British English may simply be explained in historical terms. British English provided a perceived norm, though actually localized non-native varieties have always been used in most countries formerly colonized by the British. It is true that empirical studies on this aspect of English use are lacking. However, asides by educators concerning localized varieties provide further significant attitudinal clues. Bamgboṣe (1971, p. 41), discussing the teaching of English in Nigeria, says that "the aim is not to produce speakers of British Received Pronunciation (even if this were feasible! . . . Many Nigerians will consider as affected or even snobbish any Nigerian who speaks like a native speaker of English." Similarly, in Ghana, Sey (1973:1) warns us that if an educated Ghanaian speaks the Received Pronunciation of England he "is frowned upon as distasteful and pedantic." In the Ghanaian context, as elsewhere in Africa, an educated localized variety does not mean "the type that strives too obviously to approximate to RP."

In South Asia the position of Sri Lanka (Ceylon) is not much different from that of India, as we see in the study by Passé (1947:33). He observes that,

> It is worth noting, too, that Ceylonese (Sri Lankans) who speak "Standard English" are generally unpopular. There are several reasons for this: those who now speak standard English either belong to a favored social class, with long purses which can take them to English public schools and universities, and so are disliked too much to be imitated, or have rather painfully acquired this kind of speech for social reasons and so are regarded as the apes of their betters; they are singular in speaking English as the majority of their countrymen cannot or will not speak it . . . Standard English has thus rather unpleasant associations when it is spoken by Ceylonese (Sri Lankans), . . .

This observation was made four decades ago. Today, in independent Sri Lanka where Singhala has a dominant position, and RP-sounding Singhala would be even less acceptable, as has been indicated by Kandiah (1981) and other researchers.

The countries I have cited so far have been under the political domination of Britain. Let us now take the case of the Philippines, which has been under political control of the U.S.A., and where even now that influence continues. Llamzon (1969:15) observes that "Standard Filipino English" is generally used, and it is *"the type of English which educated Filipinos speak and which is acceptable in educated Filipino circles"* (see also Llamzon, 1981).

One can go on adding to this list other areas where institutionalized second-language varieties of English have developed: Singapore, Malaysia, and Puerto Rico to name just three.[7] This list of countries makes one thing very clear: the attitudinal conflict between indigenous and external norms is slowly being resolved in favor of localized educated norms. This move is motivated more by pragmatic considerations than by a desire for linguistic emancipation. The trend is very clear, and there is a lesson in it.

Another aspect of second-language use reveals the attitude toward the functions and status of English in what may be termed utilitarian, intimate, and cultural domains. In a sense, these domains are related to what Quirk *et al.* (1972) call the "vehicular load" of English discussed in chapter 1. As noted there, this preference for English in various domains has contributed to the spread of the language, and to its retention after the end of the colonial period. It is unconsciously (and not-so-unconsciously) believed that English has an alchemy which "authenticates" a function in which it is used. That is why it is used to foster the revival or development of nationalism. It is also a preferred medium for technology and science. Let me illustrate this phenomenon by providing appropriate data from two studies, those of Fishman *et al.* (1977) and of K. Sridhar (1982).

In Fishman *et al.* (1977) we find that the use of English as a tool (or instrument) for science, technology, and other disciplines was "endorsed by the largest number of students (61 percent) as being among the three most important reasons for studying English (in Israel)." This clearly is in consonance with an earlier study by Kachru (1976) for India discussed in chapter 6. Cooper and Fishman in the above study (1977:253) assert that

> Not only did the students appear to value knowledge of English, they displayed favorable attitudes toward English vis-à-vis other languages. When asked to rate the suitability of each of five languages for each of twenty uses, English received the highest average rating on eight uses, including science, oratory, international diplomacy, philosophical treatises, and light verse. For two additional uses, novels and poetry, English received the highest average rating along with French. Thus English was the language most commonly viewed as most suitable for contexts associated with high culture and science. It was, however, also given the highest average rating for a more popular culture item, folk songs. English was even given the highest average rating for talking to babies, perhaps on the grounds that it is never too early to begin instruction in English.

Table 6 gives reasons for the study of English.

Let us now turn to the Dravidian language speakers in the south of multilingual India. Tables 7 and 8 show the functional distribution of Hindi, English, and other languages in South India.

In the non-Hindi South of India where Hindi is not the mother tongue, English is the preferred language in social interaction and professional contexts. The pan-Indian preference becomes clearer in Tables 9 and 10 taken from the above mentioned 1976 survey of English in India. Attitudinally and functionally, therefore, English is high on the language hierarchy.

The third aspect of language attitude involves the reaction of second language users toward the linguistic innovations in non-native institution-

TABLE 6. *Reasons for the Study of English in Israel*

Reason	%
1. To read textbooks assigned in universities or other institutions of higher learning	61.4
2. To get along when abroad	47.4
3. To become broadly educated	47.4
4. To pass matriculation examination	42.1
5. To read English-language books for pleasure	36.8
6. To get a job which pays more	19.3
7. To gain friends among English-speaking people	14.0
8. Yields personal satisfaction	10.5
9. To begin to think and behave as Americans do	5.3
10. To learn about foreign points of view about Israel	3.5
11. To know tourists better	1.7
12. To know English-speaking immigrants better	1.7

Source: Fishman, Cooper and Conrad, 1977:252.

TABLE 7. *South Indian Students who Use Mother-tongue, English, and Hindi/Urdu in Social Interactions (%)*

Domain	Language	Regularly	Rarely
Family	English	15	29
	Mother Tongue	87	1
	Hindi-Urdu	3	54
Friends	English	42	8
	Mother Tongue	53	12
Neighbours who can speak your language	English	17	24
	Mother Tongue	65	6
	Hindi-Urdu	4	48
Friends and relatives, during weddings, etc.	English	24	15
	Mother Tongue	71	3
	Hindi-Urdu	5	47
Teachers	English	57	3
	Mother Tongue	24	26
	Hindi-Urdu	2	57
Strangers on the bus	English	47	11
	Mother Tongue	35	11
	Hindi-Urdu	5	48
Office and bank employees	English	57	8
	Mother Tongue	26	17
	Hindi-Urdu	2	49
Political and technical discussions	English	42	8
	Mother Tongue	41	12
	Hindi-Urdu	4	50
While visiting another state in India	English	64	6
	Mother Tongue	17	27
	Hindi-Urdu	15	32

Source: K. Sridhar, 1982a.

TABLE 8. *Employees who Use English, Mother Tongue, and Hindi-Urdu in Professional Contexts in South India (%)*

Domain	Language	Regularly	Rarely
Friends	English	33	6
	Mother Tongue	66	3
	Hindi-Urdu	25	6
Colleagues and	English	64	3
Superiors	Mother Tongue	31	19
	Hindi-Urdu	16	7
Subordinate staff	English	22	25
	Mother Tongue	48	14
	Hindi-Urdu	30	5
Customers who	English	38	9
speak Mother Tongue	Mother Tongue	45	13
	Hindi-Urdu	27	6
Customers who don't	English	74	1
speak your language	Mother Tongue	5	25
	Hindi-Urdu	14	14

Source: K. Sridhar, 1982a.

TABLE 9. *Use of English in the Reading of General Literature*

| Type of material | Frequency | | | |
	Always	Frequently	Rarely	Never
Newspapers and magazines	70.74	23.40	5.03	.40
General reading	63.94	28.84	6.12	.10

TABLE 10. *Use of English in Personal Interaction*

Interaction with	All the time	Often	Rarely	Never
Family	9.11	50.34	28.97	8.29
Friends	40.81	49.65	10.6	.27
Teachers	67.48	27.75	3.53	.13

Source: Kachru, 1976b.

alized varieties. In several studies (e.g. Kachru, 1981c), the distinctiveness of, for example, American, Australian, or Canadian Englishes has actually been claimed on the basis of such localized innovations. The reaction of the users of British English toward such variations and innovations was not always one of acceptance. Such innovations were considered signals of language decay, language corruption, or language death at the hands of those who were not in touch with the "real genius" of the language. Later, this attitude was extended to the English of non-native users.

What is meant by a linguistic innovation? A linguistic innovation is one result of nativization of English (Kachru, ed. 1982:7), which in turn is the result of the new ecology in which a non-native variety of English functions. We see the influence of new linguistic, cultural, and social ecology in the *Americanness* or *Australianness* of English in the U.S.A. and Australia, respectively. It is in these ecologies that the innovations acquire their communicative "meaning." Such innovations are not only lexical but also involve distinct culture-bound strategies for writing personal or official letters, invitations, obituaries, newspaper reports, and other discourse types as I have shown in chapter 10 and in an earlier study (Kachru, ed. 1982: 325:350). As one travels in the English-using world one encounters such regional innovations in the form of local borrowings, calques, translations, and in the "mixing" of elements of English with local languages or vice versa. To the local English-using population such items are part of their linguistic repertoire and come to them as naturally as do *bull-frog, turkey-gobbler,* and *eggplant* to the users of American English. In various regions of Africa an outsider wonders what the following items mean: *kloof* "ravine, valley"; *kraal* "enclosure"; *aardvart* "ant eater"; *khang* "cloth wrapper"; *sufia* "cooking part"; *okrika* "second-hand clothing"; *okyeame* "headspokesman"; *penin* "elder"; *dunno drums* "a type of drum"; *give kola* "offer a bribe"; *cry die* "wake, funeral rites"; *throw water* "offer a bribe"; *barb* "haircut"; *head tie* "head scarf". One has the same reaction when one notices in spoken or written English in various parts of Asia innovations such as: *kampong* "a small settlement"; *makan* "food"; *tiffin-carrier* "a carrier for snack or lunch"; *ahimsa* "non-violence".

These innovations certainly are not pan-African or pan-Asian; these are localized and serve a communicative need in particular regions of South, West, and East Africa, or of South and Southeast Asia. In some cases they have a specific connotation for a religion or community as have *caste mark* and *forehead marking* to the Hindu society, and *communal question* (*-riots, -harmony,* etc.) in the relations between Hindus and Muslims. These innovations and their semantic extensions or restrictions are, therefore, indicative of acculturation of English in new sociocultural and linguistic contexts, and reflect its acceptance as a vehicle of non-native social norms and ecological needs. One might ask: Who is to judge the appropriateness and acceptance of such innovations? The actual non-native user or an idealized native speaker? The answer is not easy.

The reactions to such non-native innovations in institutionalized second-language varieties are deeply linked to linguistic attitudes. If the fundamental linguistic attitude is puristic, all innovations seem to signal decay. One tends to ignore the new cultural, social, and pragmatic contexts in which the language is embedded.[8] Each generation produces (perhaps well-meaning) linguistic alarmists whose concerns are sincere but unrelated to the pragmatics of a living language.

Lexicologists have generally demonstrated a more pragmatic language attitude which takes into consideration the non-English context, the need to use contextually appropriate lexis, and above all the importance of language as a vehicle of communication (see Kachru, 1980c).

The nativized innovations in second-language varieties of English cannot be lumped together as *mistakes*; there is a difference between what may be called a mistake and a *deviation*. From a native speaker's viewpoint both entail non-native uses, but there is an important linguistic, contextual, and pedagogical distinction between the two, as I have explained elsewhere (Kachru, ed. 1982:45).

> A "mistake" may be unacceptable by a native speaker since it does not belong to the linguistic "norm" of the English language; it cannot be justified with reference to the sociocultural context of a non-native variety; and it is not the result of the productive processes used in an institutionalized non-native variety of English. On the other hand, a "deviation" has the following characteristics: it is different from the norm in the sense that it is the result of the new "un-English" linguistic and cultural setting in which the English language is used; it is the result of a productive process which marks the typical variety-specific features; and it is systemic within a variety, and not idiosyncratic. There is thus an explanation for each deviation within the context of situation.

Why are deviations (or innovations) an essential part of the context of second-language varieties of English? Answering that question leads us to a digression concerning the new contexts in which English is used and the relationship between language form and function. It entails viewing the use of English in institutionalized second-language varieties from a different perspective. How have such innovations been viewed earlier? Again, let us consider the attitudinal history toward the South Asian variety of English. What is true of this variety is generally true of other institutionalized varieties of English as well. The attitudes typically refer to nativization of the following types: lexical or collocational changes, stylistic innovations (e.g. code-mixing), functional varieties, and lastly, reactions to the development of non-native English literatures, and to the thematic and stylistic nativization and innovations displayed in such texts.

The reactions come from four broad (and not mutually exclusive) groups: the *descriptivists*, the *purists*, the *cynics*, and the *pragmatists*. I shall discuss briefly the approaches of each group.

The descriptivists did not involve themselves with attitudinal evaluation of a variety and the innovations in it. Their studies primarily accounted for regional phonetic, lexical, and grammatical characteristics. One group of descriptivists was interested from a lexicographical point of view: the applied lexicographer's goal is very well accomplished in the monumental work of Henry Yule and A. C. Burnell entitled *Hobson-Jobson* (Yule and Burnell, 1886) discussed in chapter 3 (p. 41). The lexicographers worked in two areas: They compiled collections of essentially local (e.g. South Asian) borrowings into the localized functions of English, and they recorded some semantically nativized English lexical items. In addition, they provided purpose-specific lexical lists: these were the precursors of what later became known as English for special purposes (ESP), and they were very useful to colonial administrators dealing with alien languages and cultures (e.g. Brown, 1852; Carnegy, 1877; Roberts, 1800; Stocqueler, 1848; Yule and Burnell, 1866, and Wilson, 1955).[9] The linguists, like Schuchardt, studied Indian English as a case of language contact and language change.

Other descriptivists looked at linguistic innovations purely in terms of language change resulting from contact of two or more languages; for example, the early contact between English and South Asian languages is discussed by the German linguist Hugo Schuchardt (1842–1927) in his study of 1891. This latter group included structuralists and phoneticians—the structuralists as we understand them in the post-Bloomfield American paradigm, especially as applied to language pedagogy.

The line between descriptivists and prescriptivists has been a very fine one (especially in language teaching). When these two were blended, the result usually was linguistic purism. Once we talk of purism we invariably encounter an underlying norm. The combination of descriptivism and purism is evident in Goffin (1934), Whitworth (1907), and in a long tradition of grammars specifically produced for the second-language learner. In its more extreme form we find this position espoused by Prator (1968; for a response to it see chapter 6).

The cynics are cynical about the status of the localized varieties and of the non-native innovations. They are aware of the use of localized non-native models in education, the media, and administration, but are hesitant to consider such models "standard" for a region. With regard to the non-native literatures in English, they are not sure whether such literatures belong to the local literary traditions.

Finally come the pragmatists or functionalists who see language as part of a semiotic system in which various innovations and deviations are related to language function and change. Even the users of the transplanted first-language varieties had to wage a series of battles to establish their distinct identities, as in, for example, the United States or Australia.

A functionalist, then, views an institutionalized second language as a living and changing system, naturally acquiring new identities in new sociocultural contexts. The context provides "meaning," and as the cultural and linguistic contexts change the language acquires new meanings. In new contexts, therefore, new *uses* and *users* of English have developed appropriate linguistic tools. I shall give below the observations of two Indian linguistic realists, one an educator and linguist, P. E. Dustoor, and the other a creative writer, R. K. Narayan. Dustoor (1968:126) has made an apt observation on this phenomenon which I am tempted to quote here:

> Our mental climate will always foster plants that do not flourish in England or America; and such plants, just because they are somewhat exotic, add to the charm of a garden. All lovers of English will, therefore, encourage them to grow in the world-wide garden of English. It is only the weeds, which spring up whenever ignorance, carelessness or pretentiousness infects the air, that need to be pulled up by the roots.

Narayan is much more forthright (quoted in Press, ed. 1965:123):

> We are not attempting to write Anglo-Saxon English. The English language, through sheer resilience and mobility, is now undergoing a process of Indianization in the same manner as it adopted U.S. citizenship over a century ago, with the difference that it is the major language there but here one of the fifteen listed in the Indian Constitution.

In functional terms, then, the institutionalized second-language varieties are part of the linguistic repertoire of the users (see chapter 4). English is one linguistic tool among many, as we have seen above in Sridhar's study with reference to allocation of domains. One important domain is that of literary creativity, the results of which include *Indian* English literature, *African* English literature, and *Malaysian* English literature, to name only three. These are new—not yet fully studied—facets of English in a world context.

The spread of English—especially of its institutionalized varieties—has other dimensions which are directly related to language attitude. For example, consider the question of linguistic identity and language nationalism. The use of English by its non-native users, as one linguistic tool among many such tools, raises interesting questions: Does one necessarily lose one's cultural identity by using a non-native second language? Can one preserve one's identity and yet use a second language in intimate, professional, and cultural domains? The answer depends on how one interprets history. A pragmatist might respond affirmatively to both of these questions, and history does support such a response in the cases of West Africa, South Asia, and part of Southeast Asia. But, then, this is a controversial question, on which there are opposing views.[10]

Once national identity is associated with a second language, the question of preserving an external norm becomes difficult. We have seen this in the Nigerian novelist Chinua Achebe's attitude toward the Africanization of English, and in the Indian novelist Raja Rao's attitude toward the Indianization of English, and we find it in a Singaporean diplomat's attitude when he says:

> ... when one is abroad, in a bus or train or aeroplane and when one overhears some-one speaking, one can immediately say this is someone from Malaysia or Singapore. And I should hope that when I'm speaking abroad my countrymen will have no problem recognizing that I am a Singaporean. (Quoted in Tongue 1974:7–8.)

In the purists' view perhaps English is internationally in disarray, going through a process of decay. In reality, however, English is acquiring various international identities and thus acquiring multiple ownerships.

In the second-language varieties this acquisition of new identity sometimes occurs by design. In the foreign-language varieties, it is generally not so conscious. It is, however, difficult to say exactly when it is conscious and when it is unconscious. One has to accept the fact that humans have a way of blending the language with its functions, and thereby creating a new linguistic ecology. English has been going through this process since at least the seventeenth century. The reassurance of the British linguist J. R. Firth is still, therefore, very relevant and meaningful. He specifically addresses the question of international uses of English and says (Firth, 1956:97) that the study of English

> is so vast that it must be further circumscribed to make it at all manageable. To begin with, English is an international language in the Commonwealth, the Colonies and in America. International in the sense that English serves the American way of life and

might be called American, it serves the Indian way of life and has recently been declared an Indian language within the framework of the federal constitution. In another sense, it is international not only in Europe but in Asia and Africa, and serves various African ways of life and is increasingly the all-Asian language of politics. Secondly, and I say "secondly" advisedly, English is the key to what is described in a common cliche as "the British way of life."

These words are worthy of attention at a time when the interplay of language attitudes, especially concerning English, demands pragmatism and linguistic realism.

Notes

This chapter is based on "Institutionalized Second Language Varieties" in *The English Language Today*, edited by Sidney Greenbaum, Oxford and New York: Pergamon Press, Inc., 1985, pp. 211–226.

1. A detailed discussion of several aspects of the second-language varieties of English can be found in Smith, ed. 1981; Kachru, ed. 1982, and 1983a; and Pride, ed. 1982.
2. For references see S. N. Sridhar, 1982 and Kachru, 1983b.
3. See, for example, Gage and Ohannesian, 1974, which primarily gives the enrollment figures in school system, and Strevens, 1982. See also Kachru, 1981a.
4. See, for example, Heath, 1977 and 1980, Finegan, 1980, Baron, 1982.
5. Newman (1974 and 1976 (1980)) have already been discussed widely by the media. For attitudes toward non-native varieties, see, for example, Prator, 1968, and my response to him in chapter 6.
6. See Shaw, 1981. The survey was conducted "among final year Bachelor degree students in three locations: (1) Singapore, Republic of Singapore; (2) Hyderabad, India; (3) Bangkok, Thailand. The students in each group were from the fields of English literature and teaching, engineering, and business/commerce. 825 students from twelve universities and colleges participated in the study: 170 students from Singapore, 342 from India, and 313 from Thailand (108). The participants in the survey were asked to complete the sentence "I think that we should learn to speak English . . ." They had the following choices, (1) like the British; (2) like the Americans; (3) like the Australians; (4) in our own way; and (5) like educated non-native speakers from other countries (Shaw 1981:119). Table 5, as Shaw says (p. 120), ". . . compares the totals of the figures given for these two types of standards in the descriptions given by the students of the present English language situation as they see it, and their estimate of how they would like to see the situation develop."
7. For descriptions of such second-language varieties of English see, for example, Bailey and Görlach, eds. 1982; Kachru, ed. 1982 and 1983a, Pride, ed. 1982; and Smith, ed., 1981.
8. See Kachru, 1966 and later, collected in Kachru, 1983a. See also Kachru, ed. 1982, and Smith, ed. 1981.
9. These studies were specifically about South Asia and are discussed in Kachru, 1980c.
10. These questions have been discussed in detail in chapter 1. For a historical perspective on the attitudes toward American English and the language controversy, see, for example, Baron, 1982, Daniels, 1982, and Heath, 1977.

Chapter 3

A Nativized Variety: The South Asian Case

IN this chapter I shall use the term South Asian English to refer to the variety of English used in what has traditionally been called the Indian subcontinent.[1] The label *South Asian English*, unlike *English in South Asia*, suggests a parallelism with variety-oriented[2] terms such as *American English* or *British English* and implies a historical tradition and institutionalization, as well as distinct formal and functional characteristics. As an institutionalized variety, as discussed in chapter 2, South Asian English is distinguished from performance varieties which are used as foreign languages in highly restricted functions such as English is used in, for example, Japan and most of Europe.

In terms of language and cultures, the Indian subcontinent has several shared features, and on the basis of its shared linguistic features, South Asia has been defined as a "linguistic area" (see Masica, 1976). In political terms, however, South Asia is divided into the following countries: India (population 762.2 million), Bangladesh (101.5 million), Pakistan (99.2 million), Nepal (17.0 million), Sri Lanka (16.4 million), and Bhutan (1.4 million). The total population is 997.7 million, and of this; the largest number (76.3 percent) live in India, and the smallest (0.1 percent) live in Bhutan.[3] South Asia comprises about one-fifth of the total human population, and is culturally and linguistically pluralistic. The number of languages and dialects spoken in the region is very large, and the sociolinguistic situation is complex. Four major language families are represented: Indo-Aryan, Dravidian, Tibeto-Burman, and Munda. The two major families are Indo-Aryan and Dravidian.[4]

The Diffusion and Current Status of English

This history of British colonization of South Asia and the introduction of bilingualism in English in the region are closely linked. The initial document establishing the British contact with the Indian subcontinent was the Charter of December 31, 1600, granted by Queen Elizabeth I to some merchants of London who formed the East India Company. This charter granted them a monopoly on trade with India and the East and opened the region to British contact and domination. The introduction of bilingualism in English can be described as having three crucial phases.[5] Each phase is, in a sense, independent, and all three are important in understanding the diffusion and impact of English on South Asia.

The first phase—the missionary phase—was initiated around 1614 by Christian missionaries of various persuasions who volunteered to go to South Asia to proselytize. The second phase involved "local demand" and has been considered vital by some scholars who believe that the spread of English was the result of the demand of local people and their willingness to learn it. Chaudhuri ridicules the view that English "was imposed on a subject people by a set of foreign rulers for the sake of carrying on their alien government" (1976:89). The prominent spokesmen for English were Raja Rammohan Roy (1772–1833) and Rajunath Hari Navalkar (ca. 1770). Their aim was to persuade the East India Company to give instruction in English, since Sanskrit, Arabic, and the "Indian vernaculars" did not allow young Indians access to the scientific knowledge of the West. In a letter to Lord Amherst (1773–1857), Raja Rammohan Roy expressed disappointment in the establishment of Sanskrit schools in Calcutta and urged him to allocate funds for

> employing European gentlemen of talent and education to instruct the natives of India in mathematics, natural philosophy, chemistry, anatomy and other useful sciences, which the natives of Europe have carried to a degree of perfection that has raised them above the inhabitants of other parts of the world.

Roy's proposal set off a controversy about Indian educational policy that resulted in the third phase. This phase began after 1765 and resulted in controversy over the merits of different educational systems for India. Two principal groups were involved in the controversy: the anglicists and the orientalists. The anglicists included Charles Grant (1746–1823), Lord Moira (1754–1826), T. B. Macauley (1800–1859); and the spokesman for the orientalists was H. T. Prinsep (1792–1878). In the beginning, the colonial administrators did not agree on a simple education policy for the subcontinent, but by 1835, Prinsep and others who shared his views could not stop the far-reaching Minute of Macauley from passing, That Minute, cited on page 5, proclaimed the need to form a subculture in India which would consist of "a class of persons, Indians in blood and color, but English in taste, in opinion, in morals and in intellect". The Minute was given final approval by Lord William Bentick (1774–1839), and an official resolution was passed. This resolution is rightly considered epoch-making, and it eventually resulted in the diffusion of bilingualism in English on the Indian subcontinent.

The British Raj, or sovereignty (1765–1947), established English firmly as the medium of instruction and administration. The first three universities, modeled after British universities, were established in Bombay, Calcutta, and Madras in 1857. By the end of the century two more were added in Lahore (now in Pakistan) and Allahabad.[6]

Even after Macauley's Minute had been adopted, the debate about the medium of instruction continued in various commissions and subcommissions.[7] Now, after years of controversy and acrimony, Indians seem to have settled for what is known as the "three language formula." This formula was proposed in the 1960s with the pious hope that it would satisfy all three language pressure groups in India: the pro-English group, the pro-Hindi group, and the pro-regional-languages group. In short, this formula entails introducing English and the local regional language. It was expected that in the so-called Hindi area (the *madhya deśa* (Central India)) a Dravidian language would be introduced so that all the "school-going children" (to use an Indianism) throughout the country would have an equal language load. This formula was an attempt to use an "integrative approach" to India's language planning, but it has not been a success.

Language planning and the role and status of English in Bangladesh, Pakistan, Nepal, and Sri Lanka has not been much different from India. The literature on this topic for these countries, however, is not as profuse as that for India, but a number of studies are available to help in making a comparative study.[8]

In spite of debates and controversies about the position of English in South Asia, English has attained the status of an important intranational and international language in the area. A quantitative profile of South Asian English is not easy to provide, since figures for all the functions of English in all the regions are not available. The following figures, however, are illustrative, though in most cases these apply only to India.

In the five South Asian countries (excluding Bhutan), 24.4 million students are enrolled in English classes. The English-knowing population is distributed in practically every state of India. English newspapers are published in twenty-seven of the twenty-nine Indian states or union territories, and they command the highest circulation in terms of the total reading public (23 percent). The number of English-knowing bilinguals in South Asia is close to or larger than the number of speakers of several South Asian languages which have been recognized as "scheduled" languages—for example, Assamese (1.63 percent), Kannada (3.96 percent), Malayalam (4 percent), Oriya (3.62 percent), and Punjabi (3 percent). English is the state language of two states in eastern India: Meghalaya and Nagaland. There is a pan-South Asian reading public for English books, and in India, for example, the number of books published in English has been significant for a long time, increasing from 33 percent to 45 percent from 1969 to 1973. This percentage is higher than the percentage of books published in any other language in the area. In 1971, 74 percent of India's scientific journals and 83 per cent of the nonscientific journals were published in English. English continues to be the language of the legal system (especially that of higher courts), a major language in Parliament, and a preferred language in the universities and all-India competitive examinations for senior administrative, engineering, and foreign service positions. These examples are not exhaustive, but they certainly indicate the intranational functions of South Asian English.[9]

Varieties of South Asian English

My use of the term *South Asian English* is not to be understood as indicative of linguistic homogeneity in this variety nor of a uniform linguistic competence. It refers to several broad regional varieties such as Indian English, Lankan English and Pakistani English.

There are basically two subvarieties within educated South Asian English, each providing a continuum from Pidgin English or broken English on the one hand to educated (or standard) South Asian English.[10] Some speakers of educated South Asian English even aim at Received Pronunciation, but this goal is not always achieved in performance. Two parameters, which are not mutually exclusive, may be used to label these subvarieties: *contextual* and *acquisitional.* The contextual parameter refers to the use of categories derived from the South Asian context, for example, regional, ethnic, or occupational (see Kachru 1978b:482–84). The acquisitional parameter refers to the various linguistic performance levels acquired in the second language in a specific school system or educational setup. A tenth grade student in a rural high school does not have the same exposure to English as does, for example, a student in Colombo, Kathmandu, New Delhi, or Islamabad.

These parameters are crucial for the concept of the "cline of bilingualism."[11] The cline has three "measuring" points: the ambilingual point, the central point, and the zero point. On the basis of these three guiding points, further quantitative and attitudinal categorization is possible. The attitudinal labels such as *Babu English,*[12] *Butler English, Bearer English,*

Burger English, and *Kitchen English* refer to such categorization. The spectrum of variation is reflected in South Asian newspapers. On the one hand, highly localized newspapers—such as the *Poona Daily News* (Poona), *Kashmir Times* (Srinagar), and *The Rising Nepal* (Kathmandu)—are linguistically low on the cline. On the other, there are several national papers with an international circulation—for example, *The Statesman* (New Delhi), *Dawn* (Lahore), and *The Bangladesh Observer* (Dacca). On studying these, one is immediately struck by the range of presentation, language use, and content.

Speakers of South Asian English seem to recognize such variation within the standard (or educated) variety of their language. In my study of speakers of English from Indian universities, only 16 percent thought that Indian English constituted one uniform variety. Almost 35 percent indicated that the variability might be expressed by two to three distinct varieties, and nearly half felt that Indian English includes between four and ten varieties (see Kachru 1976:233–34, see chapter 6).

The subvarieties and registers are directly related to language function, and one must therefore consider the functions that English performs in the multilingual and multicultural context of South Asia. The importance of English and its continued use in South Asia have to be related to the complex ethnic and linguistic pluralism of this region. Each South Asian country is multilingual and multiethnic. In India there are as many as 1,652 languages and dialects, depending on whose figure one accepts (see Pattanayak, 1971).[13] The smaller South Asian countries, Nepal and Bhutan, also are multilingual. It was therefore convenient during the colonial period to use English as a "link" language, and that role of English has not changed in recent years. English has now acquired four major functions: instrumental, regulative, interpersonal, and innovative (or creative).[14] The instrumental function refers to the use of English as the medium of learning at various stages of education. As the language of the legal system and pan-Indian (or pan-South Asian) administration, English performs what might be called a regulative function. The most important role of English, however, is to provide a code of communication to linguistically and culturally diverse groups for interpersonal communication. In this capacity, English has aided regional and national mobility for a certain stratum of society. However, its use in this role also symbolizes elitism, prestige, and modernity, and the opponents of English point to this symbolism as one argument against the continued use of English (see chapter 1). The use of English has also resulted in the development of a significant body of South Asian English writing in various genres. This nativized, innovative (or creative) use of English will be discussed in a later section of this chapter.

"South-Asianness" at Formal Levels

There are three main factors which contribute to the distinct "South-Asianness" in South Asian English. First, English is primarily a second language in South Asia. A small fraction of the English-using population claims that English is their first language, but this fraction is so small that for the purpose of the present discussion it can be ignored. Most of the English users are at least bilinguals, and in a majority of cases it is even difficult to say which is their dominant language. However, all such users of English have a language repertoire in which English dominates in some functions and one or more South Asian language in others. "South-Asianness" within this group, then, is typified by features of transference.[15]

Second, English is an *acquired* language, and "South-Asianness" reflects the conditions under which it is acquired in various parts of the subcontinent. The introduction of English into the school curriculum varies from one country to another, and within a country it varies from one state to another. In acquiring English, a student is generally presented with, for example, an Indo-Aryan, a Dravidian, or a Munda model of English. The models may further by language-specific—Tamil English, Kashmiri English, Newari English, or Sinhala English. These models are not uniform, since they depend on the training, experience, and competence of the teacher. The number of schools, colleges, or universities where a native speaker of English teaches, or where technological aids are available, are negligible. Chaudhuri (1976:92) is therefore expressing the view of most South Asian users of English when he writes:

> It is my pride today that the English I write, whatever it might be—and I have my opinion of it—was not learnt from any Englishman, Scotsman, Irishman, or American in the flesh, though my debt to the great dead writers of English can never be repaid.

The third factor which contributes to the "South-Asianness" of South Asian English is the fact that English is taught through the written medium in South Asia. The curriculum does not make any special provision for spoken English. It is therefore natural that many features of "South-Asianness" in pronunciation are based on spelling (see Krishnamurti, 1978). Spoken models are exclusively Indian, and the written models are provided by the classics of English—mostly of the eighteenth and nineteenth centuries—which Indian graduate students relish.

Phonetics and Phonology

It would be impossible to provide here a detailed phonetic description of the total lectal range of South Asian English with its language-bound, area-bound, ethnic, and other subvarieties.[16] Therefore, I shall only enumerate some general characteristics of the sound system. These are mainly the features of what has been termed transparent South Asian English and, taken together, they may be used to identify a South Asian English speaker.

At the phonetic level we may identify these features on the basis of what I have earlier termed *series substitution, systemic differences, distributional differences,* and *prosodic differences.*[17] Series substitution involves, for example, the substitution of retroflex consonants for the alveolar series;

for example, [ṭ] and [ḍ] are substituted for English [t] and [d]. Systemic differences refer to the elements which constitute a phonological unit such as a syllable. In most of the South Asian languages consonant-vowel-consonant (CVC) morpheme structure is possible, as it is in English. One might then claim that this feature is shared among, say, Hindi-Urdu, Sinhalese, and Kashmiri. But this does not tell the whole story, since these languages (like most other South Asian languages) and English show differences in the elements which operated in the positions consonant, vowel, and consonant in the CVC structure. For example, South Asian language speakers do not use [f], [θ], or [ð], and they do not distinguish between the "dark" and "clear" varieties of [l]. The sounds [f], [θ], and [ð] are generally realized in South Asian English as [ph], [th], and [d] or [dh], respectively.

The identical consonant-vowel-consonant structure therefore does not pre-suppose that the inventory constituting the system is identical. Distributional differences entail a different type of transfer. A South Asian language may share items in vowel or consonant inventory, but the distribution of the item may not be identical.

The consonant clusters *sk, sl,* and *sp* are present in several South Asian languages, but do not occur in word initial position in, for example, Hindi-Urdu. Therefore there are differences in regional South Asian English pronunciation in the following lexical items: [ɪskul] *school,* [ɪsteʃan] *station,* [ɪspitʃ] *speech,* and [ɪsloth] *sloth.*[18]

Prosodic differences make South Asian English markedly distinctive, since transfer from syllable-timed South Asian languages results in a similar rhythm in place of the stress-timed rhythm of British English. Passé (1947) claims for Lankan English that it has comparatively weak stress (since stress—or force accent—is weak in Sinhalese and Tamil); no vowel reduction; and no distinction between strong and weak forms. What is true of Tamil speakers in Sri Lanka also applies to Tamil speakers in India. The stress pattern in northern Indian pronunciation is not significantly different from these Tamil-influenced varieties.

Grammar

The identification of grammatical characteristics of South Asian English inevitably leads to complexities. The attitude toward grammatical deviations is not identical to the attitude toward deviations in pronunciation. Since there has not been any serious attempt at codification of such grammatical characteristics, it is naturally difficult to distinguish a deviation from what may be considered a mistake. In grammar, therefore, the idealized norm continues to be a native prescriptive model. Perhaps the largest number of users of Fowler's *Modern English Usage* are in South Asia. South Asians are also addicts of Nesfield and Jespersen and read their grammars with delight. But in spite of such respect for linguistic authority, there are several characteristics of South Asian English which are productive and may be regarded as South Asian features. The characteristics presented here are only indicative of such tendencies, and they are not in any way codified. They also will not win general approval from a prescriptivist teacher. (For further discussion see Kachru, 1982c).

It has impressionistically been claimed that there is a tendency in South Asian English to use complex sentences which result in large-scale embeddings. One is inclined to trace this tendency to the preference of the educated South Asians for the *śiṣṭa* 'learned' style which is characteristic of literary style in South Asian languages. This trait is then transferred to South Asian English.

The transfer (or "interference") from the first languages also results in deviant constructions in, for example, interrogative sentences and the formation of tag questions. There is a tendency to form interrogative constructions without changing the position of subject and auxiliary items: *what you would like to read*? or *when you would like to come*?

In English, the structure of tag questions is composed of a statement and a tag attached to it. In such structures there is contrasting polarity; a positive main clause is followed by a negative tag and vice versa. In Hindi-Urdu, the parallel structure consists of a single clause with a postposed particle which is invariably *na*. Transfer thus results in South Asian English constructions such as *your are going tomorrow, isn't it*? and *he isn't going there, isn't it*?

Other differences in South Asian English are the result of the extension in selection restrictions in syntax and semantics as, for example, in the use of stative predicates. There are English verbs which are ungrammatical when used in the progressive form (*is having, seeing, knowing*). Therefore the following constructions, transferred from the first language of South Asian English bilinguals, are unacceptable to a native speaker of English:

> *Mohan is having two houses.*
> *Ram was knowing that he would come.*
> *I am understanding English better now.*

The use of articles in South Asian English has been discussed in detail with reference to Indian English. All three exponents of the article (i.e., definite, indefinite, and zero) are present in South Asian English, but their distribution is erratic. In his excellent studies on this topic, Dustoor has aptly classified South Asian (primarily Indian) use of the articles as "missing," "intrusive," "wrong," "usurping," and "dispossessed."

Reduplication of items belonging to various word classes is a common feature of South Asian English and is used for emphasis and to indicate continuation of a process. Raja Rao, for example, uses reduplication to create the effect of colloquial speech and to develop particular character types. Consider the following example from his short story "Javni": "With these very eyes, with these very eyes, I have seen the ghosts of more than a hundred young men and women, all killed by magic by magic . . ." (R. Rao 1978b:84). In this selection, Rao has used larger units for reduplication, but at other places he uses single lexical items: *hot, hot coffee, long, long hair*. The use of reduplication is also common in Pakistan, Sri Lanka, and

Nepal. Consider, for example, Lankan English *to go crying crying, small small pieces*, and *who and who came to the party*?[19]

Collocations

A South Asian English collocation may be defined as South Asian on the basis of its semantic or syntactic characteristics. Such collocations are the result of one or more of the following. Words or phrases of a South Asian language may be translated into South Asian English; *the confusion of caste* or *twice-born* are English translations of the Sanskrit *varṇa sankara* and *dvija*, respectively. In Lankan English the following formations entail such translations: *to buy and give, to jump and run, to run and come (home), to take and come* (Passé, 1947). In addition, there are formations which are extensions or analogies derived from English: *black money* on the analogy of *black market*. The most productive class consists of collocations which are formally nondeviant but are culture-bound, context-bound, or register-bound: *brother-anointing ceremony, co-brother-in-law, cow-worship, cousin-sister, rice-eating ceremony, nose-screw* "a decorative gold or silver ornament for the nose used by women", *military hotel* "a non-vegetarian restaurant."

Underlying regular syntactic processes are involved in forming such collocations. In one such productive syntactic process, a unit of higher rank is reduced to a lower rank. Thus, where a native speaker of English might use a clause or a nominal group, a South Asian English user prefers a formation with *modifier+head+(qualifier)* structure. Consider, for example, a preference for *welcome address* as opposed to *an address of welcome*, or for *England-returned* instead of *one who has been to England* (cf. *been-to* in African English used in the same sense). This regular tendency has been characterized as "phrase-mongering" (Goffin, 1934) and as "wrong compounding" (Whitworth, 1907). Passé considers such formations as "errors of expression that have become more or less fixed in Ceylon English and which the user would be startled and shocked to hear stigmatized as un-English" (1947, n. 4). Other such formations include *god-son* (Sanskrit, *deva-putra*), *Himalayan-blunder, nation-building*, and *dumb-millions*. Formations such as the following in Lankan English also fall in the same pattern: *to break rest, bull work*, and *to give a person bellyfull*.

Lexis

South Asian English is the only variety of non-native English in which there is a long and continuous tradition of lexicographical studies. This interest dates back to the nineteenth century, culminating in *Hobson-Jobson* (1886),[20] which has provided linguistic entertainment by its lexical explanations, ethnographic asides, apt etymological clues, and abundant citations to generations of administrators of the Raj, to Indophiles, and to Indologists.

In our discussion here, we are primarily concerned with two types of lexical items. One type comprises a comparatively small number of items, and the other a large lexical stock. The smaller group includes those lexical items which are shared with British English, and to a lesser degree with American and other native Englishes. A number of them have steadily made their way into the standard lexicons such as the *OED*, the Merriam-Webster dictionaries, and the *Random House Dictionary of the English Language*.[21]

In recent years, there has been a renewed interest in lexicographical research on South Asian English.[22] *The Little Oxford Dictionary* contains a twenty-nine-page "supplement" by R. A. Hawkins which lists about 1,500 Indian English lexical items, and in Nihalani, Tongue, and Hosali (1978) a considerable part of the book has been devoted to the usage of English in India (see Kachru, 1980c:186).

Single lexical items vary in their frequency of occurrence. They are essentially register-dependent and therefore are normally used when referring to contexts which are typically South Asian. If such references are aimed at an audience outside the region, it is normal to provide glossaries for them. Consider, for example, the following excerpts from newspapers.

> Dharmavati was chosen for Ragam, Tanam, and Pallavi. Singing with an abandon, M.S. set off the distinct character of the mode and followed with methodically improvised Pallavi. The swaraprastara was full of tightly knit figures. [*Daccan Herald*, 26 July 1977]

> Urad and moong fell sharply in the grain market here today on stockists offerings. Rice, jowar and arhar also followed suit, but barley forged ahead. [*Times of India*, 23 July 1977]

> Fish stalls in many small markets have nothing for sale. Rohu costs Rs 16 a kg. while bekti, parshe and tangra are priced between ... Hilsa, which is the most popular among the Bengalis in the rainy season. [*Statesman*, 17 August 1979]

> In Karachi Quran khawani and fateha was held at the Clifton residence of late [*sic*] Mr. Zulfikar Ali Bhutto to mark his "Chehlum" today. [*Pakistan Times*, 12 May 1979]

In South Asian English newspapers such lexical items are also used in captions or headings:

> Panchayat system upholds ideals of human rights [*Rising Nepal*, 17 December 1978; three columns]
> More subsidy for gobar gas plants [*Hindustan Times*, 5 July 1977; one column]
> Krishi bank branch needed [*Bangladesh Observer*, 21 June 1979; one column]
> Shariat courts for attack [*Dawn*, 12 March 1979; one column]
> Disbursement of zakat: law and order situation [*Dawn*, 14 March 1979; two columns]

The second type of lexical innovation, again very productive, is hybridized and contains at least one item from a South Asian language and one item from English: *janta meals, lathi charge, tiffin carrier*.[23] Hybrids may be subcategorized into two types on the basis of the constraints which apply to such formations: open-set items without grammatical constraints on the selection (*British sarkar* or *tonga-driver*)[24] and closed-system items involving bound morphemes and showing certain grammatical constraints:

-wala (vālā) in *policewala*; *-hood* in *brahminhood*; *-dom* in *cooliedom*; *-ism* in *goondaism.*[25] Some hybrid formations are semantic "reduplications"; an example is *lathi stick,* in which *lathi* (Hindustani) and *stick* (English) have identical meanings. Other such examples are *cotton kapas* and *curved kukri.*[26] A small number of formations were at first restricted to a specific area: *coconut paysam, jibba pocket,* and *potato bonda* began in the Dravidian area,[27] *yakka carriage* and *religious diwan* started as innovations in the Indo-Aryan area.[28]

Rhetorical and Functional Styles

In the cultural and linguistic network of South Asia, English is used as an additional communicative tool in a number of contexts. It is, therefore, natural that various linguistic devices are exploited to develop functional or communicative styles relevant to social, literary, and cultural contexts of South Asia. These devices are then organized into what speakers of South Asian English consider appropriate rhetorical styles. Appropriateness is determined by several factors, the native literary and cultural traditions being very important. Above all, the notion of a "proper" style in a particular context is derived from languages such as Sanskrit, Persian, and Arabic. In all these languages, stylistic embellishment is highly valued. These *native* rhetorical styles are then imposed on an "alien" language which results in functional and communicative varieties in South Asian English distinct from other Englishes. The reaction of native English speakers to such "deviant" communicative styles and rhetorical devices has not been one of acceptance or understanding, as exemplified by the use of attitudinally marked terms such as *Latinity, phrase-mongering, polite diction, moralistic tone,* or *bookishness.* Such labels, however meaningful, ignore the fact that in South Asian English the *text* and the *context* are nativized in order to make the text "meaningful" in new situations in which it functions. As standards of appropriateness and acceptance develop for discourse types in South Asian English, native norms emerge. One consequence of such acculturation for South Asian English is that the more culture-bound it becomes, the more distinct it grows from other varieties of English (see Kachru 1965:409; see also chapter 10).

The range of South Asian English text types is large. The texts vary primarily on two dimensions: their contextual range and acquisitional range. For each context, texts may be differentiated on the basis of the English used in them, ranging from educated South Asian English to Pidgin English.

The following examples illustrate some typical South Asian English functional texts. I will first consider matrimonial advertisements, since these provide an example of highly contextualized English lexical items with semantic nativization in reference to the caste, color, region, and sub-caste (see also Mehrotra 1975). I have discussed this aspect of non-native Englishes in more detail elsewhere (see Kachru, 1982b).

Well-educated settled Kayastha boy around 28 for Srivastava M.A. Wheatish fair slim girl. [*Pioneer*, 31 December 1978]

Wanted suitable match for fair-complexioned, good looking Christian girl (Protestant) knowing ... educated Christian (Protestant) youths to apply. [*National Herald*, 31 December 1978]

Wanted well-settled bridegroom for a Kerala fair, graduate Baradwaja gotram, Astasastram girl ... Subsect no bar. Send horoscope and details. [*Hindu*, 1 July 1979]

Non-Koundanya well qualified prospective bridegroom below 20 for graduate Iyengar girl, daughter of engineer. Mirugaserusham. No. dosham. Average complexion. Reply with horoscope. [*Hindu*, 1 July 1979]

Match for my younger son Khanna. Khatri noble family ... girl main consideration of respectable family. Highly educated, homely, gracefully [*sic*.], attractive, sweet tempered, smart, fluent English, well-versed in household, cooking, tailoring. Talented in fine arts, crafts, painting, music and driving. [*Hindustan Times*, 20 May 1979]

Announcements of deaths are just as culture-specific. The *Hindustan Times*, for example, announces "the sad demise" or "the sudden and untimely demise of" persons who have "left for heavenly abode," adding that there will be "kirtan and ardasa for the peace of the departed soul" or that a "uthaoni ceremony will take place on" a specified day.[29] If the dead person is a Muslim, "his soyem Fateha will be solemnized" and "all the friends and relatives are requested to attend the Fateha prayers" (*Dawn*, 14 March 1979). These are specimens of highly restricted culture-dependent uses of a non-native language.

Personal letters in South Asian English often exemplify transfer of rhetorical style. The structure of such letters involve not only the "etiquette" of the first language, but also re-creation of the situation from one's own culture into another language. These letters are often read by users of native Englishes with great amusement, and often the intent of the letter is misunderstood. For example, the relationship in a letter is established by phatic communion, as in the following:

I am quite well here hoping the same for you by the virtue of mighty god. I always pray to God for your good health, wealth and prosperity. [*Tribune*, 22 November 1978]

Typically South Asian functional styles will be made clearer by the following three Indian English texts, which represent three distinct register types. The first is an example of Indian legal language (from Hyderabad) and is taken from what Indians call a "surety bond":

Know all men by these presents that _____ s/o _____ resident of H. no. _____ in the District of Hyderabad at present employed as a permanent _____ in the Department of _____ (hereinafter called the surety) bind myself firmly to the Registrar, Osmania University (hereinafter called "the Osmania University" which expression shall unless excluded by or repugnant to the subject or context include his successors in office and assigns) in the sum of Rs _____ (Rupees _____ only), to be paid to the Osmania University for which payment to be and truely made I hereby bind myself, my heirs, executors, administrators and representatives firmly by these presents and witness my hands this _____ day of _____ 1980.

Legal language in Indian English has a shared characteristic with that of other Englishes in the sense that it is practically unintelligible to the layman.

The second specimen, a letter published in the *Indian Express* (Madurai, 19 March 1962), is—according to Dustoor (1968:122)—an "average" specimen of "English as written in India today":

> Sir—I am one of those poor devotees who are touched on the raw by the way the police handled the crowd at the Krithigai festival in Triuvannamalai. I have visited many pilgrim centres in the North as well as South during festival times, but nowhere have I witnessed such a scene.
>
> The huge temple gates at the foothill are kept open till 5:30 p.m. and whoever comes after that has to wait at the entrance. After the lights are lit at the hilltop the doors are flung open and the crowds from inside and outside the temple dash against each other in the most disorderly fashion. Neither the police nor the temple authorities had made any arrangements for separate entrance and exit of the devotees and being unable to control the crowd, the police began to lathi-charge without any warning.
>
> It was a terrible scene to witness the devotees seeking dharsan of the Lord being meted out a raw deal at the hands of the police. It is most unbecoming of both the police and the devasthanam not to have made any proper arrangements. [N. Rangaswami]

The third specimen is from the administrative register still in use by the Indian bureaucracy:

> H. E.'s P. A. has written D. O. to the A. S. P. about the question of T. A.'s. The D. C. himself will visit the S. D. O. P. W. D. today at 10 A. M. S. T.

Such profusion of "initialisms" in administrative language has not changed since Goffin (1934) first noticed it. The letter intends to convey the following message:

> His Excellency's Personal Assistant has written a demi-official letter to the Assistant Superintendent of Police about the question of Travelling Allowances. The Deputy Commissioner himself will visit the Sub-Divisional Officer of the Public Works Department today at 10 a.m. Standard Time.

South Asian English Literature

A wide range of stylistic experimentation is found in creative writing in South Asian English, and one's understanding of South Asian English will be limited without considering its large and growing body of literature.[30] Many studies during the last decade have overemphasized either the linguistic or literary aspect of South Asian English. This artificial dichotomy prevents one from viewing South Asian English as a living language functioning as any other nativized language in the South Asian socio-linguistic context. An integrative approach provides a more realistic view of the relationship of language and its use. Such an approach is desirable for South Asian English, since, as an institutionalized variety of English, it has developed a *local* body of writing in various literary genres. In South Asia, English, and to a lesser degree Sanskrit, are the only two pan-South

Asian languages. In functional terms Sanskrit is, of course, highly restricted and therefore does not compare favorably with the present functional range of English. English has provided an important pan-South Asian link language, and South Asian English writing is the only writing which has some market (and a reading public, however restricted) in the whole of the subcontinent and outside of it. South Asian English writers still stand out in the literary mosaic of South Asia, since they have more than their share of enthusiastic supporters and equally vocal critics.

Among the South Asian countries, the most active, productive and well-discussed group of writers in English is in India. I will therefore discuss South Asian English writing with a focus on India; however, selected references will be provided for other countries, especially Sri Lanka and Pakistan.[31]

"South Asian English literature" refers to the fast-developing body of literature written by South Asians who use English primarily as a second language. Their writing is now recognized as one of many manifestations of South Asian creative talent and literary aspirations. What Iyengar says about India is certainly true of Sri Lanka and Pakistan:

> Indian writing in English is but one of the voices in which India speaks. It is a new voice, no doubt, but it is *as much Indian as the others.* [Emphasis added, Iyengar, 1962:3]

That this voice is "as much Indian as others" has upset the nationalistic sensibilities of some Indians and has therefore resulted in great polemics. The study of such polemical writing is useful for understanding the relationship between language and nationalism, language and ethnicity, and language and development.[32]

The short history of South Asian writing in English, particularly that of Indian writing in English,[33] has been one of controversy and search for identity (see Lal, 1969:i–xliv). Two early writers, both from Bengal, are Kashiprasad Ghosh and Sochee Chunder Dutt. Ghosh's collection, *The Shair and Other Poems*, was published in 1830 and is considered "the earliest work of Indian poetry in English to have been reviewed in England and which, presumably, is the earliest extant work of its kind" (Bose, 1968:31). In the *New Monthly Magazine* (June 1831), published in England, Ghosh received the following commendatory notice:

> Our new poet, Kasiprasad Ghosh [*sic.*] describes himself as the "first Hindoo who has ventured to publish a volume of English poems." ... The Shair (the Persian term for minstrel) is a poem of considerable length and of varied merit.... A great deal of poetical feeling may be discerned in parts of the poem, richness of imagery, and elegance of language, the whole requiring polish and cultivation, but evincing considerable natural powers, and exciting throughout a strong feeling of interest for the writer. [Quoted by Bose, 1968:3]

The first fiction in English by an Indian writer was published by Sochee Chunder Dutt in 1845. In him we have one of the first creative writers who "translated Indian terms instead of their pure English equivalents to maintain the Indian local color as well as to add a distinct Indian flavour" (Sarma, 1978:329).

A few years after Dutt, another Bengali, Lal Behari Day, excelled his predecessor in Indianizing the English in his novels. The following passage is a stylistic precursor of, for example, Mulk Raj Anand or Khushwant Singh:

> "Come in," said Badan, and jumped out of the verandah towards the door. "Come in, Acharya Mahasaya; this is an auspicious day when the door of my house has been blessed with the dust of your honour's feet. Gayaram, fetch an *asan* (a small carpet) for the Acharya Mahasaya to sit on." [Day, 1913:48; quoted by Sarma, 1978:330]

Day is apologetic for making his Bengali peasants speak "better English than most uneducated English peasants" in 1874, and explains to his "gentle reader":

> Gentle reader, allow me here to make one remark. You perceive that Badan and Alanga speak better English than most uneducated English peasants; they speak almost like educated ladies and gentlemen, without any provincialisms. But how could I have avoided this defect in my history? If I had translated their talk into the Somerset or the Yorkshire dialect, I should have turned them into English, and not Bengali, peasants. You will, therefore, please overlook this grave though unavoidable fault in this authentic narrative. [Day, 1913:61; quoted by Sarma, 1978:332]

The predicament of creating a style range in South Asian English fiction continues even now.

The initial attempts at creative writing in South Asian English not only gave rise to literary traditions but gradually developed a significant body of writing. Among the earlier poets to achieve an international reputation were Aurobindo Ghosh (1872–1950), Manmohan Ghosh (1869–1924), Toru Dutt (1859–77), and Sarojini Naidu (1879–1949). The use of a colonial, "alien" language for expressing local sensibility and native contexts has been suspect, and even the integrity of such South Asian writers has been challenged. But, in spite of suspicion, polemical controversies, and a restricted although growing reading public, the body of South Asian English writing has been steadily increasing in poetry,[34] fiction,[35] literary criticism,[36] and drama.[37]

Political writing is another important genre with a tradition dating back to Rammohan Roy (1772–1833). In chapter 1 I have mentioned that English continued to be a medium which various political leaders used for national awakening and the freedom struggle. It was used effectively during the struggle against colonialism and continues to be used now for any issue which has an "all-India" or "pan-South Asian" implication. Such writers include Mohandas K. Gandhi (1869–1948), Bal Gangadhar Tilak (1856–1920), Mohammed Ali Jinnah (1876–1948), Jawaharlal Nehru (1889–1964), and C. Rajagopalachariar (1879–1972).

The story of South Asian English writers in the 1970s is much different from what it was in the 1930s—both in the attitude toward them and in their impact. In 1934 Singh was not only indifferent to the Indian writers in English, but also rather apologetic about their performance:

> Indian writers and story-tellers, on the whole, do not compare favourably with Anglo-Indian writers. That they write in a foreign tongue is a serious handicap in itself. Then few of them possess any knowledge of the art of fiction. . . . In plot construction they are weak, and in characterization weaker still. [Singh, 1934:309]

Contrast this with an observation made exactly thirty years later by Gokak, a critic, creative writer, and an eminent educationist:

> Indo-Anglian [Indian English] writing is direct and spontaneous,—like creative writing in any other language. It is conditioned in many ways by the peculiar circumstances of its birth and growth. . . . Gordon Bottomley is said to have described typical Indo-Anglian poetry as "Matthew Arnold in a *sari.*" He should rather have referred to it as Shakuntala in skirts. [Gokak, 1964:162]

Why do educated South Asians write in English when their own languages provide fine means of expression with a rich literary tradition? The question is naturally most vocally asked by those South Asians who are creative writers in their first languages and has been debated in South Asia with various degrees of intensity at literary and political forums. One such debate of interest to sociolinguists, language scholars, and literary critics is presented by Lal in his *Modern Indian Poetry in English.* In this 594-page anthology of 132 (mostly post-1947) "practising poets," we have specimens of "two decades of revolt, experimentation, and consolidation by the younger poets" (1969:iii). The poets' responses to the following questions are also included in the anthology: (1) What are the circumstances that led to your using the English language for the purpose of writing poetry? and (2) Do you think English is one of the Indian languages? I shall consider the answers of some of the more prominent and esablished poets. They have understandably answered these questions with varying degrees of seriousness and detail. A. K. Ramanujan does not think that it is a matter of controversy "whether people can, will, or should write in a particular language." In his view, "people who write (in a particular language) don't have a choice in the matter" (Lal, 1969:444–45). For Kamala Das, "Why in English?" is a "silly" question: "English being the most familiar, we use it. That is all." And she rightly adds, "The language one employs is not important. What is important is the thought contained in the words" (Lal, 1969:171). Kamala Das previously articulated her feelings about her choice of language in an often-quoted poem:

> . . . I am Indian, very brown, born in
> Malabar, I speak three languages, write in
> Two, dream in one. Don't write in English, they said.
> English is not your mother-tongue. Why not leave
> Me alone, critics, friends, visiting cousins,
> Every one of you? Why not let me speak in
> Any language I like? The language I speak
> Becomes mine, its distortions, its queerness
> All mine, mine alone. It is half English, half
> Indian, funny perhaps, but it is honest,
> It is as human as I am human, don't
> You see? It voices my joys, my longings, my

Hopes, and it is useful to me as cawing
Is to crows or roaring to the lions, it
Is human speech, the speech of the mind that is
Here and not there, a mind that sees and hears and
Is aware. . . .

[Das, 1973:128]

More than South Asian English poetry, fiction from this region demonstrates the formal and functional nativization of the English language, Raja Rao's fiction provides a good example of such nativization. He has been successful in transferring the "rhythm" of his mother tongue—Kannada—into his English, and the devices he uses are much more subtle than the linguistic devices used by Mulk Raj Anand, Khushwant Singh, and others. Consider the following passage from his novel, *Kanthapura*:

> The day rose into the air and with it rose the dust of the morning, and the carts began to creak round the bulging rocks and the coppery peaks, and the sun fell into the river and pierced it to the pebbles, while the carts rolled on and on, fair carts of the Kanthapura fair—fair carts that came from Maddur and Tippur and Santur and Kuppur with chilies and coconut, rice and ragi, cloth, tamarind, butter and oil, bangles and kumkum, little pictures of Rama and Krishna and Sankara and the Mahatma, little dolls for the youngest, little kites for the elder, and little chess pieces for the old—carts rolled by the Sampur knoll and down into the valley of the Tippur stream, then rose again and groaned. . . . [1963:39]

The novelist Mulk Raj Anand (among others) "transcreates" native situations into English by using native lexical items, hybridization, new collocations, and contextually marked translations of Punjabi or Hindi-Urdu clauses and sentences. Although Anand's Punjabi characters (e.g., a coolie, an untouchable, and a washerman) would be distinguished from one another by their dialects, style ranges, and diction in Punjabi, they lose these distinguishing features in the translation to South Asian English. Because of this uniformity and because such individuals do not actually speak English, Anand's characters sound artificial, a little unreal, and almost comic to an Indian, but that is the price one pays for using an "alien" language in contexts in which it does not ordinarily function. Consider the following as a typical example of Anand's stylistic device:

> "Ari, you bitch! Do you take me for a buffoon? What are you laughing at, slut? Aren't you ashamed of showing your teeth to me in the presence of men, you prostitute?" shouted Gulabo, and she looked towards the old man and the little boys who were of the company.
>
> Sohini now realized that the woman was angry. "But I haven't done anything to annoy her," she reflected. "She herself began it all and is abusing me right and left. I didn't pick the quarrel. I have more cause to be angry than she has!"
>
> "Bitch, why don't you speak! Prostitute, why don't you answer me?" Gulabo insisted.
>
> "Please don't abuse me," the girl said, "I haven't said anything to you."
>
> "You annoy me with your silence, you illegally begotten! You eater of dung and drinker of urine! You bitch of a sweeper woman! I will show you how to insult one old enough to be your mother." And she rose with upraised arm and rushed at Sohini.
>
> Waziro, the weaver's wife, ran after her and caught her just before she had time to hit the sweeper girl.
>
> "Be calm, be calm; you must not do that," she said as she dragged Gulabo back to her seat. "No, you must not do that." [Anand, 1935:37]

The Muslim novelist Ahmed Ali provides an example of such contextualization in a typical middle-class Muslim family:

> Dilchain had, in the meantime, discovered a small earthen doll buried under the oven
> when she was cleaning it one day. She went and showed it to Begam Kalim and Begam
> Habib.
> "It is the effect of witchcraft," she said, "which is responsible for Mian's illness."
> The tender hearts of the women were filled with dread. They sent Dilchain to
> Aakhoonji Saheb, who wrote verses from the Koran on seven snow-white plates in
> saffron water. The plates were to be washed with a little water, and the water from one
> plate was to be taken for three days, a drop in the morning. . . .
> But strange things happened inside the zenana. A pot full of ill-omened things came
> flying in the air and struck against the bare trunk of the date palm whose leaves had all
> fallen. Another day some cooked cereal was found lying under the henna tree. . . .
> Poor women from the neighbourhood came, fluttering their burqas and dragging
> their slippers under them, and sympathized. . . .
> Thus they came and sympathized and suggested cures and medicines. One said to
> Begam Habib:
> "You must go to the tomb of Hazrat Mahboob Elahi and pray. . . ."
> "You must give him water from the well at Hazrat Nizamuddin's tomb," another
> suggested. "It has magical qualities and has worked miracles. . . ." [Ali, 1966:278–79]

Anthologies of South Asian poetry include a wide range of styles and
genres (see Gokak, 1970 and Parthasarathy, ed. 1976). The following
poets, among others, have not only contributed to anthologies but have
also published one or more individual collections in South Asia or the
West: Keki N. Daruwalla (born 1937). Kamala Das (born 1934), Nissim
Ezekiel (born 1924), Shiv K. Kumar (born 1921), P. Lal (born 1931), R.
Parthasarathy (born 1934), and A. K. Ramanujan (born 1929). There are
more than half a dozen novelists in South Asia who have created a small
but slowly increasing reading public for themselves, both nationally and
internationally.[38] South Asian English writing is now hesitatingly but
definitely being recognized as part of the indigenous literary traditions in
South Asia. It is one of the important voices in which South Asian creative
writers express themselves. This body of writing has over the years developed an interested reading public outside South Asia, and it constitutes an
important part of what is termed "Commonwealth writing in English" or
"world writing in English."

Attitudes Toward South Asian English

The labels which speakers of native Englishes attach to non-native
Englishes are often attitudinally revealing. Such labels have been applied
to, for example, Indian English (as in the case of Prator, 1968 discussed
in chapter 6) and to particular South Asianisms.[39] Equally interesting,
however, are the attitudes of South Asian English users toward their own
variety of English. Have South Asian English users accepted what has
been termed the "ecological validity" of their local or native English?

In South Asia, there has been a traditional conflict between linguistic
behavior and linguistic norm. The hypothetical norm continues to be

British English, especially RP, although this norm is seldom available and even more seldom attained. Actual linguistic behavior shows use of characteristic South Asian English features varying according to the competence of the user.

In chapter 2 I have provided tables, based on a survey, to show the attitude of students majoring in English, and of their teachers toward various models of English (see Tables 1–5 on pp. 22–24). In the study of langauge attitudes, "self labeling" of one's variety provides an important indication about the attitude of a user of a variety toward other varieties. This survey shows that the graduate students (majoring in English) used the following "identity-marking" terms for their own varieties of English: Indian English, 56 percent; British English, 30 percent; American English, 3 percent. The rest used labels such as "mixture of all three," "I don't know," and "good English."

South Asian English and Other Englishes

In presenting a variety-oriented description, one tends to focus on the differences between the variety in question and other native (or non-native) varieties. The differences at various linguistic levels are part of each variety and have resulted in variety-specific labels such as *Americanisms, Australianisms, Canadianisms,* or *Indianisms.* On the other hand, the non-shared differences in the non-native Englishes have either been viewed pedagogically with reference to second-language acquisition or in a pejorative sense.

Little research has been done on the shared features among the non-native Englishes—for example, African English, South Asian or Southeast Asian English. A number of such productive and shared processes in grammar, lexis, and in communicative and functional styles are present in several non-native Englishes, specifically in African and South Asian English (see Richards 1979). The reasons for linguistic and contextual nativization of English in these two areas also seem to be identical. A few examples intended to illustrate the point follow.

The deviant use of such function words as definite and indefinite articles is shared by several non-native Englishes.[40] In grammar, several tendencies—especially in the uses of the verb phrase—are common to African, South Asian, and Southeast Asian English. One feature common to African English and South Asian English, for example, is what has been called "yes-no confusion" (see Kachru, 1969:652–53): the response of *no* where a native speaker would expect *yes.* In several languages (e.g., African, South Asian, Russian, and Japanese), the choice of *yes* or *no* in response to a question depends on the *form* of the question and the *facts* of the situation. If the form and the facts have the same polarity (both positive or both negative), the answer is positive. If the polarity is not the same, (i.e., if the question is in the positive and the situation is in the negative), the answer is negative (and vice versa). In standard English, on the other hand, the response *yes* or *no* depends only on the facts of the situation: in a positive situation, the answer is *yes*; in a negative situation the answer is *no*. (For illustrations from African English see Bokamba, 1982:84).

Lexis, collocations, and semantic extension and restrictions in the non-native Englishes are even more similar in the underlying processes they use and in the motivations for using them. The goal of such nativization is to contextualize the language.

Two other similarities between South Asian and African English deserve mention here. The first refers to what constitutes a "grand" style in South Asian English. "Appropriateness" in various rhetorical and communicative styles is conditioned by the native literary traditions and cultures. The African and South Asian concepts of style therefore conflict with the current western notion of "good" style. In Africa, as Sey says, "flamboyance of English prose style is generally admired" (Sey, 1973:7). The speaker or writer

> who possesses this style is referred to in the vernaculars in such terms as 'the learned scholar who, from his deep mine of linguistic excellence, digs up on suitable occasions English expressions of grandeur, depth and sweetness.' [1973:7]

The same is true of South Asia. Gokak observes that those

> who are true to Indian thought and vision cannot escape the Indian flavour even when they write in English. Their style is, in a great measure, conditioned by the learned vocabulary of the subject on which they write,—philosophy, sociology, literary criticism and the like. Even when they write fiction, they depend, for their effect, on picturesque Indian phrases and their equivalents in English. [1964:162–63]

The "Indianized" style is found in the creative writing of, among others, Mulk Raj Anand, Raja Rao, and G. V. Desani. Anand has argued that the King's English is inadequate for an Indian writer (Anand, 1948). But Raja Rao is emphatic that "English is not really an alien language to us": his often quoted words are worth quoting here again:

> It is the language of our intellectual make-up—like Sanskrit or Persian was before—but not of our emotional make-up. . . . We cannot write like the English. We should not. We cannot write only as Indians. We have grown to look at the large world as part of us. Our method of expression therefore has to be a dialect which will some day prove to be as distinctive and colorful as the Irish or the American. Time alone will justify it. [1963:vii]

Rao's position is identical to the position of esteemed African writer Chinua Achebe (1965), which I have quoted in chapter 1 (p. 11).

The second characteristic which cuts across non-native Englishes is the development of code-mixed varieties of English. Code mixing is a result of language contact and code switching and has to be distinguished from lexical borrowing. By code mixing I mean the use of one or more languages for consistent transfer of linguistic units from one language into another which results in a new restricted—or not-so-restricted—code of linguistic interaction (see Kachru, 1978c; see also chapter 4).

The implications of code mixing are important from the point of view of language attitude, elitism, and language change.[41] The code-mixed varieties of English are part of the verbal repertoire of the non-native users of English and play an important role functionally and formally in various contexts. The process of mixing is not restricted to one unit, but ranges from lexical items to full sentences and embedding of idioms from English. There are various motivations for code mixing with English, the main ones being role identification, register identification, elucidation, status indication and elitism.

The study of such cross-variety features of non-native Englishes is of both theoretical and pedagogical interest. There are at least three areas of research on which such studies may throw some light: second-language acquisition, the nativization of English and the processes used for it, and the impact of English on native languages and literatures. A number of these points are discussed in detail with illustrations in the following chapter.

Conclusion

In this chapter the characteristics of South Asian English have been related to the linguistic and cultural aspects of the South Asian countries. In spite of the apparently overwhelming complexity of linguistic and cultural pluralism and varied political systems, there is an underlying linguistic and cultural unity in the region and, as shown in this chapter, it reflects in the use of English, too.

The growing body of South Asian writing in English has been considered here as an integral part of the literary tradition of the region—native and non-native. Given the shared range of features and styles, it is not surprising that two prominent creative writers from two separate continents—one African and the other Indian—have almost identical attitudes toward English and its nativization. The West African novelist Chinua Achebe, as stated in chapter 1 (p. 11), asserts that he wants English to express his African experience. In order to use English in African contexts, Achebe is willing to alter the English language to suit the "African surroundings" (1965:222), and rightly feels that the language will be able to carry the "weight" of his African experience. In chapter 2 (p. 30) I have cited the position of Indian novelist R. K. Narayan who clearly emphasizes that "we are not attempting to write Anglo-Saxon English" (1965:123).

As this chapter has demonstrated, the English language is already successfully carrying the "weight" of the South Asian "experience" which manifests itself in the South Asianization of its form and functions.

Notes

This chapter is a revised version of "South Asian English" in *English as a World*

Language, edited by Richard W. Bailey and Manfred Görlach, Ann Arbor, MI: The University of Michigan Press, 1984, pp. 353–383.

1. This chapter draws heavily on my earlier research on this topic, especially from Kachru, 1965, 1966, 1969, and 1978b (a revised and updated version of the 1969 article). There is a large body of scholarly and popular literature on various aspects of South Asian English, especially Indian English. Readers are encouraged to consult the following bibliograhies for references pertaining to specific areas of South Asian English: Aggarwal, 1981; Kachru, 1978b pp. 523–37, and 1983a; Central Institute of English and Foreign Languages 1972. Terms such as *rank, register, system,* and *structure* have been used in systemic linguistics and are explained in Kachru, 1983a.
2. The term *variety* has been used in the same sense in which it is used in Kachru, 1965, 1966, 1969, and 1978b. See also Kachru, 1983a.
3. These figures are taken from 1985 World Population Data Sheet: Population Reference Bureau, Inc. Washington DC.
4. For details, see Pattanayak, 1971.
5. For references on the history of English in South Asia, see Aggarwal, 1982 and Kachru, 1983a.
6. Pakistan was part of undivided India until 1947, and Bangladesh was part of Pakistan until March 1971, when it was proclaimed an independent state.
7. There is a large body of literature supporting and opposing the use of English in present and future language planning in South Asia. For detailed bibliographical references, see Aggarwal, 1982, Kachru, 1978b:514–21, and 1983a.
8. See, for example, for Nepal: Kansakar, 1977 and Malla, 1977: for Pakistan: Dil, 1966: for Sri Lanka: Kandiah, 1964.
9. See also Kachru, 1980b, Mehrotra, 1977, and Sridhar, 1979 and 1982a. As we know, it is difficult to define *bilingual person.* Therefore, one cannot provide a clear definition of an "English-knowing bilingual" in South Asia. One may tentatively define such a person as one who can use English (more or less) effectively in a situation. The intelligibility with a native speaker of English is not necessarily the main criterion. The educational level can also provide some indication about the competence of a person (see Kachru, 1978b:488–89). It is generally believed that South Asia has an English-knowing population of approximately 3 percent. This figure naturally varies with area and country. Sri Lanka has a higher percentage than other parts of South Asia. At present no reliable statistics are available. (For further discussion see Kachru, 1983a, chapter 1).
10. The term *Indian English* has been used to refer to the educated variety in several earlier studies; see Kachru, 1983a, Masica and Dave, 1972; Passé, 1947. Passé says, "For practical and other reasons the almost certain course will be the teaching of the Ceylonese [Sri Lankan] variety of 'Modified Standard' English" (p. 34).

    Note that almost a century ago, when English was a highly restricted *foreign* (not *second*) language in India, the German scholar Hugo Schuchardt developed a cline of "Indo-Englishes" ([1891] 1980). I am grateful to Glenn Gilbert for bringing this valuable work to my attention in 1978.
11. This term was first used in this sense with reference to Indian English by Kachru, 1961, and further explained in Kachru, 1965, pp. 393–96 and 1978b, pp. 485–86.
12. The term *babu* (Hindi-Urdu *bābū*) is mainly used for clerks who have reasonable competence in various administrative registers of South Asian English. (For full discussion see Kachru, 1981c).
13. The "family affiliation" of these languages is as follows: unclassified, 601; Indo-Aryan, 532; Austric, 53; Dravidian, 148; and Tibeto-Chinese, 227. This list also includes nine languages of Sikkim. See Pattanayak, 1971, p. v. Note that the itemized figures given in Pattanavak do not add up to the total figure of 1,652.
14. I have borrowed these terms from Basil Bernstein (1971) but have used these in a slightly different sense from his. See also Kachru, 1981c.
15. The term *transference* is used in the sense of *interference* or *transfer* from the mother tongue (L_1) to an additional language (L_2), in this case L_1 being a South Asian

language, and L$_2$ English. It is interesting that the transplanted varieties of South Asian English continue to show such transference even in places such as South Africa. In South Africa (see Lanham, 1978:24–25), "the Indian South African needs an Indian ... language for religious ritual—and that not always—and possibly for communication with his elders, but English for all the other needs of his daily life. His children are taught in the English medium, his newspapers are printed in English, his legal affairs are conducted in English; if Hindi speaking, he converses with his Tamil- or Gujarati-speaking neighbour in English, and in his employment he is utterly dependent on English."

It is claimed that in pronunciation South African Indian English has "many of the features which mark general Indian English of India ... South African Indian English is further marked by peculiarities of grammar, vocabulary, idiom and turn of phrase, many with an obvious source in Indian languages" (Lanham, 1978:24–25; see Bughwan, 1970).

16. A selected list of such studies is given in Kachru, 1978b:523–37.
17. See Dustoor, 1968, especially pp. 180–263, and Kachru, 1978b.
18. This statement applies primarily to the South Asian English speakers whose first language is Hindi-Urdu.
19. See Passé, 1947 and Kachru, 1978b:502–3.
20. See Yule and Burnell [1886] 1968. The phrase *Hobson-Jobson* "... may be taken as a typical one of the most highly assimilated class of Anglo-Indian *argot*, and we have ventured to borrow from it a concise alternative title for this glossary" (1968:419).
21. A detailed story of South Asian borrowings in South Asian English and native varieties of English is given in Kachru, 1975 and G. Rao, 1954. (See also Kachru, 1983a, especially chapters 5 and 6). According to the following sources, the extent of South Asian lexical items in English varies from 188 items to 26,000 items depending on the size and focus of a dictionary: (1) Fennell (1892:xi) lists 399 words. These are divided among Hindoo [sic.] (336), Sanskrit (32), and Dravidian (31). (2) The *Oxford English Dictionary* includes 900 words of South Asian origin. This number does not include many thousands of derivatives from these words. (3) Wilson ([1855] 1940) lists 26,000 words. (4) Serjeantson (1935:220–60) lists 188 words. The *Random House Dictionary of the English Language* includes over two hundred words of Indian origin. The largest group involves the nonshared items. They are nonshared in the sense that they belong to South Asian English registers (e.g., those of agriculture, caste, or rituals), and are therefore culture-bound. Wilson is correct in his observation about such items:

> Ryot and Ryotwar, for instance, suggest more precise and positive notions in connection with the subject of the land revenue in the South of India, than would be conveyed by cultivator, or peasant, or agriculturalist, or by an agreement for rent or revenue with the individual members of the agricultural classes. [(1855) 1940:1]

22. For a detailed discussion of the history of the dictionaries of South Asian English see Kachru, 1973c and 1980c (revised versions in Kachru, 1983a, chapters 5 and 6).
23. *janta* "the people, the masses". *lathi* "long iron-bound stick, baton" (used to control a mob, usually by police); *tiffin* "snack, light meal".
24. *sarkar* "government"; *tonga* "two-wheeled horse-drawn open carriage".
25. *vala*, used as an agentive suffix in Hindi-Urdu; *coolie* "hired labor"; *goonda* "a hooligan, a rowdy person".
26. *kapas* "cotton"; *kukri* "curved".
27. *paysam* "pudding" (a dish made of coconut); *jibba* "loose shirt"; *bonda* "savory fritters".
28. *yakka* "pony-trap"; *diwan* "religious recitation common among the Sikhs".
29. See the *Hindustan Times*, 20 May 1979; 20 June 1979; 28 June 1979; and 30 June 1979.

30. For a detailed discussion and bibliographical references, see Kachru, 1983a.
31. For India; see Narasimhaiah, 1976, pp. 47–53 and Kachru, 1982b for Sri Lanka; see Abeysinghe and Abeysinghe, 1970, Goonewardene, 1970, Halverson, 1966, Kandiah, 1971 and 1981, and Obeyesekere and Fernando, 1981.
32. For anti-English comments and articles see, for example, *Organiser* (Delhi): for pro-English views see *Swaraj* (Madras).
33. In the literature a number of terms have been used to refer to this body of writing, e.g., *Anglo-Indian, Indo-Anglian, Indo-English,* and *Indian English.* See Kachru, 1978b: 504–5.
34. See Lal, 1969 and Parthasarathy, 1976.
35. See Makherjee, 1971.
36. See Naik, Desai, and Amur, 1968, and Ramakrishna, 1980.
37. See Naik and Mokashi-Punekar, 1977.
38. For example, Mulk Raj Anand, Anita Desai, Manohar Malgonkar, R. K. Narayan, Raja Rao, Khushwant Singh, and Nayantara Sehgal.
39. As in, for example, Goffin, 1934, and Whitworth, 1907.
40. See Bokamba, 1982, Kachru, 1981c, Kirk-Green, 1971, and Sey, 1973. The reduplication of word classes is extensive in several non-native Englishes and is also used in some native varieties of English such as Black English in North America. In Kenyan English, reduplication is used the same way as in South Asian English: *small small one*; *small small whiskey*; *long long one.*
41. The West African and the Philippine situations have been discussed by Ansre (1971) and Bautista (1977), respectively.

Chapter 4

English in the Bilingual's code Repertoire

RECENT research on bilingualism,[1] especially during the last two decades, has significantly contributed to our understanding of two rather neglected areas of this topic: the neurolinguistic study of a bilingual's brain (Paradis, 1979), and formal and functional analyses of the linguistic (or verbal) repertoire of a speaker of a language (Kachru, 1981b; Wald, 1974).

The focus on the functional aspects of bilingualism has shown that functionally (and formally), bilingualism does not invariably entail "the native-like control" of two languages (Bloomfield, 1933:56). Nor is it necessarily an "alternate" use of two or more languages (Weinreich, 1953:1). The bilingual's (or plurilingual's, if we prefer this term) use of languages may also be viewed from the perspective of possessing a linguistic or verbal repertoire functional within a specific societal network (Gumperz and Hernandez-Charez, 1972). The focus on the repertoire—within the context of the speech community—leads to a functional realism of our understanding of a bilingual's use of languages.

The terms "linguistic repertoire", "code repertoire", and "verbal repertoire" are used more or less identically to refer to the total range of codes which members of a speech community have available for their linguistic interaction.[2] But no speaker necessarily controls all the codes which constitute the verbal repertoire of a speech community. Each code in the repertoire has markers[3] (clues[4]) which provide various types of identities essential for understanding how individuals function in a wider societal context: for example, class (Robinson, 1979), caste (Brown and Levinson, 1979; Giles, 1979), religion and ethnicity (Kachru, 1973b; Miranda, 1978a, 1978b), sex (Smith, 1979), and region (Allen and Underwood, 1971). In this sense then the concept "linguistic repertoire" is not restricted to a bilingual's or a multilingual's competence in distinct "languages"; it may also be used to refer to the repertoire of styles and registers, or dialects. Thus this concept applies both to a monolingual and to a bilingual, though the constituents (or the set) which comprise the repertoire are not necessarily identical. Functionally, both a monolingual and a bilingual can be distinguished on the basis of *code range, code confusion, code-extention, code-switch*, and *code-mix*. The differences between the two are in the types of choices made, their linguistic characteristics and the contextual meanings. Gumperz (1968:381) refers to this similarity when he points out that "in many multilingual societies the choice of one language over another has the same signification as the selection among alternates in linguistically homogeneous societies."

The monolingual's repertoire will not be discussed here. Rather, this study is concerned with some linguistic aspects of code repertoire within the broad framework of three approaches to the study of language in societal context. One might use the following cover terms to identify these approaches: "context of situation" (Kachru, 1980d; Mitchell, 1978); "ethnography of communication" (Hymes, 1962, 1964, and 1974); and "linguistic repertoire" (Gumperz and Hernandez-Charez, 1972). These three approaches have been chosen because they share some underlying assumptions about language and its function in society. For example, they emphasize (a) the study of language in functionally determined contexts, (b) the heterogeneity and variation in codes as a characteristic of a speech community, and (c) the relationship between the structure of code and the structure of social context.

Within the framework of such approaches, this chapter discusses the following six aspects related to a bilingual's repertoire of codes and their functional implications. First, the concept of repertoire of codes is viewed in terms of a *functional hierarchy,* which is related to the "context of situation" in terms of what I have earlier called *contextual units* (Kachru, 1966, 1981d), participants, etc. Second, the role of language *shift, switch,* or *alteration* is considered within the total repertoire range of a bilingual as a member of a speech community. Third, a formal and functional distinction is suggested for separating the linguistic strategies of *switch* and *mix.* Fourth, the process of "mixing" is shown to be not a random but a rule-governed process, with constraints on "mixing" the units of two or more codes. Fifth, the effects of repertoire range, and the process of *switch* and *mix* are studied in a wider context, that of initiating structural changes in the linguistic systems of a language at various linguistic levels. Finally, in a minor digression, I have listed some of the educational implications of code repertoire, code hierarchy, and code-mixing.

Vernacular, Code Repertoire and Code Hierarchy

I shall use the term "code repertoire" in roughly the same sense in which the terms "verbal repertoire", "linguistic repertoire", and "communicative repertoire" have been used in earlier literature (Gumperz, 1964, 1972:20; Hymes, 1972a:xxxiv).

Code repertoire refers to the total range of codes available to a bilingual including his or her *vernacular.* A vernacular is defined here, for the lack of a better term, as the mother tongue (or L_1). One need not distinguish the use of the term "vernacular" from that of literary (or formal) language used in literature or the school system. Actually, the dichotomy is not so neat; the status of a vernacular and the use of this term varies from one bilingual context to another, and the attitudinal responses to "What is a vernacular?" are not identical in all contexts. European scholars have generally used this term to refer to all the modern South Asian or African languages, in a sense distinguishing these from the classical languages and the "prestigious" (literary) Western languages. In such a use, "vernacular" becomes a cover term, on the one hand for Bengali, Tamil, or standard Hindi (Kharībolī), and on the other hand for Magahī, Maithilī, or varieties of Kashmiri. These cases are not identical in terms of their literary traditions, functions, and the native speakers' attitudes toward them. Therefore, the use of such a cover term must be redefined with reference to each speech community.[5]

The set which comprises the repertoire range is also not identical in all bilingual contexts. Consider, for example, the following possibilities which might be included in the "repertoire range". (a) dialects or "styles" of a language (Gumperz, 1964); (b) a variety of distinct languages, from a closely related language family to a not-so-closely related family (Annamalai, 1971, 1978; Kachru, 1978a, 1978c); and (c) languages from two distinct language families (e.g. Sanskrit and Tamil).

The *code hierarchy* is essentially determined on the basis of function, that is, in terms of what a particular code accomplishes for the user in terms of status, identity, mobility, advancement. It may also depend on the attitude of a caste, class, or society at large toward a code. Such pragmatic considerations determine the functional allocation of vernaculars or other codes in the bilingual's repertoire. Therefore, the attitude toward a code and its ranking on the code hierarchy are not necessarily permanent. Consider the emerging dialect conflict in the so-called Hindi area, which is the result of postindependence reconsiderations of the dialect speakers (such as of Maithilī and Rājasthānī) toward Kharībolī Hindi (see Y. Kachru and Bhatia, 1978).

Dimensions of Code Repertoire

The code types which constitute a code repertoire of a bilingual may be identified in terms of their formal features and the functional domains. In formal terms, generally two devices are used: *foregrounding* and *neutralization* (or *backgrounding*).[6] The term "foregrounding" is used here in the Prague School sense, referring to the use of language in such a way that the formal devices attract attention. The attempt, then, is to *deautomize* language use, (Fried, ed. 1972:125). This then entails "conscious" use of phonological, grammatical, and lexical devices. The *registral function* may be marked by a specific type of lexicalization. In India, for example, Persianization has traditionally been used for the legal and court registers in the Hindi, Kashmiri, Kannada, or Telugu areas. On the other hand, the process of Englishization is evident in the registers of science, technology, and the social sciences.

The *style function* is a dimension of "register classification" (Halliday *et al.* 1964:92–3). It refers to the relations among the participants, and thus characterizes a formally determined choice. Again considering the Indian situation, the style function may be identified by choosing a "high code" from the available codes, e.g. high Hindi (Sanskritization), and Persianization, or by Englishization. The presence or absence of the "high code" marks styles such as *grānthika* "classical" and *vyāvahārika* "colloquial" in Telugu, and *sādhu bhāṣā* "literary" and *calit bhāṣā* "colloquial" in Bengali.

The *identity function* establishes an "in-group" relationship, a village identity (e.g. by switching to Magahī, Maithilī, or Braj (see Gumperz, 1964)), a religious identity (see Dil, 1972; Kachru, 1973b), a caste identity, or an elitist identity.

"Neutralization" is a device for not drawing attention to some of above-discussed "identities". It is a linguistic strategy to "unload" a linguistic item from its traditional, cultural, and emotional connotations by avoiding its use and choosing an item from another code. The borrowed item has referential meaning, but no cultural connotations in the context of the specific culture. Thus a borrowed item is used not because it fills a "lexical gap", but because for the user it has certain neutrality and specificity.

In chapter 1 (p. 9) this point has been illustrated with several examples from Tamil. In these examples, Annamalai (1978) has shown that one function of code-mixing with English is to avoid revealing social, regional, or caste identity. An English-educated Tamil speaker avoids lexical items from Tamil because they are not free from such connotations while English lexical items have no caste or regional undertones. The result is that English lexical items *brother-in-law, wife,* and *rice* are preferred to their Tamil equivalents. The same is true of educated Hindu Kashmiris who, for example, prefer to use English *widow* to Kashmiri *vedvā*.

Neutralization may also be used for establishing a linguistic identity to convey the idea that "I am one of you." The participants in a speech act know that this linguistic device is artificial, and they use it as a means of accommodation. Let me illustrate the switch of this type from Kashmiri, in which traditionally two religious varieties have been recognized, i.e. Hindu Kashmiri and Muslim Kashmiri (Grierson, 1911) or Sanskritized and Persianized (Kachru, 1973b:7–11).

Set 1	Set 2	Gloss
athɨ pəthrun	athɨ čhalun	"to wash hands"
khɔdā	bagvān	"God"
patīlɨ	bohgun	"cooking vessel"
kəhvɨ	čāy	"tea"
nāṭɨ	nʼeni	"meat" (lamb)
āb	pōnʼ	"water"
yēzārɨ	pəjāmɨ	"pajama, trousers"

Almost all of these lexical items are intelligible to speakers of both varieties.[7] The users of the above two sets can be marked as Muslims (set 1) or Hindus (set 2). In many situations a lexical switch takes place to de-emphasize the religious separation. Neutralization, then, is a linguistic attempt to achieve "accommodation", and "almost in-groupness". Note, however, that even when a lexical switch is made one may clearly retain the "separatenes" at the phonetic level. "Phonetic switches" seem more difficult to accomplish than lexical switches. Some phonetic "markers" of two religious groups are given below. In these examples the first phonetic markers refer to "Hindu Kashmiri" and the second to "Muslim Kashmiri".

1. central vowel → front vowel (e.g. *rikh* → *rikh* "line"; *ṭikh* → *ṭikh* "run")
2. high central vowel → low central vowel (e.g. *gə̃ṭh* → *gə̃ṭh* "eagle", *dəh* → *dah* "ten")
3. central vowel → back vowel (e.g. *mə̄j* → *mō̄j* "mother")
4. initial back vowel → central vowel (e.g. *ōlav* → *ə̄lav* "potatoes")
5. v → ph (e.g. *hohvur* → *hohphur* "wife's parents")
6. initial Cr → Cˡ (e.g. *brōr* → *bˡōr* "cat", *krūr* → *kˡūr* "well")
7. r → ṛ (e.g. *gur* → *guṛ* "horse"; *yor* → *yoṛ* "here")

The phonetic "accommodation" is, however, acquired by those who want to switch to the "urban/educated" variety of Kashmiri. (See Elias-Olivares, 1976:182 for a Chicano example; see also Scotton, 1976.)

In functional terms, the bilingual's codes may be viewed either as *inclusive* or *exclusive*. The inclusive codes are "free access" codes, and conscious efforts may be made to increase the number of their users. Such codes may be termed, for example, *national language, official language, lingua franca, koine,* or *creole.* These codes generally cut across language and/or dialect boundaries. The use of such a code may be sought for nationhood, educational status, political unification (e.g. the case of Hindi in India, Swahili in parts of Africa, English in non-native contexts). The exclusive codes tend to have a restricted membership. These may be termed "limited access" codes, and they mark an "in-group identity". Such codes are used for *trade, secrecy, caste, religion,* and *initiation* (Halliday, 1978). The membership of each type is not necessarily mutually exclusive. In a sense, the literary codes have the characteristics of restricted codes. For example, Sanskrit has traditionally been a literary code and by and large an "exclusive code". The dichotomies, therefore, do not always provide a clear picture.

It seems that in bilingual communities—and even in monolingual communities—attitudes toward codes (generally termed "language attitudes") are based both on the formal and functional characteristics of a code. On the basis of these attitudes loyalty toward a code is expressed. Consider, for example, the use of the following attitude-marking terms toward various types of codes:

a. *aesthetic/unaesthetic:* The attitude toward Italian in Europe, or toward Bengali, Tamil, and Punjabi in India. (Note the use of "musical" in this context.) In India, Bengali is considered "musical" and "melodious", and Tamil and Punjabi "harsh".
b. *correct/incorrect:* The dichotomy of literary/nonliterary. This refers to the mixing of style, e.g. "formal" vs. "informal". One is therefore not expected to use contracted forms in formal English.

c. *cultivated/uncultivated:* In terms of the literary traditions.
d. *developed/undeveloped:* English vs. Indian languages; Tamil/Bengali vs. Hindi (see also *c* and *g*).
e. *dialect/nondialect:* Attitude shown in both the mediums, i.e. written and spoken.
f. *educated/uneducated:* See Quirk's (1960) analysis of "Educated British English".
g. *effective/ineffective:* Attitude toward English (or French) in South Asia, Africa (justification: register range).
h. *primitive/nonprimitive:* An attitude which developed with colonization.
i. *proper/improper:* Languages of rituals or liturgy, e.g. Sanskrit or Latin.
j. *religious/nonreligious:* Attitude common in South Asia, for example, toward Sanskrit and Arabic.
k. *regional/nonregional:* Essentially based on phonology, lexis and syntax (see also *e*).
l. *sacred/nonsacred:* Arabic for the Muslim world and Sanskrit for Hindus (see also *j*).
m. *slang/nonslang.*
n. *standard/nonstandard.*
o. *u/non-u:* A dichotomy based on class, *u* (upper class) and *non-u* (lower class). A. C. Ross provided the illustrations and Nancy Mitford made it popular.
p. *vigorous/nonvigorous:* Attitude toward literary forms; for example, Urdu is considered "vigorous" and suitable for "forceful" poetry as opposed to Hindi which is considered suitable for *bhakti* "devotional" poetry.

The attitudes toward codes have serious linguistic implications. To a large extent, the concept of code-standardization is based on "language attitude", and such attitudes are indirectly responsible for the rise of academies (e.g. in Italy in 1600; France, 1635; Spain, 1713; Sweden, 1739). In a number of bilingual contexts one task of such academies is *code purification*, a linguistic activity aimed at curtailing linguistic change.

Code Alteration

In the literature a variety of terms have been used to describe types of code alteration, so terminological "untangling" is not easy (Baker, 1980). It has, however, been shown that out of the total code repertoire the bilingual tends to make two types of code alterations, termed here *code-switching* and *code-mixing*. The strategy of switching tends to be used, for example, as an aside for explanation, for establishing communicative "intimacy", or as a bond of identity. Formally, such switches result in embedding one or more sentences in a verbal interaction. Consider the following two examples from the written texts of Nigerian English and Hindi.

1. "Good! See you later." Joseph always put on an impressive manner when speaking on the telephone. He never spoke Ibo or pidgin English at such moments. When he hung up he told his colleagues: "That na my brother. Just return from overseas. B.A. (Honors) Classics." He always preferred the fiction of Classics to the truth of English. It sounded more impressive.

"What department he de work?"
"Secretary to the Scholarship Board."
"'E go make plenty money there. Every student who wan' go England go de see am for house."
"'E no be like dat," said Joseph. "Him na gentleman. No fit take bribe."
"Na so," said the other in unbelief.

[Chinua Achebe, *No Longer at Ease*, 1960]

2. [Standard Hindi] maĩ sab samajhtā hũ. tum bhī khannā kī tarah bahas karne lage ho. maĩ sātvẽ aur navẽ kā pharak samajhtā hũ. [switch to Awadhi] hamkā ab prinspalī kare na sikhāv bhaiyā. jonū hukum hai, tonū čuppe [switch to English] kari auṭ [switch] karo, samjhyo nāhī.   [Srilal Shukla, *Rāgdarbārī*, 1968:31]

[Kharīboli; standard Hindi] I understand everything. You have also started arguing like Khanna. I understand the difference between seven and nine. [switch to Awadhi] Don't teach me, dear, how to be a principal. Whatever is the order you carry it out quietly. Do you understand or not?

In (1), the West African novelist Chinua Achebe switches from English to pidgin; the contextual appropriateness of the text is maintained. In (2), the switch is from Kharīboli (standard Hindi) to a dialect (Awadhi). There is also a sprinkling of English lexical items to convey the effect of authority (*principal, carryout*). In switching, then, the units from another code are essentially sentences which are preserved with a clear function in the discourse. Code alteration of this type indicates the bilingual's facility with several codes, and their use in appropriate contexts with relation to the participants, setting, and for specific effect (e.g. the use of Awadhi in the above). Further, consider the following interaction in a typical educated Kashmiri family:

A. Hello, how are you, Kaul Sahib?
B. *vāray mahrā* [Kashmiri]
   "well, sir"
A. *vɔliv bihiv* [Kashmiri]
   "come in (hon.), sit down (hon.)"
A. *zarā cāy lānā, bhāī* [to a servant, in Hindustani]
   "some tea bring, brother" [mode of address]
   I will be back in a minute.

In these five sentences three codes are represented (English, Kashmiri, Hindustani), but each unit is a complete utterance in a specific code. The switching is at the intrasentential level, and becomes meaningful within the context of "greetings". If understood in that specific context, there is a cohesiveness in the text.
Another example entails a slightly different use of switching:

(On the telephone) When will you come?
(To his wife) *me dītav kāgaz pensaǐ*
    [Kashmiri: "Please give me some paper and a pencil."]
(On the telephone) What is your address?
(To his children) *šŏr mat karo bhaī, zara čup karo.*
    [Hindustani: "Don't make noise, keep quiet."]
(To his wife) *talay yim kar nāvukh tshɔpi*
    [Kashmiri: "Please keep them quiet."]
(On the telephone) All right, I will write to you. Thank you.

One should add here that the speaker could have used only English but instead chose to use three different codes. We still understand very little about such switches by bilinguals, especially when there is one *shared code* between the participants in a speech event and no *status* or *identity* questions seem to be involved.

The functional and attitudinal dependence of such switches—versus the one discussed above—is illustrated by Gumperz (1964) in the code repertoire of a typical villager in Khalapur. Khalapur, a small town 80 miles north of Delhi, has a population of about 3,000. The profile of the population's code repertoire is as follows. The local dialect is used for "local relations" and as a code of identity by the educated people. The standard language, Hindi, is used as a symbol of status and for commerce, etc. The other varieties of the local dialect are *motīboli* "rough/coarse dialect", *sāf boli* "refined/pure dialect" the market style, and the oratorial style. The "linguistic bounds" are marked by the appropriate choice of the code from this code repertoire. There are formal differences which mark the local varieties from standard Hindi, but I shall not discuss these here.[8]

In Kashmir such context-dependent code switches may entail a switch from Kashmiri to one or more other languages, such as Urdu, Hindi, Panjabi, English, Persian, Arabic, or Sanskrit. On paper, such a situation appears rather complicated, but in actual interaction, given the appropriate role and situation, this is a normal verbal strategy used in multilingual contexts. In fact, in traditionally bilingual societies, a mark of an educated or cultivated speaker of a language is to have this competence in switching. Creative writers have made very effective use of such strategies, as we saw in the examples from Achebe and Shukla.

In terms of linguistic units, "mixing" entails transfer of the units of code *a* into code *b* at intersentential and intrasentential levels, and thus "... developing a new restricted—or not-so-restricted—code of linguistic interaction" (Kachru, 1978a:79, see also 1978c; Sridhar, 1978; Warie, 1978). It seems that a user of such a code functions, at least, in a disystem. The resultant code then has formal cohesion and functional expectancy with reference to a context.

In such a situation there is an "absorbing" code and an "absorbed" code. The absorbed code is assimilated in the system of the "absorbing" code. There is rarely a situation in which the user of such a mixed code can not identify the "absorbing" and "absorbed" codes. The transferred units may be morphemes, words, phrases, clauses, sentences, and what are traditionally called "idioms".

At the lexical level, then, such "mixing" may result in having a choice of several *lexical sets* which function in identical contexts. The choice of a particular set may be made for functional, attitudinal, or registral reasons. Consider, for example, the following lexical sets available to a Hindi bilingual.

Set 1 (Sanskritization)	Set 2 (Persianization)	Set 3 (Englishization)	Gloss
āgyā denā	ijāzat denā	permission denā	"to grant permission"
parikšā denā	imtihān denā	examination denā	"to take an examination"
krodhit honā	gussā honā	angrī honā	"to be angry"

A code-mixed variety, as mentioned elsewhere (Kachru, 1978a, 1978c), often acquires a new name which refers to its hybrid characteristics. The name may be attitudinally derogatory (as in the case of Tex-Mex (Gumperz, 1970)), or not so derogatory, e.g. Bazār Hindi (Apte, 1974), Englañol (Nash, 1977), Hinglish (Kachru, 1979a), Singlish (Fernando, 1977), Spanglish (Nash, 1977).

The devices of "switching" and "mixing" have traditionally been used for stylistic effects in literature. In Sanskrit, the switch to Prakrit was specifically used for women, the nonelite, and clowns. In Indian poetry, *bhāṣā sankar* "language mixture" is an accepted linguistic device for stylistic effects and was used successfully by the Hindi poet Amīr Khusru (12th century) and the Kashmiri poet Parmānanda (1791–1874), to name just two. The use of such a device in literature is discussed in Kachru (1978a), Pillai (1974), and Timm (1975).

Code alteration and speaker-hearer

Code-switching refers to the alteration in which the speech event does not necessarily require that the speaker and hearer share identical code repertoires. The user may be bilingual and the receiver a monolingual.

On the other hand, in code-mixing, the codes used and the attitudinal reactions to the codes are shared both by the speaker and hearer.

Hypotheses for "mixing"

The main hypotheses for explaining the phenomenon of mixing are as follows:

1. *"Borrowing" hypothesis.* This hypothesis treats "mixing" (or switching) as a manifestation of what has been traditionally termed "borrowing" (Baker, 1980:4–5; Gumperz and Hernandes-Charez, 1971:320). It seems that it is difficult to explain mixing as merely borrowing (Kachru, 1978a). First, the items borrowed in mixing are not always motivated by the "lexical gaps" in the "mixer's" L_1, although traditionally that is considered one of the main arguments in favor of borrowing. Second, the absorbed items are not restricted to one unit, for example, a lexical item; "borrowing" extends to phrases, clauses, and sentences. In addition, collocations

and idioms are "absorbed". Third, "mixing" provides parallel lexical sets which are marked for register, style, or for identity functions, as illustrated by the parallel sets in Hindi or Kashmiri. Furthermore, as Pfaff (1979:195) shows, "the use of borrowing does not presuppose bilingual competence since 'borrowing' may occur in the speech of those with only monolingual competence." Bautista (1975:85) argues that "the term 'code-switching' is not appropriately applied to the instances of the use of loanwords, for instance, lexical items from lexicon L_2 in L_1 utterances. Although there is a branching into the lexicon of L_2, there does not seem to be a switch in code or linguistic system—the linguistic system is still that of L_1." (See also Leap, 1973, esp. p. 286).

2. *Pidgin hypothesis.* The pidgin hypothesis as an underlying motivation for "mixing" certainly does not apply to "educated mixing". Pidgins are characterized by their restricted functional range, structural simplicity, and inability to express abstract ideas (Kachru, 1978a:110–11). The users of pidgins generally do not share a mutually intelligible code of communication, so a pidgin is the only code of communication available to them. In contrast, users of "mixed" codes generally share mutually intelligible codes and use a mixed variety for various functional, attitudinal, and socio-cultural reasons.

3. *Distinct code hypothesis.* The code-mixed texts clearly show formal cohesion and functional dependency (Kachru, 1978c:31), despite the fact that constituent features of the resultant code are from two or more codes. The cohesiveness is the result of certain types of lexicalization and pattern symmetry (adjustment). The contextual appropriateness of a code-mixed text is the result of such lexicalization (e.g. Persianization, Englishization, or Sanskritization in South Asia). Extended borrowing is only one component. The appropriateness (or *expectancy*) of a code-mixed text must be judged within the context of situation. (See also Kachru, 1978c:29–31).

This view is not necessarily in conflict with the preoccupation of linguists with the notion of "a language" and its description. The vital question is: When do we know that we have a *new* code? Ferguson asserts that "linguists, by and large, have put that problem aside" (1978:98). But one is still compelled to consider how one code can be separated from another code. Ferguson provides three criteria for "delineating" the "natural unit" of language, i.e. *autonomy, stability,* and *functional range. Autonomy* refers to the "structural" and functional distinctiveness of a code in comparison to other codes. *Stability* is the degree of internal variation and the *functional range* is "the degree of restriction in semantic range". It might be useful to apply these criteria to the code-mixed varieties, too.

Toward a typology of repertoire types

At present, we have very limited cross-linguistic and cross-cultural empirical data on the types of code alteration. These are some of the possibilities in the repertoire range of a bilingual:

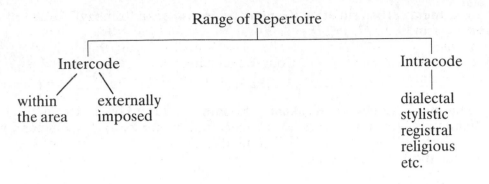

It seems that the more intercode mixing there is, the more structural "conflicts" are possible which might create problems of cohesion in code-mixed texts (Bautista, 1975; Gingrás, 1974). Let us consider some of the typical situations discussed in literature.

1. Chicano situation (Elías-Olivares, 1976):

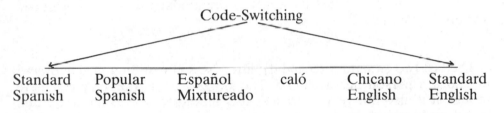

In this situation the repertoire range comprises standard varieties of both Spanish and English, and other "mixed" or "not-so-mixed" codes which have distinct functional roles.

2. North Indian rural situation (e.g. Srivastava *et al.*, 1978; see also Gumperz, 1964 for the situation in Khalapur):

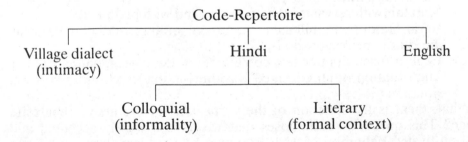

This presents the range of a typical educated Hindi speaker from a village of the *madhya deśa* (Central India). The range comprises the village dialect, the colloquial and literary varieties of Hindi, and English. In a number of cases Sanskrit may be used as a language of religion. The switching and mixing may take place in all these codes, depending on the participants and the context.

3. Indian urban situation (Gujarati businessmen in Bombay) (Pandit, 1972, 1977):

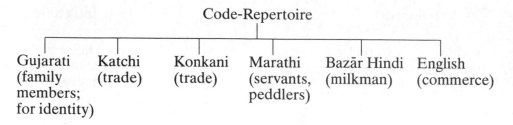

4. Kashmiri situation:

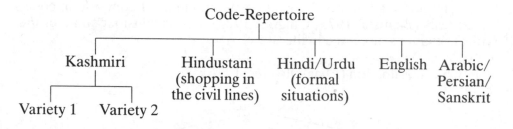

The last two situations (3 and 4) differ basically in the range and types of codes a person has available. The situation 3 is not very extensive, though it is also not very restricted. It is an impressive example of functional multilingualism, further seen to a lesser degree in the repertoire range of an educated Kashmiri (situation 4).

Pandit (1972, 1977) shows that a Gujarati businessman in Bombay has the following functional repertoire range:

(a) Gujarati (with family members for identity and as a family language);
(b) Katchi (as a trade language);
(c) Marathi (with servants in the business and with peddlers);
(d) Bazār Hindi (with milkmen who are generally from Uttar Pradesh, the Hindi-speaking region);
(e) English (used in interstate commerce, trade, correspondence, etc.). The situation of an educated Kashmiri is not much different from situation (3).

What, then, is the function of the vernacular in the above repertoire range? This question presupposes that we have a widely accepted and well-motivated definition of what we mean by the term "vernacular". As we know, that is not the case. It is even not clear that such a term is useful for providing a classification of various code types. But that is another story.

It has been suggested that a vernacular may be identified as a code with which one feels close identity, emotional attachment, and which one uses in intimate contexts. The problem is that this definition can not be generalized. In terms of a hierarchy of prestige, a code immediately next to the code one is using is generally termed a vernacular. It is an attitudinally loaded concept. An English educated Hindi speaker considers Hindi a vernacular (so did the European scholars), a Khaṛibolī (standard Hindi) speaker thinks of a dialect (e.g. Awadhī, Braj) as a vernacular. A speaker of a dialect of Hindi considers the rural varieties as vernaculars. As I mentioned earlier, the distinction between literary vs. nonliterary does not seem to apply in this context. In the above Gujarati situation, for example, the functional allocation of code types seems to be more important than the vernacular vs. nonvernacular distinction. It is, however, clear that functionally restricted codes seem to be labeled "vernaculars".

Manifestations of "Mixing"

The manifestations of "mixing" range from the use of lexical items to units up to a sentence or more, and embedding of idioms from the other codes. Kachru (1978a; 1978c) shows how this process works with reference to Hindi and English.[9] The borrowing code makes the use of "mixing" in such a way that the resultant text has both formal cohesiveness and functional appropriateness. In fact, it is due to such cohesiveness and appropriateness that such codes are functionally relevant in bilingual situations. Consider, for example, the following illustrations in which "mixing" is not restricted to only one unit.

1. *ṭank* [tank] *va reḍār* [radar] *prāpt karne kī bhī yojnā*
   "tank and radar procure do of also scheme"
2. *sarkas* [circus] *aur numāyiš yahā̃ phēl* [fail] *haĩ*
   "circus and exhibition here fail are"
3. *purānī hai to kyā huā, phāin* [fine] *to hai.* But I do not like Rajesh Khanna
   "old is what happened fine however is. But I do not like Rajesh Khanna."
4. *aur maĩ parivartan ghar se šuru karū̃gā kyũki* charity begins at home.
   "and I change home from begin will do because charity begins at home."
5. *akṭing vekṭing maĩ kyā jānũ re*
   "acting and the like I what should know hey"
6. mujhe is bat mẽ bilkul *doubt* nahī̃ hai, *rather I am sure* ki *this year* B.Sc. *examination* ke *results* bahut kharāb haĩ. kuch to *examiners* ne *strictness* kī aur kuch papers bhī aise *out of way* āye ki *students* to *unexpected questions* ko *paper* mẽ *set* dekh kar *hall* kī *ceiling* hī *watch* karte rah gaye. itnā *failure* to *last three or four years* mẽ kabhī huā hi na thā abkī *admission* mẽ bhī *difficulty* uṭhānī paṛegī. *Last year* bhī *in spite of all attempts* kuch *applicants* ke *admission almost impossible* ho gaye the. *After a great stir registar* ko *move* kiyā jā sakā, jisse kuch *seats* kā *extra arrangement* kiyā gayā. (Bhatia, 1967:55)

The English rendering of illustration (6) is as follows. The italicized items are present in both texts.

> I have no *doubt* in this matter, *rather I am sure* that *this year* the *B.Sc. examination results* are very bad. To some extent the *examiners* used *strictness* and the *papers* also were *out of the way.* On seeing *unexpected questions set* in the *papers* the *students* kept *watch*(ing) the *ceiling* of the *hall.* This much [high percentage of] *failure* had not taken place in the *last three or four years.* This time, too, we will have to face *difficulty* in *admission. Last year,* too, *in spite of all attempts, admission* of some *applicants* became *almost impossible. After a great stir* the *registrar* could be move(d), which helped in making *extra arrangement*(*s*) for some additional *seats* [places, openings].

In the illustrations we find the following types of units from English mixed with Hindi: (a) a noun phrase (in 1); (b) a hybrid noun phrase (in 2); (c) a sentence (in 3); (d) an idiom (in 4); (e) reduplication (in 5); and (f) an extreme case of code-mixing with English, with appropriate cohesion within the text (in 6). In the last text, out of 113 lexical items, counting both content words and function words, 44 percent are from English.

We now have a large number of studies which show that the device of "mixing" is used almost in all bilingual contexts and is not specific to any particular bilingual society. The following examples of code-mixing represent several language families in a variety of cultural contexts.

Ansre (1971a) provides examples from West African languages:

1. *Mele* very sorry, *gake mena* every conceivable opportunity -*i hafi wò* let-*m* down (Ewe).
   "I am very sorry, but I gave him every conceivable opportunity and yet he let me down."
2. *Se wɔbɛ*-report *wo ma me bio a mebe-* dismiss *wo* without further warning. (Twi)
   "If you are reported to me again I shall dismiss you without further warning."
3. *Ne* phoneme *nye* minimal phonological unit *eye* morpheme *nye* minimal grammatical unit, *lo, ekena* lexeme *anye* minimal lexical unit. (Ewe)
   "If the phoneme is the minimal phonological unit and the morpheme is the minimal grammatical unit, then lexeme will be the minimal lexical unit."

Bautista (1977) gives ". . . instances of language 1 NPs [Tagalog] appearing as subjects and complements in language 2 [English] units." Consider the following illustrations.

1. *Dito po sa atin . . . ang intensyon po talaga ng tinatawag na* national parks is to set aside an original area *na tinatawag po natig may magandang tanawin*
2. *Ang* family planning *po dito* is really the most crucial at the moment.
3. They are given *ivong tinatawag na* academic appointments.

Warie (1977) considers the case of contact of Thai and English:

> . . . *khɔ̌ɔkhwvan cam kiaw kàp* income effect *kɔ̌ɔkhɨ̀ wâa man pen bùak sàmɔ̌ɔpay čên nay kɔɔ-ra-nii kìawakàp khɔ̌ɔŋleew* inferior goods *nán* income effect *àat pen lóp dây.*

> ". . . things to remember about income effect is that it is not always positive, for example in case of inferior goods, the income effect can be negative."

Nash has discussed "language mixture" in Puerto Rico and gives the following examples of what she terms "midstream code switching" (1977:214):

1. Buy your home in Levittown Lakes, *donde la buena vida comienza.*
2. *Yo y mi* Winston-*porque* Winstons taste good like a cigarette should.
3. If the boss calls, *digale que no estoy.*

One may add to this list studies such as Annamalai, 1978; Gingras, 1974; Jacobson, 1978; Lawton, 1980; Lindholm and Padilla, 1978; Marasigan, 1983; McClure, 1977; Pfaff, 1976; Poplack, 1981; Sridhar, 1978; Valdes-Fallis, 1978; and Zentella, 1978.

Constraints on "Mixing"

A number of language-specific studies have shown that the receiving code does not mix units from another code without certain formal constraints. Code-mixing is clearly a rule-governed and function-dependent phenomenon; in terms of function in some multilingual situations it is almost a sign of language dependency.

There seems to be a range between acceptable "code-mixing" and what may be termed "odd-mixing". On the basis of the types of "mixing", one notices a cline on which the code-mixed varieties (within a variety) may be marked. There is, on the one hand, "educated" code-mixing (e.g. registral, or style-specific) and, on the other hand, the type which is characteristic of codes such as *butler English* (or *butler Hindustani*), and what are called *boxwallah* varieties in Indian English (Kachru, 1981c).

We lack any study which gives us a typology of constraints found across such codes. In what may be termed "educated" code-mixing with English by Hindi-Urdu speakers, the following constraints are found, but at this stage of empirical research one has to make generalizations with reservations.

1. Rank shift constraint:
   (a) *merā skūl which is in *bosṭan bilkul acchā nahĩ hai*
       "My school which is in Boston is not at all good."
In this case the rank shift clause cannot be from English.

2. Conjunction constraint: the conjunctions "and", "or", etc. from English are not used to conjoin nonEnglish NP's or VP's.

(a) *pustak and čābī bhī lānā
   "book and key also bring"
On the other hand, conjoining two sentences from two codes is acceptable.
(b) čāy jaldī piyo and let us go
   "tea quick drink ..."
(c) You must eat some food aur dūdh bhī pīnā
   ".... and drink some milk, too."
As I have said earlier (Kachru, 1978a:40), if the code-mixing in a language
has been assimilated, this constraint is not applicable, for example, Persian
and Sanskrit conjunction markers in Kashmiri.
   3. Determiner constraint:
   (a) *maĩ five sundar laṛkiyõ ko jāntā hũ
                        (numeral)
   "I five beautiful girls know."
   (b) *āp that makān kī bāt kar rahē haĩ?
                        (demonstrative)
   "You (hon.) that house of talk doing are."
   "Are you talking of that house?"
   4. Complementizer constraint:
   (a) *maĩ sočtā hũ that ham ko jānā hogā
   "I thinking am that we going will be."
   "I think that we will have to go."
   For a discussion of other languages see, for example, Annamalai, 1971;
Bautista, 1975; Gingras, 1974; Marasigan, 1983; Pfaff, 1979; Poplack,
1981; Sridhar, 1978; Timm, 1975; Warie, 1977; McClure and Wentz,
1976.

"Constraints" and "cohesiveness"

The syntactic constraints provide only part of the picture. One must
extend the concept of "cohesiveness" (or "integration") both to formal
cohesiveness and to contextual appropriateness. Cohesiveness refers to
"the integration of the units of another code into the systems of the receiving code, and organizing the units from two codes into a semantic
relationship" (Kachru, 1978c:112–113). "Semantic relationship" entails
integrating the L_2 items in such a way that the contextual appropriateness
is maintained without "violating" the rules of formal cohesion. As is well
known, this is achieved by various means, e.g.
   1. the use of productive grammatical processes of L_1 to nativize the
items of L_2. Consider the following examples of Hindi:
   Number: filmẽ "films"; ajensiyã "agencies"; moṭarẽ "motors".
   Gender: māsṭarin (f) "master".
   Abstract nouns: ḍākṭarī from "doctor"; aphsarī from "an officer". (See
also Pandharipande, 1980).
   2. the use of syntactic "equivalence" (Annamalai, 1971; Sridhar and
Sridhar, 1980).

Convergence of Codes and Code Change

It is evident that "mixing" and "switching" are a consequence of code contact or convergence. In earlier literature (Clyne, 1972; Weinreich, 1953) a number of examples illustrate the impact of language contact on language change. The contact has two manifestations: first, in terms of the extension (or addition) of the verbal repertoire of bilinguals; second, in terms of the structural changes initiated at one or more levels of language.

An extended code normally acquires a label which may in some cases indicate the processes involved in developing the code, for example, the case of the so-called Hindi area and Nagpur in central India. In the Hindi area the code repertoire includes the following, among others:

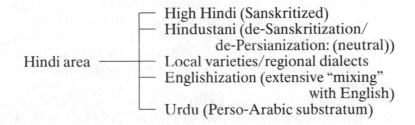

Hindi area
- High Hindi (Sanskritized)
- Hindustani (de-Sanskritization/ de-Persianization: (neutral))
- Local varieties/regional dialects
- Englishization (extensive "mixing" with English)
- Urdu (Perso-Arabic substratum)

One can recategorize these on a different dimension with reference to function, using terms such as *formal, informal,* and *register-specific.* The Nagpur situation is not identical to that in the Hindi area (Pandharipande, 1980). Nagpur has a bilingual speech community *within* the borders of Maharashtra (the Marathi-speaking state of India), and parts of the state border on the Hindi dialect area. The result is that some syntactic features in Nagpur Marathi (NM) are shared with Hindi and not with the standard variety, Puṇerī Marathi (PM). The situation is somewhat as follows:

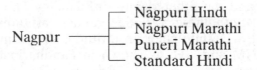

Nagpur
- Nāgpurī Hindi
- Nāgpurī Marathi
- Puṇerī Marathi
- Standard Hindi

NM is the language of *bahujan samāj* "the majority of the people". In informal situations NM and NH are used, and in the formal situations the switch is to PM and Standard Hindi. In creative literature, NM is used primarily for local color, for marking character-types, and for informal conversation. In formal or what the newspaper editors consider "serious situations" NM is not used, since, as one editor commented, "the readers" opinion about the news is affected by the type of language used in the newspapers (Pandharipande, 1980:32). Therefore, some lexical borrowing and loan shifts are used from NH, but "syntactic constructions which reveal the influence of Hindi on Marathi are rarely found in the newspapers."

The contexts for structural changes, especially syntactic, are not always identical. Let us consider the following cases. First, two language families influence each other and thus, over a period of time, contribute to the development of a language *area* comprising various language families (Emeneau, 1956; Masica, 1976). In this situation the change either is initiated in a *contact area*, or the contact is indirect (Gumperz and Wilson, 1971; Nadkarni, 1975; Sridhar, 1978). Second, two speech communities have lived together using two codes, and the linguistic implication is the development of two distinct varieties of *contacting* languages. In Nagpur, NM and NH are the result of such contact. Third, there may be a contact with an "imposed" language associated with elitism, power, administration, mobility, advancement, and access. The cases of Persian and English in South Asia provide good examples of this.

We shall not consider the influence of language contact at all linguistic levels, since a large body of literature on this topic discusses the implications of such contact in phonology and lexis. However, we still have limited evidence for the influence of such contact on syntax, especially in Asian and African bilingual contexts, one reason being that syntax is generally resistant to such change. The following case studies will illustrate the point.

In Dravidian languages, as Sridhar says, "the influence of Indo-Aryan is least pronounced on the level of sytnax" (1981:208–9). There are, however, several traces in "modes of compounding", which are not typically Dravidian in structure since the determiner is placed "before the determined and are probably due to the influence of Sanskrit", (e.g. *yatha śakti* "according to one's ability"), the passive construction (e.g. "the door was opened by the girl"), which is "also likely to have developed under the influence of Sanskrit, a tendency further reinforced by the influence of English", and finally, "the clausal mode of relative-clause formation" (Sridhar, 1981:209, Nadkarni, 1975).

On the other hand, the Nagpur situation has two faces, one deeply influencing Marathi, and the other deeply influencing Hindi at all linguistic levels. However, both these varieties remain attitudinally low on the language hierarchy. Despite such an attitude, the "transfer" in syntax is present both in NM and NH, as shown in Pandharipande (1980). I will present a few examples from both varieties. NM has several syntactic features which it does not share with PM but which it does share with Standard Hindi (or NH). The following are illustrative.

1. Progressive construction:
   (a) PM: *ti   gānā mhaṇat   āhe*
            she song say-prog.   is
            "She is singing a song."
   (b) NM: *ti   gānā mhaṇūn ṝahilī   āhe*
            she song say   prog.   is
            "She is singing a song."
   (c) Hindi: *vah gānā gā   rahī   hai*
            she song sing prog. is
            "She is singing a song."

Note that in PM, the progressive aspect of a verb is indicated by adding /t/ to the verb stem, which is followed by the relevant form of the verb *as-ṇe* "to be" (Damle, 1911, quoted in Pandharipande, 1980).

2. Negation:
   (a) PM: *āmhī udyā   mumbailā zāṇār nāhī*
             we   tomorrow Bombay to will go not
             "We will not go to Bombay tomorrow."
   (b) NM: *āmhī udyā   mumbailā nāhī zāū*
                                      zāṇār nāhī
             we   tomorrow Bombay to will not go
                                       will go not
             "We will not go to Bombay tomorrow."
   (c) Hindi: *ham kal   bambaī nahĩ jāẽge*
             we   tomorrow Bombay not   will go
             "We will not go to Bombay tomorrow."

Note that, in (b) above, NM allows both constructions (i.e. PM-type and H-type), but the H-type (c) seems to be preferred. Further evidence for the preference for H-type constructions is the NM speakers' use of another type of negative construction. In PM, the verb *pāhije* "to want" when negated is deleted and replaced by *nako* "to not want". Consider the following:

   (a) PM: *malā cahā pāhije*
             I-dat. tea   want
             "I want tea."
   (b)   *malā cahā nako*
             I-dat. tea   do not want
             "I do not want tea."
   (c) NM: *malā cahā nako* (or)
             malā cahā nāhī pāhije
             I-dat. tea   do not want
             "I do not want tea."
   (d) Hindi: *mujhe cāy   cāhiye*
             I-dat. tea   want
             "I want tea."
             mujhe cāy   nahĩ cāhiye
             I-dat. tea   not want
             "I do not want tea."

In NM, then, the variation is a result of the extended code repertoire, as compared to PM.

On the other hand, as Pandharipande (1979) has shown, NH clearly has syntactic transfers from Marathi. Consider the following examples:

1. Conditional sentence:
    (a) NH: *(agar) vah āyā   rahtā to   māĩ usse   milā rahtā*
         if   he   came aux. then I   he-with met   aux.
         "If he would come, I would meet him."
    (b) Hindi: *(agar) vah ātā   to   māĩ usse   miltā*
         if   he   came then I   he-with meet
         "If he would come, I would meet him."
2. Coercive causative:
    (a) NH: *māĩ ne   uskō   kām   karnekō lagāyā*
         I   Ag. he-dat. work to do   made

In Hindi this construction is not possible.

3. Quotative construction:
    (a) NH: *māĩ āũga karke bol rahā   thā*
         I   will come thus say prog. aux.
         "He said that he would come." ("'I will come,' thus he
         said.") (See also Y. Kachru, 1979).
4. *Have-to* construction:
    (a) NH: *mujhe bambaī jānekā   hai*
         I-dat. Bombay go-possessive is
         "I have to go to Bombay."
    (b) Hindi: *mujhe bambaī jānā hai*
         I-dat. Bombay to go aux.
         "I have to go to Bombay."

The next case is that of the Englishization of South Asian and African languages. The switching and mixing with English has contributed to syntactic innovations as well. I have discussed some of these processes with examples in chapter 9 (p. 151). (See also Tiwari, 1966:290–305). The number of examples at various levels can be multiplied, as can the sources responsible for the influence. However, the important point to recognize is the far reaching linguistic significance of code alteration in syntax.

Code Repertoire and Linguistic Description

Let me now revert to the bilingual's code repertoire within the context of a linguistic description. The centrality of variation within a code, and its implications for synchronic and diachronic descriptions, have been convincingly demonstrated by Labov (1966, 1972b) and other "variationists". But equally exciting and at the same time more complex questions have yet to be faced by linguists. One might ask: "What goes on in a speech community that uses—let us say—four languages?" In other words, can one write a grammar of bilinguals' complex linguistic roles? This is the type of investigation Ferguson (1978) would like linguists to undertake. After all, that is how bilinguals use languages for *living*, and in their use of codes they always show an awareness and concern for *appropriateness*. Those who have observed how traditional multilingual societies work with their code repertoire have clearly seen that the codes function as "one system" with formally and functionally definable subsystems. The challenge is, to quote Ferguson again, to "try the job of writing grammars of such complex systems" (1978:104). This statement will surely cause jitters, because the task is enormous and methodologically complex, as Ferguson admits: "I know it is hard enough to write grammars, anyway, and what I am suggesting makes it even harder. But I still think this is the job of the linguist." This is a call to take the next step from Gumperz' and Hymes' notion of "linguistic (or verbal) repertoire". The aim is to build this concept into a linguistic description, and to structure the exponents of such repertoire. There are, as Ferguson mentions, several fragmentary attempts already available; Denison (1968), Scollon (1979), Trudgill (1976–77). This new demand may entail taking a new theoretical and methodological direction, perhaps within the existing theoretical frameworks which have shown concern for accounting for such formal complexity in linguistic behavior.

The complexity of the task is obvious, as is the desirability for such descriptions of bilingual's code repertoires. This is perhaps the only way to establish meaningful relationships between the formal and functional aspects of the bilingual's linguistic interaction.

One need not go too far to see that, functionally, a code repertoire is used as "one system" of linguistic behavior by bilinguals or multilinguals. One notices this in classrooms with bilingual or bidialectal children, in creative writing where such verbal strategies are constantly exploited for their stylistic effect or for distinguishing various character types, and in the personal interaction of the members of bilingual communities in performing their roles as parents, husbands, buyers, sellers, and as participants in other social and religious interactions. The task, then, is to account for this linguistic reality.

Implications

As indicated earlier, I shall use this digression merely to list some of the areas in which our better understanding of the role of the vernacular in a bilingual's code repertoire has serious implications. The range of such implications is far-reaching, and a complete picture is not possible without more interdisciplinary and cross-cultural research. Consider areas listed below which are illustrative and not exhaustive:

(a) Literacy planning
(b) School instruction
(c) Curriculum development
(d) Codes in professions and their intelligibility
(e) Code modernization

(f) Code and media
(g) Attitudes toward codes
(h) Codes as markers of styles and registers

Theoretical and empirical research in some of these areas has already been initiated, but it still is limited and restricted to selected parts of the world (Cazden *et al.*, 1972; Cicourel *et al.*, 1974; Ferguson and Heath, 1981; Freed, 1978; Robinson, 1978; Sinclair and Coulthard, 1975; Srivastava *et al.*, 1978; Tough, 1977; Valdes-Fallis, 1978).

Conclusion

In recent years substantial data has been collected to prove that speech communities—monolingual or multilingual—are not homogeneous users of single codes. A speech community tends to use a network of codes which are functionally allocated in terms of their social uses. The type and range of such codes, however, vary from one community to another. Contextually, the codes alternate in several dimensions, e.g. status, sex, region, setting, age. And each context has its formal exponents which mark the context specification of a code. In some contemporary approaches to language description, such as Labov, Hymes, Halliday, Firth, and Gumperz, to name just a few, understanding of such societal functions of codes has become pivotal. However, one can not deny that some paradigms of linguistics still continue to treat such societal and functional concerns as marginal or secondary. In these approaches, there is not only hesitation to go into these areas, but even a clear indifference toward developing such concerns for linguistics. In this respect, Hymes (1972a:xi) has described the attitude of linguists well when he says ". . . some linguists whether in disgust, disdain, despair, or some combination of matters, saying that the present state of linguistic theory is so confused that linguists can tell teachers nothing useful at all."

However, one cannot deny that concepts like contextualization, functionalism, ethnography of communication, and pragmatics have increasingly been used in linguistic descriptions and the pedagogical concerns of linguists, as for example, in the work of Candlin (1981), Gumperz (1970), Halliday (1970, 1973), Kachru (1980c), Munby (1981), Paulston (1971), Widdowson (1978), and Wilkins (1978). The internal (structural) organization of a bilingual's codes is better understood now than it was only two decades ago. The result is that code-mixing and code-switching are now seriously studied in terms of their formal constituents and constraints, and their functional and pragmatic uses. It is true that the attitudinal reactions to some mixed varieties of codes have not yet changed, as in, for example widespread attitudes towards Tex Mex, Bazār Hindustani (Kalkatiyā Hindi; Bambaiyā Hindi), or Nāgpurī Marathi. Reference to these or some other varieties are still made in a pejorative sense, even tending to some types of "linguistic deprivation."

On the basis of the last two decades of empirical research we can now give less ambiguous answers to questions such as the following: What is meant by the functional allocation of codes? What are the processes which result in code-mixing? What constraints separate "code-mixing" from what may be termed "odd-mixing"? and What are the functional and attitudinal criteria for establishing hierarchies of codes? The change may be slow; language habits are slow to change and least prone to legislation. But they do change. During the last thirty to forty years there has been a clear change in popular attitudes toward the caste dialects in the South of India, toward the Received Pronunciation in the English-speaking world, and some discernible change in attitudes toward what is termed the Black dialect in America, and toward the non-native varieties of English (Kachru, ed., 1982). What is more important, we have begun to take seriously the "socially realistic" linguistic frameworks and their methodology (Kachru, 1981d; see also Chishimba, 1983; Lowenberg, 1984 and Magura, 1984). That, in itself, is a sign of new awareness and a new direction.

Another important question is how linguists'—or educators'—understanding of the formal and functional characteristics of bilingual speech communities has been related to the bilingual/bidialectal educational system. This is, of course, a double-edged sword, with a pedagogical side and a linguistic side. An applied theoretician must accept a planner's role with ramifications which touch upon more than one discipline. And one therefore treads on many sensitive toes. That makes applied linguistics (or its sub-field "educational linguistics") a difficult area to work in . Its methodology has yet to be sharpened and its concern highlighted. But there is no doubt that the underlying theoretical framework must be based upon a paradigm concerned with "socially realistic linguistics."

Concern about such an approach to a bilingual speech community, and its educational ramifications, is not restricted to the U.S. context. It is a pervasive concern with international implications. In a restricted sense one might see it as Coballes-Vega (1979) sees it in the context of the Chicano and Puerto Rican children in Chicago, or as Warie (1978) sees it with reference to the Thai-speaking speech community. But the concern is larger, very vital, and with significant implications in education. After all, most speech communities in the world are not monolingual. A majority of language users have multicodes of communication, whether we see such codes in terms of bidialectism, bilingualism, or plurilingualism.

Another significant phenomenon of our times is that one code functions across such linguistic and cultural pluralism: the English language. In functional terms bilingualism in English is historically unprecedented, and provides the first example of the role of a natural language as an almost universal language. The non-native users of English contribute toward its further role-extension and actual expansion. But we still have far to go to understand the pragmatics of non-native varieties of English (see Kachru, 1981c). The professions which train teachers of English for various parts of the world, and other supporting agencies, have so far shown indifference to such issues and concerns.

In understanding the role of English in a non-native English user's linguistic repertoire, the need is to recognize three types of clines. First, the range of *Englishes* which such a user commands can vary from pidgin English to what may be termed a "standard" English. Second, such varieties are used in different roles for *intranational* and *international* functions. Third, there is a relationship between the variety and the participant in a linguistic interaction. This, then, is an attempt toward the contextualization of *Englishes* within a context of situation. Through such contextualization the underlying reasons for the acculturation or nativization of English in Asia or Africa will be understood. I shall not elaborate on this point here, since several studies on this topic have just been published or are forthcoming. A number of these are listed in the bibliography in this volume.

This chapter has merely attempted to highlight some of the manifestations of code repertoire, its theoretical implications, and its relevance to our understanding of various societal, educational, and literary concerns. This is only a fragment of the uninvestigated linguistic "iceberg". A significant part of it has yet to be uncovered.

Notes

This chapter is adapted from "The Bilingual's Linguistic Repertoire" in *Issues in International Bilingual Education: The Role of the Vernacular,* edited by Beverly Hartford, Albert Valdman and Charles R. Foster, New York: Plenum Publishing Corporation, 1982, pp. 25–52.

1. I have incorporated in this chapter several ideas and illustrations—either modified or without modification—presented earlier in Kachru (1978a; 1978c). I have used "bilingualism" as a cover term to include the concepts of "multilingualism" and "plurilingualism".
2. Hymes (1972:xxxiv) also uses the term "communicative repertoire" in this context.
3. See Scherer and Giles (1979:xii): ". . . the term 'marker' should be taken in a fairly general sense to mean speech cues that potentially provide the reader with information concerning the sender's biological, psychological, and social characteristics".
4. See Trudgill (1974:14).
5. The term is primarily used to refer to a "language" or a "dialect" spoken by the people of a particular country or district. It is generally a native or indigenous "language" or a "dialect" (see *OED*). A vernacular is traditionally distinguished from the literary language.
6. It has been suggested, for example, by Christina Paulston (personal communication) that in this context the term "backgrounding" may be more appropriate.
7. However, there are other lexical items which are not necessarily mutually intelligible since these are register-restricted.
8. The main differences between the local dialect and the standard variety are, e.g. retroflex vs. nonretroflex /n/ and /ṇ/,/l and /l/; retroflex flap /ṛ/ and retroflex stop /ḍ/; diphthongs with an upglide *uī, aī, oī; s* and *š, ø*; consonant gemination in medial position *loṭṭā* 'jug'ʼ*loṭā;* differences in inflectional endings; and the infinitive suffix (*bōlnā*ʼ*bōlan* "to speak"). There are also substantial lexical differences.
9. A partial list of such studies on several other Western and non-Western languages is given in Kachru (1978a, 1978c).

PART II
Models, Norms and Attitudes

Chapter 5

Regional Norms

IN discussing the norm for localized varieties of English around the world, we are in a sense faced with the situation described in the entertaining Eastern fable about the elephant and the four blind men.[1] Each blind man, the story tells us, tries to describe the animal on the basis of touching one part of the large animal. One, after feeling the animal's leg, claims that an elephant resembles a gnarled tree trunk; another compares it with a thick rope, since that is how the elephant's trunk appears to him; feeling the circular belly of the animal, the third blind man exclaims, "Aha, an elephant is like a smooth round drum." and so on. Clearly, each blind man has a correct perception about an individual part of the elephant, but that part itself is not the totality termed "elephant." It is all these parts together, and various types within these species, that constitute the "elephant-ness." And this analogy applies to languages, too. When we use an identification label for a variety (e.g., American, British, Canadian, Indian, Malaysian, Nigerian), we are actualy thinking in terms of what linguists have called "common core" analysis, "over all" analysis, or a "nucleus." These terms are as abstract as the "elephant-ness," or using another example, "dog-ness," aptly suggested by Quirk *et al.* (1972:13):

> The properties of dog-ness can be seen in both terrier and alsatian (and, we must presume, equally), yet no single variety of dog embodies all the features present in all varieties of dog. In a somewhat similar way, we need to see a common core or nucleus that we call 'English' being realized only in the different actual varieties of the language that we hear or read.

The global spread of English and its various functions in the sociolinguistic context of each English-speaking country make generalizations about the language almost impossible. Because each regional variety of English has its distinct historical, acquisitional, and cultural context, the genesis of each variety must be seen within that perspective. The generalizations from one localized variety are as deceptive as the blind men's description of the elephant. At the same time, each description contributes to our understanding of the *Englishness* of world Englishes, and their specific sociolinguistic contexts.

Before further elaborating on this and related points, let us first discuss the terms "model," "standard," and "norm" as these are used with reference to English.

Model, Standard, and Norm

These three terms are generally used as synonyms in literature related to language pedagogy or in prescriptive texts on pronunciation and usage. In language evaluation these terms refer to proficiency in language acquisition, and attitudinally they indicate acceptance in certain circles.

What are the norms for English?

In the case of *non-native* speakers of English, when we talk of a norm, we imply conformity with a model based on the language used by a segment of the native speakers. The language use of this segment attains the status of a preferred norm for mainly extralinguistic characters (for example, education, class, and status).

In English the prescribed norm does not refer to the use by a majority. The motivations for such a preferred norm stem from pedagogical, attitudinal, and societal reasons, and are not due to any authoritative or organized move for codification, as is the case with some other European and non-European languages.

The imposed norms for English lack any overt sanction or authority; whatever norms there are have acquired preference for social reasons. These are indirectly, or sometimes directly, suggested in dictionaries of English, in pedagogical manuals, in preferred models on television and radio, and in job preferences when a particular variety of language is attitudinally considered desirable by an employer, whether it is a government agency, private employer, or a teaching institution. Through such imagined or real societal advantages of a norm, parents develop their preferences for the type of instruction their children should get in the school system. The case in point is Black English in the United States. On linguistic (or logical) grounds one cannot consider it a *deficient* variety (see, for example, Burling, 1973 and Labov, 1970), but for current attitudinal reasons it certainly restricts access to the cherished spheres of activities that all enlightened parents want their children to enter and succeed in. The same is true of various local varieties of British English. Thus members of a speech community share the belief that adherence to a certain preferred norm provides advantages for mobility, advancement, and status. In Britain, what are called "public" schools became the centers fostering adherence to such norms, and conscious efforts were made there to cultivate and preserve them.

The lack of an organized agency for language codification did not dampen the enthusiasm of the proponents of such norms for English. It is a fact—and a well-documented one (see, for example, Heath, 1977b and 1980; Kachru, 1981a; Kahane and Kahane, 1977; Laird, 1970)—that the "guardians of language" failed to provide such codification as has been provided by the Academies for French, Spanish, Italian, or, more recently, Hebrew. It was, however, not for want of such effort. Attempts to establish an academy for the standardization of English were made on both sides of the Atlantic in the eighteenth century, just sixty years apart. In 1712, Jonathan Swift wrote an often-quoted letter to "the Most Honourable Robert, Earl of Oxford and Mortimer, Lord High Treasurer of Great Britain," outling "A Proposal for Correcting, Improving and Ascertaining the English Tongue". The proposal was both a complaint and a plea:

> My Lord; I do here, in the Name of all the Learned and Polite Persons of the Nation, complain to your Lordship, as *First Minister,* that our Language is extremely imperfect; that its daily Improvements are by no means in proportion to its daily Corruptions; that the Pretenders to polish and refine it have chiefly multiplied Abuse and Absurdities; and, that in many Instances, it offends against every part of Grammar.

What did Swift have "most at Heart"? He wanted codification with the aim "that some Method should be thought on for *ascertaining* and *fixing* our Language for ever, after such Alterations are made in it as shall be thought requisite." The persons undertaking this task "will have the example of the French before them, to imitate where they have proceeded right, and to avoid their mistakes." The proposed goal then would be to provide linguistic watch-dogs.

> Besides the grammar part, wherein we are allowed to be very defective, they will observe many gross improprieties, which, however authorized by practice, and grown familiar, ought to be discarded. They will find many words that deserve to be utterly thrown out of our language, many more to be corrected, and perhaps not a few long since antiquated, which ought to be restored on account of their energy and sound. [Swift, reprinted 1907:14–15].

The second such proposal, submitted by John Adams, came before the Continental Congress of another major English-speaking country, the United States, in 1780. This proposal, somewhat more precise than its predecessor, asked for a "public institution" for "refining, correcting, improving, and ascertaining the English language" (1856:VII:249–50). This proposal is almost an echo of Swift's. Swift's proposal did not go very far because of Queen Anne's death, and Adam's proposal was disapproved, as Heath states (1977:10), since "the founding fathers believed the individual's freedoms to make language choices and changes represented a far more valuable political asset to the new nation than did a state decision to remove these freedoms from the individual." It was therefore "*a policy not to have a policy.*"

In retrospect, the failure to establish such an academy for English had its advantages. Since there was no authorized establishment for linguistic codification, no organized resistance to a norm could develop. It is not so easy to fight against the subtle and psychologically effective means of codification that were used for establishing a norm for English (see, e.g., Baron, 1982).

One might, therefore, say that each identifiable native variety of English can provide a norm for English. The identification may be in terms of some characteristic formal features that are realized in pronunciation, lexicon, or grammar. These features may then be associated with the localized variety of English. In linguistic terms, one may identify the *Americanness* in American English; and in a geographical (political) sense, one might use terms such as "Canadian English" or "Australian English." One is, of course, aware of further subvarieties within these broad categories. The natively spoken varieties are: American, Australian, British, Canadian and New Zealand. In chapter 2 (p. 20) I have given the 1985 population figures for these nations. These figures give some idea about the total number of speakers of each variety.

But in reality the question is not that simple. The native varieties of English also have a long history of debate concerning the desirability of having an exo-normative (external) or an endo-normative (local) model. This controversy developed into a fascinating debate in, for example, America (see Kahane and Kahane, 1977; Mencken, 1919), and is of specific interest to a student of language loyalty and language attitudes. Once that controversy was settled, two main models (norms) remained: Received Pronunciation (RP), and General American (GA) English.

These models gained currency for two reasons. Attitudinally, the prestige of the speakers of such varieties resulted in their emulation by others. Pedagogically, they served as two well-documented models of pronunciation. For example, in the works of Jones for RP and Kenyon for GA (see also Krapp, 1919), we have earlier valuable manuals and descriptions of pronunciation and dictionaries.

Received Pronunciation has alternately been termed "BBC English" (standing for the British Broadcasting Corporation), "educated English" and "public school English." (The term "public" school, when used in the British sense, traditionally means a "private" school.) "Public schools" refers to the old typically British institutions which, as Abercrombie says (1951:12), "are themselves unique." Received Pronunciation is by and large acquired unconsciously; therefore, as Abercrombie observes, "there is no question of deliberately teaching it." (See also Gimson, 1962 and Ward, 1929). It has, however, been treated as the main pedagogical norm for the *export* variety of British English, especially for tapes, records and pronunciation manuals used in classrooms.

But the status of this accent, and the term used for it, has been controversial. The "social judgment" that gave it a predominant position and prestige is now being challenged—after all, it had no official status. However, RP was considered a proper and desirable "accent" for government assignments and diplomatic services, and it was widely used by the ubiquitous BBC. But within the changed British context Abercrombie (1951) has provided three valid arguments against RP. First, recognition of such a standard variety is "an anachronism in present-day democratic society" (p. 14); second, it provides an "accent bar" reminiscent of the color bar and "to many people, on the right side of the bar, it appears eminently reasonable" (p. 15); lastly it is also debatable whether RP represents "educated English," since RP speakers are "outnumbered these days by the undoubtedly educated people who do not talk RP" (p. 15).

On the other side of the Atlantic, the use of "General American" is misleading, since the term covers parts of the United States and most of Canada. GA is spoken by 90 million people in the central and western United States and Canada. Kenyon's motivations for describing GA were almost opposite to those of his British predecessor Jones. As I have stated elsewhere (Kachru, 1982c:34), Kenyon is "conscious of the harm done by the elitist, prescriptivist manuals for pronunciation," and his concern is that "we accept rules of pronunciation as authoritative without inquiry into either the validity of the rules or the fitness of their authors to promulgate them" (1924:3). He is, therefore, attacking the shibboleth of correctness, the validity of prescriptive "judgements" and "advice" concerning pronunciation. He rightly believes that the underlying cause for such judgements is that people tend to be "influenced by certain types of teaching in the schools, by the undiscriminating use of textbooks on grammar and rhetoric, by unintelligent use of the dictionary, by manuals of 'correct English,' each with its favorite (and different) shibboleth' (1924:3).

Kenyon clearly expresses the evident disparity between linguistic norm and behavior and rightly asserts that "probably no intelligent person actually expects cultivated people in the South, the East, and the West to pronounce alike. Yet much criticism, or politely silent contempt, of the pronunciations of cultivated people in other localities than our own is common" (1924:5). In his perhaps too simplistic view, the remedy for such an attitude is the study of phonetics, since a student of phonetics "soon learns not only to refrain from criticizing pronunciations that differ from his own, but to expect them and listen for them with respectful intelligent interest."

What, then, is the generally accepted norm for English? There are several ways of answering this multifaceted and attitudinally loaded question. Ward (1929:1) has taken one extreme position concerning a standard when she says, "No one can adequately define it, because such a thing does not exist." It is clear that Daniel Jones would not necessarily agree. Strevens (1980:70) answers this question very differently. In his view, in the case of English, "standard" does not mean "imposed," or a language "of the majority"; he believes that an interesting aspect of Standard English is "that in every English-using community those who habitually use *only* Standard English are in a minority: that is to say, over the global population of English-users monodialectal Standard English-users are in a very small minority" (1980:70). The situation seems to be that "the phenomenon of Standard English exists and maintains itself without any conscious or coordinated programme of standardization" (Strevens, 1980:70).

Despite these positions, the dictionaries and manuals do indicate preferred pronunciation as well as the use of certain grammatical forms and lexical items. The "minority" use in such cases does not necessarily refer to the numerical use, but may refer to preference in attitudinal terms, too. A frequent usage is not always the usage that is attitudinally or socially accepted.

Teaching materials and teacher training programs do not generally present a "linguistically tolerant" attitude toward non-native localized varieties, or toward the speakers of varieties considered different from the "standard" ones. As mentioned earlier, in the United States one notices this attitude toward Black English (or other ethnic Englishes). In Britain such an attitude has traditionally been present toward the speakers of regional varieties. Therefore, it is not only the non-native users of English who suffer from this attitude.

Norm for non-native Englishes

The historical development of non-native varieties of English is closely related to colonization. Attitudinally, the colonizers' English became the preferred norm once English was introduced in the linguistic network of a country. But actually, the "norm" provided by the representatives of the Raj was not always the "standard" variety of English. In a number of cases, English teachers were not even native speakers of the language, especially in convent schools, or in other missionary establishments using Belgian, French, or Irish teachers. (The native speakers were very rarely RP speakers; for instance, a significant number of them came from Scotland, Wales, or Ireland.)

We thus have, broadly speaking, two models for non-native Englishes. The largest population of non-native English speakers considered English as their model in large parts of Asia, Africa and the Caribbean. On the other hand, American English served as a model where American influence reached because of colonization (the Philippines, see Llamzon, 1969; Samonte, 1981; Puerto Rico, see Zentella, 1981), trade and commerce (Japan, see Stanlaw, 1982), or geographical proximity and other impact (Mexico, Cuba, or other parts of Latin America).

There was, however, a mythical quality about the native models. In reality, it is doubtful that one homogeneous model was ever introduced in the colonies. Colonial administrators, teachers, and military personnel provided a confusing spectrum of varieties of English. Thus the native speakers of English never formed more than a fraction of English instructors in a majority of the colonies; certainly in South Asia their numbers were insignificant, and their impact on the teaching of English was negligible.

Types of non-native Englishes

The varieties of non-native Englishes cannot be presented in terms of misleading and unrealistic native—versus—non-native dichotomy. In an earlier study I have suggested (1982c:37) that one must consider these varieties in the following four contexts: *acquisitional, sociocultural, motivational,* and *functional.*

A further division is possible; for example,

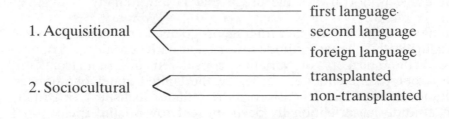

1. Acquisitional
    first language
    second language
    foreign language

2. Sociocultural
    transplanted
    non-transplanted

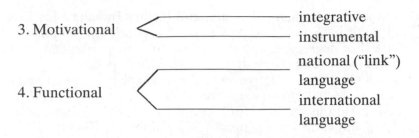

3. Motivational <——————————— integrative
                                instrumental

4. Functional <——————————— national ("link")
                                language
                                international
                                language

In literature another well-motivated distinction has already been introduced (see Catford, 1959; Halliday *et al.* 1964) between the *first-, second-,*
and *foreign*-language varieties of English (see also Kachru, 1982c). Alternately, the second- and foreign-language varieties have been termed the
institutionalized and *performance* varieties (see particularly Kachru and
Quirk, 1981; Kachru, 1981c and 1983a). This is an important distinction,
because it brings us to the question of exo-normative (external) and endo-
normative (local) standards for the non-native Englishes.

A non-native variety generally acquires an identity in terms of either
political boundaries (e.g., *Indian* English, *Lankan* English, *Kenyan*
English) or a larger geographical area (e.g., African English, South Asian
English, or Southeast Asian English).[2] The identification labels of the first
type (Indian, Lankan), which provide clues to the political boundaries, are
not necessarily instructive. The impression of divisiveness in world
Englishes that such labels present does not actually exist in real-life contexts. The variety-marking clues are determined, by and large, by the
underlying linguistically and culturally shared characteristics of an area. In
this sense, then, terms such as "African English" or Africanization (see
Bokamba, 1982) or South Asianization (see Kachru, 1983a) are more
appropriate. But these terms, too, are useful only to the extent that they
provide insights about the shared characteristics at various levels within
various regional varieties. They are only as reflective of the true situation
as are the terms "American English" or "British (or English) English." They
mask the linguistic heterogeneity within a region, and to some extent serve
to reassure those who are alarmed by what is considered divisiveness
within the English-speech community.

We then have, on the one hand, a "standard" or "educated" variety for a
larger region, and within it several subvarieties. There is thus a cline in
bilingualism in English (Kachru, 1965). Subvarieties are identifiable on the
basis of region, ethnic identity, education, function, etc. In each region we
have studies that identify such subvarieties—e.g., in Nigeria (Bamgboṣe,
1982); Kenya (Zuengler, 1982); India (Schuchardt, 1891 [1980]; Kachru,
1969 [1978] and 1983a; Singapore and Malaysia (Platt and Weber, 1980;
Wong, 1981; Tay and Gupta, 1981); and the Philippines (Llamzon, 1969
and 1981).

A speaker of a non-native variety may engage in a variety-shift, depending on the participants in a situation. An educated Indian English speaker
may attempt to approximate a native-English model while speaking to an
Englishman or an American, but switch to the localized educated variety

when talking to a fellow Indian colleague, and further Indianize his English when communicating with a shopkeeper, a bus conductor, or an office clerk. There are thus degrees of approximation to a norm, depending on the context, participants, and the desired end result of a speech act.

The concept of cline in non-native varieties of English has been recognized for almost a century now (see Schuchardt, 1891 (1980)), and has been illustrated in various studies (for example, for South Asian English see Kachru, 1965 and later; for a general bibliography see Kachru, 1983a and 1982d). Strevens (1977:140–141) sums up the situation well with references to Indian English:

> The Indian (or Pakistani) doctor who communicates easily in English with professional colleagues at an international medical conference is using a type of 'Indian English' . . . in which Standard English dialect is spoken with a regional accent. The Indian clerk who uses English constantly in his daily life for communicating with other Indians, by correspondence or telephone, may employ an 'Indian English' in which the dialect is not Standard English and the accent is regional or local. The lorry-driver who uses English occasionally, as a lingua franca, may be using an 'Indian English' which is for all practical purposes a pidgin. It is the second of these three examples which constitutes the typical 'Indian English' and which most frequently attracts the criticism of the teaching profession. But is criticism justified? The ultimate test of effectiveness of a variety of language is whether it meets the communication needs of those who use it. Clearly, 'Indian English' of this second type would not be adequate for the professional man to communicate with an international audience, but it probably does serve local needs well enough, just as all local dialects and accents do.

It is difficult to say how many people use various types of Englishes (say, as standard localized varieties or pidgins) as non-native varieties across cultures and languages. One has no reliable way of knowing it since English is learned around the world in unimaginable situations. On the one hand, people learn it in "English teaching shops" in bazārs from people who can hardly use the language. On the other hand, those who have resources learn English from highly accomplished teachers in ideal language learning situations. Whatever the actual statistics, the number of bilinguals who know English is fast increasing, and English has already acquired the status of a universal language (see chapter 1). This status is essentially due to the use of English in non-native contexts. The spread of English continues, and is now controlled by its non-native users; it is their initiative that is planning and coordinating the role of English in the developing world.

Development of localized norms

The various historical phases involved in the development of localized models for English cannot be traced precisely. Instead, one must trace the changing attitudes toward such varieties. It is like recognizing the presence of a linguistic behavior that was there all along but that attitudinally lacked status. The Indians, the Africans, the Malays, or the Filipinos have struggled with the myth and reality since English first became part of their educational system and linguistic repertoire. University teachers generally defended the exo-normative standard, often not realizing that they themselves used and taught to their students a transparent local accent. More important, the ever-present localized innovations in lexis and grammar (e.g., Africanisms, Indianisms) gradually gained currency.

But then the conflict in attitudes toward local varieties was also always present. Therefore, when we discuss the development of a model, we are not focusing on the distinct stages through which a norm passes before it gains some kind of ontological status. These attitudinal stages have been presented in Kachru, 1982c, and we shall briefly summarize them here with a note of warning (see also chapter 2, pp. 50–51). These stages are not clear-cut and mutually exclusive; they are primarily related to the extent of the diffusion of bilingualism and to the institutionalization of a variety. The first stage seems to be non-recognition of a localized variety and clear indifference to it. This is followed by a stage in which the localized variety is recognized (e.g., Indian, Lankan, Kenyan); but it is always the *other* person who uses it. Again, there is a clear disparity between the norm and behavior. The third stage shows a reduction in such an attitude. A controversy develops between the defenders of the localized variety and those who prefer an exo-normative standard (see Kachru, 1982c:39–40).

In the final stage, teaching materials for English are prepared with nativized contexts; English is not used just with an integrative motivation involving another culture, but essentially as an instrument for exposing students to their own culture. It is like turning an "external" language around for an "inward" look. The "window on the world" or "library language," becomes a window on one's own culture, history, and traditions. Furthermore, the variety develops its own nativized registers and is used in imaginative or creative contexts (see Kachru, 1981c, 1982b and 1983a), albeit by a small group of people. In this sense, English becomes part of the local literary and cultural traditions (see, for example, Sridhar, 1982).

Norm at various levels

The term "norm," as is generally discussed in literature, does not apply only to the phonetic/phonological levels. A language user may reveal his or her variety by lexical, grammatical, or discoursal features. However, the largest number of attitudinal comments—or displays of intolerance—concern pronunciation (generally discussed in terms of a person's "accent.") This is the aspect of use discussed in various manuals. The variety's lexical, collocational, grammatical, and discoursal features are often looked upon as "mistakes." This aspect has been discussed in several studies, and I shall not reiterate it here (see Kachru, 1982c and 1983a).

In linguistic literature, it was in the 1960s that attention was first drawn to the distinction between a "mistake" and a "deviation" in the context of non-native Englishes. (For references and discussion, see particularly Kachru, 1982a.) The deviation at various levels is directly related to the degree of nativization (see Kachru, 1983a and Kachru and Quirk, 1981). The attitude toward nativization is determined by the extent of a variety's institutionalization; the institutionalization, in turn, depends on the *range* and *depth* of a variety in a particular setting. The range of a variety refers to its extension into various cultural, social, educational, and commercial contexts. The greater the range of functions, the more subvarieties a variety develops. The term *depth* relates to the penetration of bilinguilism into various strata of society.

The attitude toward variety-specific characteristics (for example, lexical and grammatical; see Smith, 1981; Bailey and Görlach, 1982; see also chapter 2) is largely determined by whether a variety is used as a first or a second language. Labeling a word or a formation an Americanism, Australianism, or Canadianism is one way of characterizing it as deviant from "mother English." The history of attitudinal conflict even toward the native transplanted varieties is fascinating and has been discussed in a variety of popular and scholarly works.[3] The case of institutionalized non-native varieties has been much more difficult. Any deviation in such varieties has been termed a "mistake" or an "error". The "native speaker" has traditionally determined the extent of acceptable deviation, both linguistic and contextual (see also chapter 2, p. 29).

It is clear that, for English, the concept of "native speaker" has doubtful validity.[4] Since English is used across cultures and languages in a multitude of international and intranational contexts, the "deviations" must be seen in those functional contexts. This, then, leads us to another question that is crucial for understanding the relationship of the localized (or regional) varieties and the norm: What are the motivations for deviations?

The deviations in localized non-native varieties cannot in every case be characterized as linguistic aberrations because of acquisitional inadequacies. That rash generalization would miss serious underlying reasons for such innovations and would thus imply negating the context in which a language functions. The acculturation of a variety occurs over a period of time in a distinctly "un-English" context.[5] (A number of such case studies have been presented in Kachru, ed., 1982). The English language has now ceased to be a vehicle of Western culture; it only marginally carries the British and American way of life. This point is very effectively made by J. R. Firth almost thirty years ago. I have quoted his words in chapter 2 (pp. 31–32).

English is thus a medium that in its various manifestations, East and West, results in cultural adaptations. In South Asia it connotes the Indian, Lankan, or Pakistani ways of life and patterns of education and administration. The nativized formal characteristics acquire a new pragmatic context, a new defining context, culturally very remote from that of Britain or America. I have provided a number of illustrations in various studies (see Kachru, 1965 and later, included in 1983a) in which deviations have been related to the "social meaning" of the text peculiar to the culture in which English is used as a non-native language. I am taking the liberty of quoting the relevant parts below (1982b:329–330).

In terms of acculturation, two processes seem to be at work. One results in the *decultu-ration* of English, and another in its *acculturation* in the new context. The latter gives it an appropriate identity in its newly acquired functions. The Indians have captured the two-faceted process by using the typical Sanskrit compound *dvija* ("twice-born") for Indian English. (The term was originally used for the Brahmins who, after their natural birth, are considered reborn at the time of the caste initiation.) Firth (1956: [in Palmer, 1968:96]) therefore is correct in saying that "an Englishman must de-Anglicize himself"; as must, one could add, an American "de-Americanize" himself, in their attitudes toward such varieties, and for a proper appreciation of such acculturation of Englishes.

This initiation of English into new culturally and linguistically depend-ent communicative norms forces a redefinition of our linguistic and contextual parameters for understanding the new language types and dis-course types. Those who are outside these cultures must go through a *variety shift* in order to understand both the written and the spoken modes of such varieties. One cannot realistically speaking, apply the norms of one variety to another variety. I am not using the term "norm" to refer only to formal deviations (see Kachru, 1983b); rather, I intend to refer to the underlying universe of discourse which makes linguistic interaction a plea-sure and provides it with "meaning." It is the whole process of, as Halliday says, learning "how to *mean*" (1974). It is a very culture-bound concept. To understand a bilingual's mind and use of language, one would have, ideally, to be ambilingual and ambicultural. One would have to share responses to events, and cultural norms, and interpret the use of L_2 within that context. One would have to see how the context of culture is manifest in linguistic form, in the new style range, and in the assumptions one makes about the speech acts in which L_2 is used. A tall order indeed!

This redefined cultural identity of the non-native varieties has not usually been taken into consideration. There have been primarily three types of studies in this area. The first type forms the main body—under-standably so, since these are devoted to pedagogical concerns. In such studies, any deviation has been interpreted as violating a prescriptive norm and thus resulting in a "mistake." The urge for prescriptivism has been so strong that any innovation which is not according to the native speaker's linguistic code is considered a linguistic aberration. If one makes too many such "mistakes," it is treated as an indication of a language user's linguistic deprivation or deficiency. Second, some linguistic studies focus on formal characteristics without attempting to relate them to function, or to delve into the contextual needs for such innovations. This separation between *use* and *usage* has masked several sociolinguistically important factors about these varieties. The third group of studies deals with the "contact literature" in English, perhaps used on the analogy of "contact languages." Such literature is a product of multicultural and multilingual speech com-munities, and it extends the scope of English literature to "literatures in English." Most such studies are concerned with the themes, rather than with the style. (For further discussion, see, e.g., Sridhar, 1982.)

Norm vs. intelligibility

One major motivation for having a norm is that it maintains intelligibility (see Smith and Rafiqzad, 1979)[6] among speakers of distinct localized varieties of English. According to this view, a prescriptive norm is vital for communication. At least three problems exist in using the concept of intelligibility with any rigor. First, although one always encounters this term in pedagogical literature and in studies on second-language acquisition, it is unfortunately the least researched and least understood concept in cross-cultural and cross-linguistic contexts. Second, whatever research is available on the second-language varieties of English primarily focuses on phonetics, specifically on the segmental phonemes. (The limitations of such research have been discussed in Nelson, 1982.) The interference in intelligibility at other levels, especially in communicative units (see, for example, Nelson, 1984) has hardly been understood. Third, in the case of English, we must be clear about whom we have in mind when we talk of participants in a linguistic interaction. What role does a native speaker's judgment play in determining the intelligibility of non-native speech acts that have intranational functions in, for example, Asia or Africa? The variety-specific speech acts are vital for communication, as has been shown in Chishimba (1983) and various studies in Kachru (ed. 1982). In international contexts certainly one might say that an idealized native speaker could serve as a model. But in the cases of institutionalized varieties, a *native* speaker is not a participant in the actual speech situation. Localized uses are determined by the context of each English-using country, and the phonetic approximation is only part of the language act. The nativized lexical spread and the rhetorical and stylistic features are distinctly different from those of the native speaker.

How many users of the institutionalized varieties use English to interact with *native* speakers of English? I have shown in the following chapter (pp. 110) that, out of all users of Indian English, only a fraction have an interaction with native speakers of English. For example, among the graduate faculty of English in the universities and colleges I surveyed, 65.64 percent had only occasional interaction with native speakers, and 11.79 percent had no interaction with them. Only 5.12 percent claimed to have daily interaction with native speakers. I should, however, warn the reader that this survey was restricted to a highly specialized segment of the English-using population of India—professionals involved in teaching English at the graduate level. The results for those not involved in the teaching of English, especially at the graduate level, will be different. My experience in Singapore has shown that the situation there is not much different from India. What, then, is the issue? The issue is more complex than has been presented in literature.

There can be no one "mononorm" approach to this concern (see also chapter 7). As is true with native varieties, the intelligibility of the non-native institutionalized varieties of English forms a cline. The intelligibility within the extended group depends on various sociolinguistic parameters of region, age, education, and social role. Ward (1929:5) gives some indication of the situation in Britain:

> It is obvious that in a country the size of the British Isles, any one speaker should be capable of understanding any other when he is talking English. At the present moment, such is not the case: a Cockney speaker would not be understood by a dialect speaker of Edinburgh or Leeds or Truro, and dialect speakers of much nearer districts than these would have difficulty in understanding each other.

This observation, made over half a century ago, is still valid. One might add that, given the ethnic, cultural and linguistic pluralism of the United States, the situation has become even more complex there (see Ferguson and Heath, 1981). Once we move to the second language contexts of English in Africa, Asia, or the Pacific, the situation appears to be perplexing.

But there is a pragmatically refreshing side to all these situations. What appears to be a complex linguistic situation at the surface, in Britain, in American, in Africa, or in South Asia, is less complex if one attempts to understand it from another perspective. In his cone-shaped diagram (reproduced in Ward, 1929:5; see below), Daniel Jones has graphically

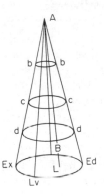

shown that "as we near the apex, the divergencies which still exist have become so small as to be noticed only by a finely trained ear" (Ward, 1929:6). Ward rightly provides the argument of "convenience or expediency," (p.7), suggesting that "the regional dialects may suffice for those people who have no need to move from their own districts."

In this I find a clear case of parallelism between the native and institutionalized non-native varieties of English. The intelligibility is functionally determined with reference to the sub-region, the nation, political areas within the region (e.g., South Asia, Southeast Asia), and internationally. True, educated (standard) Indian English, Singapore English, Nigerian English, or Kenyan English is not identical to RP or GA. It is different; it *should* be different. Do such educated varieties of non-native Englishes create more problems of intelligibility than does, for example, a New Zealander when he or she talks to a midwestern American?

In some situations, the markers of *difference* may establish a desirable identity. Such formal markers provide a regional and national identity and help in establishing an immediate bond with another person from the same region or country. The desire for retaining such markers has been well presented in the following observation by T. T. Koh, Singapore's former Representative to the United Nations:

> ... when one is abroad, in a bus or train or aeroplane and when one overhears someone speaking, one can immediately say this is someone from Malaysia or Singapore. And I should hope that when I'm speaking abroad my countrymen will have no problem recognizing that I am a Singaporean [cited in Tongue, 1974:iv].

Attitudes Toward Localized Norms

What are the attitudes toward the localized norms of English? I have merely hinted on this point in chapter 2 (pp. 28–30). Let me, therefore, discuss it briefly here. One has to consider the attitudes of two distinct groups: One group consists of the *native* English speakers who traditionally have been considered crucial for such judgment. This group's attitude is reflected in three ways—first, in the teaching materials produced for non-native users. Until recently, such texts attempted primarily to introduce the reader to Western (British or American) culture; this is, however, slowly changing now. Second, one notices the native speaker's attitude in the books specifically written to train teachers of English as a second language. Such books make no attempt to show the institutionalization of English in other cultures, or to portray the non-Western contexts in which English is nativized. Third, practically no mention is made of the development of non-native English literatures, and of the uses one can make of this body of literature. In this discussion of English across cultures we find on the one hand the extreme position of, for example, Prator (1968), versus the position typified in Smith 1981 (see especially the Introduction by Kachru and Quirk). The position presented in Smith (1981) or in Kachru (1982c) is still held by only a small group of people and does not represent the view of the profession.

The fact that non-native users of English have demonstrated no unified identity and no loyalty toward localized norms, does not, however, imply that there has been no serious thinking in this direction. One does not notice a shift from earlier conflict between the actual linguistic behavior and the norm; attitudinally now there is a realization about the pragmatics of language use. The discussion is either directly related to the question or indirectly related to this issue. This debate, however, is not recent; rather, it started when the institutionalization of English was recognized, and the English language—in spite of the attitude toward the British Raj—was being considered an important member of the local linguistic repertoire. In India, for example, the educator and a distinguished English scholar Amar Nath Jha said, in 1940, almost with tongue in cheek:

> May I . . . venture to plead for the use, retention, and encouragement of Indian English? . . . . Is there any reason why we need to be ashamed of Indian English? Who is there in the United Provinces [Uttar Pradesh] who will not understand a young man

who had enjoyed a *freeship* at college, and who says he is going to join the *teachery* profession and who after a few years says, he is engaged in *headmastery*? Similarly, why should we accept this English phrase *mare's nest,* and object to *horse's egg,* so familiar in the columns of *Amrita Bazar Patrika*? Why should we adhere to *all this* when *this all* is the natural order suggested by the usage of our language? Why insist on *yet* following *though* when in Hindustani we use the equivalent of *but*? Must we condemn the following sentence because it does not conform to English idiom even though it is literal translation of our own idiom? *I shall not pay a pice what to say of a rupee.* Is there any rational ground for objecting to *family members* and adhering to *members of the family*? . . . A little courage, some determination, a wholesome respect for our own idioms and we shall before long have a virile, vigorous *Indian English.*

Dustoor (reproduced in Dustoor, 1968:126; see also Kachru, 1982c) makes a firmer claim by saying that there will always be a more or less "indigenous flavor about our English. In our imagery, in our choice of words, in the nuances of meaning we put into our words, we must be expected to be different from Englishmen and Americans alike."

We lack in-depth empirical studies concerning the opinions of teachers, students, and educators about an exo-normative standard. But educators in those areas where English has been institutionalized (e.g., Africa, Asia, the Pacific) have commented on this question in asides, or in discussion of other issues related to the localized varieties. In Nigeria, Bamgbose (1971:41) clearly indicates that "the aim is not to produce speakers of British Received Pronunciation (even if this were feasible). . . . Many Nigerians will consider as affected or even snobbish any Nigerians who speak like a native speaker of English." In Ghana, an *educated* Ghanaian is expected to speak, the localized *educated* variety of English, and it does not mean, as Sey writes (1978:8) "the type that strives too obviously to approximate to RP. . . ." An imitation of RP "is frowned upon as distasteful and pedantic."

In South Asia, one notices the same reaction to the imitation of exo-normative standards such as RP or GA. In the case of Sri Lanka (Ceylon) Passé comments (1947:33), "It is worth noting, too, that Ceylonese [Sri Lankans] who speak 'standard English' are generally unpopular." During the last half-century the tendency in Sri Lanka is more toward favoring the localized norm (see Kandiah, 1981). In the Philippines, "Standard Filipino English" is *"the type of English which educated Filipinos speak, and which is acceptable in educated Filipino circles"* (Llamzon, 1969:15).

In such observations one notices that an unrealistic adherence to an exo-normative standard is clearly not attitudinally desirable. In most cases such discussions are specifically addressed to the spoken norm for English. Localized lexical innovations have always been recognized as legitimate and as a manifestation of nativization. But the nativization is not restricted to phonology and lexis. As stated in an earlier study (see Kachru, 1982c:7), it also shows in "collocational innovation, in syntactic simplification or overgeneralization, and in the use of native rhetorical and stylistic devices. In short, nativization creates a new ecology for a non-native language.

Conclusion

The question of norms for localized Englishes continues to be debated, though the tone is becoming more one of realism and less one of codification. Furthermore, the *educated* non-native varieties are now being increasingly recognized and defended, both on attitudinal and on pedagogical grounds. The national uses of English are being separated from the international uses, and the nativized innovations are now being considered as essential stylistic devices for non-native English literatures. One notices a shift of opinion toward considering such localized varieties *different*, not necessarily *deficient*.

One has to realize that there are several tendencies in the current spread of English. First, as stated earlier, English already has more non-native users than native users. The non-native users show a wide range of proficiency, almost ranging from ambilingualism to broken English. But functionally, each variety within a variety serves its functional purpose. Second, the planning for the spread of English is steadily passing into the hands of its non-native users. These users have developed their own norms that are not identical to the norms labeled RP and GA. In some cases the deviation from the native norm is the result of economic and other reasons, for example, a lack of good teachers, non-availability of teaching equipment and materials. Thus the British or American norm actually is never presented to students learning English. In other situations, the recognition of a localized norm is used as a defense mechanism to reduce the "colonial" and "Western" connotations associated with English. Such an attitude is one way of expressing what may be termed "linguistic emancipation." But that is only part of the story. There are other more significant reasons, too. First, this is how human languages seem to work. After all, the example of Latin is before us which eventually evolved into Romance languages. And, in spite of strict codification, Sanskrit has developed into numerous regional varieties in South Asia. Second, there is no doubt that the development of non-native literatures in English (contact literatures) have contributed to the "norm-breaking" trend in English around the world. The most interesting nativized innovations are the result of such contact literature.

The complex functions of English across cultures and languages make it very clear that whatever is said about it internationally will present only part of the picture. Therefore, the moral of the Eastern story of the elephant and the four blind men should serve as a warning; it should encourage us to undertake more empirical work across cultures to comprehend the totality. That type of research has yet to be initiated in a serious sense.

Notes

An earlier version of this chapter was published in French with the title "Normes régionales de l'anglais" in *La Norme Linguistique,* edited by Édith Bédard and Jacques Maurais, Québec: Conseil de la Langue Français, Gouvernement du Québec, 1983 pp. 707–730. An

English translation was published in *Initiatives in Communicative Language Teaching: A Book of Readings,* edited by Sandra J. Savignon and Margie S. Berns, New York: Addison-Wesley Publishing Company, 1984, pp. 55–78. This chapter is a revised version of the 1984 English translation.

1. A selected bibliography on this topic is given in Kachru, 1982c and in Smith, 1981.
2. For further discussion, see Kachru, 1983a and "Introduction: The Other Side of English" in 1982, ed.
3. See, for discussion and references, among others, Finegan, 1980; Heath, 1977; Kahane and Kahane, 1977; Kachru, 1982c; Mencken, 1919.
4. Note, for example, C. A. Ferguson's observation (in Kachru ed. 1982:vii): "Linguists, perhaps especially American linguists, have long given a special place to the native speaker as the only true valid and reliable source of language data, whether those data are the elicited texts of the descriptivist or the intuitions the theorist works with. Yet much of the world's verbal communication takes place by means of languages which are not the user's mother tongue, but their second, third, or nth language. . . . In fact, the whole mystique of native speaker and mother tongue should probably be quietly dropped from the linguists' set of professional myths about language."
5. See Kachru, 1983a for discussion of this phenomenon in the case of South Asian English; for African English, see Bokamba, 1982 and Chishimba, 1983 and Magura, 1984.
6. A comprehensive list of references on this topic is given in Nelson, 1982, 1983 and 1984.

Chapter 6

Native and Non-native Norms

IN the last century a substantial body of linguistic literature has been written presenting language attitudes of those speakers of English who use English as their first language, for example, the speakers of American English, British English, and Australian English. (For discussion see, e.g., Read, 1933, 1935, 1936 and 1938; Mencken, 1919.) These attitudes and reactions form a spectrum which vary from hilarious attitudinal epithets to a plea for linguistic tolerance (Quirk, 1972:14–31). In recent years the language war between cousins speaking the same language and living on different continents seems to have subsided. In America it has, however, taken the shape of a family feud in which the members of the same speech community, say, for example, the speakers of American English, have started evaluating attitudes toward the various dialect speakers of their variety of the language. On this side of the Atlantic the last decade has produced a great deal of literature presenting conflictive points of view on the *colored* varieties of English, i.e. Black and White. (See, e.g. Burling, 1973; Dillard, 1972; Labov, 1972a; and Shuy, 1967.)

In this chapter I propose to discuss another linguistic feud, primarily one of language attitudes, between the native speakers of various varieties of English (and some non-native speakers, too) and the speakers of the non-native varieties of English, such as Filipino English, West African English, Indian English, etc. In the available literature on this topic only one side of the picture seems to have been presented, that of the native speakers of English. I shall first discuss these attitudes and then focus on certain pragmatic questions related to a particular non-native variety of English used in a Third World country. Since in these countries a large spectrum of colors is involved, it is not possible to categorize these varieties as Black English, White English, or Brown English. No one color category can include all these varieties.

It would be appropriate first to clear away a few attitudinal cobwebs which we find in some recent literature, about non-native varieties of English. I do not want to give the impression that I am out to destroy an imaginary linguistic straw man; therefore, as an illustration of such linguistic attitudes, I shall use this chapter as a belated response to a paper of Clifford H. Prator, a distinguished and active scholar in the area of the Teaching of English as a Foreign Language. His paper "The British Heresy in TESL" (Fishman, *et al.,* 1968:459–76) provides my starting point for several reasons. First, it demonstrates a typical language attitude which continues to be nurtured by several educated native speakers and educators of English. Second, it reflects the attitude of one important segment of our profession toward those varieties of English which are not used as first languages; this interdisciplinary profession has several acronyms depending on which aspect of it is under focus, but the ones generally used are TESL and TEFL. In the TESL operation, as is evident from Prator's paper, an unrealistic and unpragmatic attitude toward the non-native varieties of English seems to have developed. The reasons for this are several, but one main reason is that, as yet, the role of English in the socio-linguistic context of each English-using Third World country is not properly understood, or is conveniently ignored. The consequences of this attitude are that the Third World countries are slowly realizing that, given the present attitude of TESL specialists, it is difficult to expect from such specialists any theoretical insights and professional leadership in this field which would be contextually, attitudinally and pragmatically useful to the Third World countries. Third, since Prator's attitude is shared by other influential people in the profession, it is important that a user of a Third World (transplanted) variety of English, like myself, attempt to present the other side of the picture. My side of the picture is naturally based on my Indian experience and Indian data; but it seems to me that one can make several generalizations on the basis of this experience which may apply to most of the Third World (English-using) countries.

The paper under discussion was presented by Prator in 1966 and published in 1968. This paper provides a good example of linguistic purism and linguistic intolerance, in which Prator has naturally associated himself, as he says, with the French attitude to language, and dissociated himself with what he terms "the British group." He discusses a doctrine which is "unjustifiable intellectually and not conducive to the best possible results in practice" (459). The heresy which has provoked Prator's puritanic wrath is summed up by him in the following words:

> . . . the heretical tenet I feel I must take exception to is the idea that it is best, in a country where English is not spoken natively but is widely used as the medium of instruction, to set up the local variety of English as the ultimate model to be imitated by those learning the language. (459)

I shall, therefore, first discuss briefly some of the points raised by Prator in his paper and then turn to the question of the pragmatics of the English language in a Third World country, namely India. By the term "pragmatics" I mean the roles and uses of English in the overall societal network of India, in which *Indian* English is used as a language of interaction, for maintaining *Indian* patterns of administration, education, and legal system, and also for creating a pan-Indian (Indian English) literature which forms part of the world writing in English.

Seven Attitudinal Sins

Since Prator's paper, both in its title and its tone, introduces us to the world of *heresies* in TESL, it might not be inappropriate to divide his attitude into seven parts and term these "the seven attitudinal sins." His paper is a sociolinguistically important document, as it exhibits the language attitude of an educated speaker, and his perception of how *his* language should be used by those who use it as a foreign or second language. It demonstrates much more than just that; it also establishes an identity with the speech community of another language based on the identical language attitudes (in his case, with the French). Prator then develops a set of fallacies to mark as separate those members of the English speech community who (he would like to believe) do not have language attitudes identical to his, namely the British.

It is easy to demonstrate that the linguistic tolerance attributed to my former colonial masters is undeserved. But I will not go into that digression here.[1] It is true that David Abercrombie, M. A. K. Halliday and Peter Strevens, among others, have adopted the position condemned as "heretical" by Prator. But the position of these scholars has developed partly as a reaction to those British scholars or organizations who hold views identical to those of Prator. However, I will go along with Prator's assumption about the British linguists working in the field of TESL and take the position that I am in good company with several British linguists in the stand which I adopt here. An analysis of Prator's paper shows that he has committed the following "seven attitudinal sins"—that is, if we follow his own use of the terms.

1. *The sin of ethnocentricism:* Prator has adopted (rather perversely) an intellectually and empirically unjustified view concerning the homogeneity and speech uniformity of American society. Consider, for example, his statement that "Social classes are difficult to distinguish in the United States, and social dialects show relatively little systematic variation" (471). This view is, of course, contrary to the empirical linguistic research undertaken in America for over two decades (see, e.g., Allen and Underwood, 1971; Currie, 1952; Labov, 1966; Marckwardt, 1958; Williamson and Burke, 1971). Consider, for example, the following observation in Wolfram and Fasold (1974:27):

> It is obvious that throughout the history of the English language in America, the layman has recognized that social differences were often reflected in language differences. Scholars of the English language in America have also been quite aware of these differences. Terms such as *vulgar, uncultivated, common* or *illiterate* speech all refer to what we now call Nonstandard English. For the most part, English scholars viewed these language varieties as deviations from acceptable usage, reflecting the same linguistic prejudice as the layman.

In earlier literature, too, the social parameter of language variation has been well documented and discussed (see, e.g., Babbitt, 1896 and McDavid, 1948). It is obvious, therefore, that this incorrect view has been adopted by Prator in spite of the empirical evidence contrary to it; in turn, it is this view which makes him adopt an unrealistic attitude to homogeneity and linguistic conformity in non-native varieties of English.

2. *The sin of wrong perception of the language attitudes on the two sides of the Atlantic:* Prator has attempted to structure the language attitudes of the speakers of English on the two sides of the Atlantic in a neat dichotomy: The British attitude is presented as one of ". . . deep-seated mistrust of the African who presumes to speak English too well" (471). This hypothesis has been built on the evidence of "at least one well known British linguist." The corollary of this "one British linguist's" observation is:

> A man who consciously regards language as a symbol of social status is naturally suspicious of one who appropriates the symbol but clearly does not belong to the social group that it typifies. If an Englishman is himself a proud speaker of RP, he may find each encounter with a person who obviously does not speak his language well a pleasantly reassuring reminder of the exclusiveness of his own social group. (471)

On the other hand, the attitude of the French and Americans is presented thus:

> The mistrust of French and Americans seems rather to be directed toward the outsider who does *not* speak French or English well. (471)

The reason for this attitude of the American English speaker, says Prator, is:

> . . . the American's greater experience with large numbers of immigrants, whose presence in his country he has felt as an economic threat and a social problem, undoubtedly helps to explain his greater antipathy toward foreign accents. (471)

The sociological asides supposed to provide bases for the two types of language attitudes, unfortunately, are not only counter-intuitive, but without any empirical basis.

3. *The sin of not recognizing the non-native varieties of English as culture-bound codes of communication:* It is evident from Prator's paper that he ignores the inevitable process of acculturation which the English language has undergone in Third World countries, for example, in the Indian sub-continent, Southeast Asia and Africa (see, e.g., Bailey and Görlach, ed. 1982; Kachru, ed. 1982 and 1983a; Pride, ed. 1982 and Smith, ed. 1981). In these countries the English language is not taught as a vehicle to introduce British or American culture. In these countries, English is used to teach and maintain the indigenous patterns of life and culture, to provide a link in culturally and linguistically pluralistic societies, and to maintain a continuity and uniformity in educational, administrative and legal systems. Again, let us consider the case of India as an example. In their almost two hundred years of not-so-peaceful stay on the Indian sub-continent, the Britishers left several legacies in India. One legacy which the Indians slowly accepted, and then in their typical Indian way acculturated, is the English language. The outcome of this long process of Indianization of the English language is what is now termed "Indian English" (see Kachru, 1983a). In the linguistic history of India this phenomenon is consistent with the past linguistic assimilations of this country—for example, the

Indianization of Persian, the Dravidization of Sanskrit, and the Indo-Aryanization of the Dravidian languages. (See, e.g., Gumperz and Wilson, 1971; Kachru, 1979). In this acculturation of languages, India is not unique, since this phenomenon is typical of a situation of language contact and language convergence.

4. *The sin of ignoring the systemicness of the non-native varieties of English:* The claim that there is a system to the non-native varieties of English, say, e.g., Indian English or West African English is not taken seriously by Prator. Though he agrees that the "mother-tongue varieties of English also lack complete consistency, and idiolects vary with circumstances" (46), he is obviously concerned that among the non-native English speakers

> ... very few speakers limit their abberrancies to the widely shared features: each individual typically adds in his own speech a large and idosyncratic collection of features reflecting his particular native language, educational background, and personal temperament. (464)

His concern develops into a serious worry when he proclaims no "specific meaning" for a definition such as "Indian English is the English spoken by educated Indians" (465).

However, it turns out that in linguistic research or preparation of pedagogical materials it is not uncommon to use identical "impressionistic," or what Prator calls "scientifically meaningless" concepts. Consider, for example, the use of the term "educated English" by Randolph Quirk for his Survey of English Usage, an outcome of which is the latest *A Grammar of Contemporary English*. When the project was initiated, Quirk presented the goal of the survey as follows: (Quirk, 1968:79)

> The Survey is concerned with 'educated' English: that is, no account is taken of dialect or sub-standard usage. But it is necessarily acknowledged that these terms are relative and that the varieties of English so labelled are by no means entirely contained within hard and fast boundaries. It is an important feature of a language's 'style reservoir' that there should be a periphery of relatively dubious usage which the timid avoid, the defiant embrace, and the provocative exploit; we may compare our mild fun with 'he didn't ought to have ate it' or 'who-done-it'. . . . A working definition like 'Educated English is English that is recognized as such by educated native English speakers' is not as valueless as its circularity would suggest . . .

In presenting the structure of the non-native varieties of English a more or less identical procedural concept was used. (See, for example, Bansal, 1969; Masica and Dave, 1972.) The concept of "cline of bilingualism" is crucial in this context. Consider, again, in this context the observation of Quirk (1972:49).

> In the Indian and African countries, we find an even spectrum of kinds of English, which extends from those most like Pidgin to those most like standard English, with imperceptible gradations the whole way along.

5. *The sin of ignoring linguistic interference and language dynamics:* There are several reasons why the non-native varieties of English deviate

at the phonological, grammatical and lexical levels. First, as is well known, the presence of a substratum. Second, the impact of cultural parameters. Third, resistance to the impact of linguistic change which influences the native varieties of English. Fourth, attaching primary importance to written sources, especially those of the eighteenth and nineteenth centuries. This manifests itself in what has been labeled "bookishness" in Indian English (Kachru, 1983a:41).

The impact of contextual parameters has been equally important in marking the distinctness of the native varieties of English, and in their innovations at various levels. This is well documented in Baker (1945) for Australian English, and Mencken (1919) and Marckwardt (1958:21–58) for American English.[2] In the same way, a large number of innovations in Indian English or West African English are contextually determined.

The English language has functioned in India for two hundred years; it would obviously be "intellectually unjustifiable" to expect it to function there in a socio-cultural vacuum. Probably it demonstrates the strength of the English language that the pragmatic parameters of India have molded it to Indian needs and functions. In other words, it has slowly gone through a process of Indianization. This is a process which is normal for a human language which is used for day to day interaction. Prator seems to attach too much importance to the "model" of the spoken word.

6. *The sin of overlooking the "cline of Englishness" in language intelligibility:* In whatever little research has been done heretofore on language intelligibility we find that this concept has yet to be related to the concepts of *appropriateness* and *effectiveness* in a speech situation (Catford, 1950:7–15; Nelson, 1982 and 1984). In understanding the pragmatic use of language it is essential that the concept intelligibility be explained in these terms and that it be related to the context of situation (Kachru, 1980d). The little we know about intelligibility convinces us to accept the cline of intelligibility more or less parallel to and related to the cline of bilingualism as suggested earlier. In fact, the cline of bilingualism makes sense only if intelligibility is used as the primary criterion. Note, however, that the cline of intelligibility is not a concept related only to the phonetic level of language, as Prator suggests, but extends to all the levels. It applies to the first language varieties of a language, to the second language varieties and also to intelligibility between dialects of the same language. Consider, for example, Quirk's observation (Quirk, 1972:36):

> It is in fact impossible to read the Lallans poetry of contemporary Scotland without believing them independent, or the novels of Alan Sillitoe without sharing his belief that the working class substandard speech of contemporary Nottingham is capable of the fullest sensibilities and range of expression. And you may recall that although Mellors was perfectly fluent in standard British English, he felt that only his Derbyshire dialect was adequate to loving Lady Chatterley.

Thus, the problem, as Prator perceives it, is not necessarily one of intelligibility between the speakers of the *native* varieties of English and the non-native varieties of English. Rather, the question is one of recognizing that there is a *cline* in intelligibility *among* the members of the speech community who speak different varieties. In the case of non-native speakers, the higher a person is on the cline of bilingualism, the higher intelligibility he attains with a person of identical background and education.

There are two other points which need enumeration here. First, in language learning, it is not only appropriate but crucial to relate the model of language to the attitudes and reactions of the actual learners. One wonders how sensible it is to present a speaker of RP as a model of spoken English to a class full of Black students in America, or a Midwestern speaker in a junior college in a village in India. Second, overemphasis on the role of the phonetic level for language intelligibility is also questionable. This question has two angles: One is a pedagogical one, the other is a pragmatic one. Pedagogically one might ask: Do *all* the Indian learners of English really need to concentrate on the spoken forms? The uses of English in India are so varied and so medium-restricted that a large percentage of learners, perhaps, need only a reading knowledge of English. In overemphasizing the spoken form of a language for intelligibility, we still seem to be under the hangover of the structuralist tenets of language pedagogy.

It seems to me that the whole concept of intelligibility is open to question if we do not include the appropriate parameters of the context of situation as relevant to intelligibility at various levels. J. R. Firth, a proud Englishman and a supporter of English as a world language, has put this point well in the following words (Firth, 1930:177 (quoted from 1966 reprint)):

> In the primary speech situation 'meaning' is as much a property of the situational context of people, things, and events as of the 'noise' made by the speaker. The noise is important, but not nearly so important as purists and others believe.

7. *The sin of exhibiting language colonialism:* An enthusiastic defender of the non-native varieties of English will not be too wrong if he detects traces of linguistic and cultural colonialism in Prator's arguments. If this attitude does not manifest itself in the imposition of a particular language, it shows in an unrealistic prescription with reference to a model.

Prator mentions the current research in language learning in which various types of motivations for achievement in language learning are discussed, for example, Lambert's research at McGill University. Out of the two motivations in language learning, namely *integrative* and *instrumental,* Prator seems to recommend an "integrative" orientation to the language teaching as opposed to an "instrumental" orientation. In an approach based on the integrative orientation a learner wants ". . . to identify with members of the other linguistic-cultural group and be willing to take on very subtle aspects of their behavior such as their language *or even their style of speech* (Prator's italics, 474). On the other hand, in the instrumental orientation, a language is used primarily as a tool and ". . . corresponds to the typically British attitude toward the teaching of English" (474).

In presenting these two motivations in language learning Prator seems to set up a preferential order with an embedded language attitude which ignores the realities concerning the uses of English and elevates the integrative approach to the level of cultural colonization. The "insistence on aiming toward a mother-tongue type of pronunciation is an essential part" in the teaching of French, German or Russian in India, but the case of English in India is entirely different from those of these languages.

In suggesting—even indirectly—the "integrative approach" to the teaching of English in India Prator is committing several fallacies, viz. (a) neglecting the roles of English primarily as an *Indianized* link language for use in Indian culture and society; (b) failing to see the role of English as identical to that of Sanskrit in earlier Indian history, or that of Indian Persian in the North of India during the Muslim period. It is true that the areas of function of Sanskrit and English are not identical. However, the parallel between the use of these languages in the Indian socio-cultural network remains; and (c) failing to make a distinction between *second* language learning and *foreign* language learning at various levels of bilingualism in a culture where over 23 million people are English-knowing bilinguals (that is, approximately 3 percent of India's 1985 population.)

In India, as in other Third World countries, the English language is used to "integrate" culturally and linguistically pluralistic societies. "Integration" with the British or American culture is not the primary aim. It might not be out of place to mention here that this "outer language colonialism" seems to manifest itself in "internal colonialism"[3] within the U.S.A. too, especially with reference to the attitude toward Black English and such other varieties of English.

From "Sins" to "Heresies": the Case of Indian English

Prator's language attitude is clearly shown in the preceding statements which I have labeled "attitudinal sins." In addition, the list of "heresies" reflecting his attitude toward one specific non-native variety of English, namely Indian English, is equally impressive.

I shall discuss some of these "heresies" below, since Prator has made claims which are subjective and without any empirical basis. It is not uncommon to find Prator's claims on Indian English quoted by others without verification. These claims, and many other such claims, have gained a snowball effect and generated several myths about Indian English.

The first claim Prator makes is that ". . . *the doctrine of local models of English are championed more often and more vehemently in India than anywhere else*" (473, emphasis added).

In chapter 2 (pp. 22–23), I have presented the results of a survey of the attitudes toward various models of English among the faculty and graduate students in English in Indian Universities (see Tables 1–3 in chapter 2). I shall not repeat the results here. On the basis of this survey it is evident that Prator's above claim is not justified.[4]

It is interesting that Indians still consider the British model to be the preferred model (66.66 percent first preference). It is only after British English that they rank Indian English. Perhaps Prator is not aware of the fact that the struggle for recognition of the term and concept "Indian English" has as eventful a history as that for the terms "American English" and "Australian English." The opposition to the concept Indian English came from both British educators and highly educated Indians. It is only recently that the term has gained currency in India (Kachru, 1983a).

The second claim Prator makes is that ". . . *for the rest of the English-speaking world the most unintelligible educated variety is Indian English*" (473; emphasis added). It is obvious that in making this statement Prator has been carried away by emotions and by his language attitude. It is not even clear what Prator has in mind when he uses the term "Indian English." Indian English has a cline of intelligibility the same way as does any other variety of a language. A distinction therefore, has to be made between the *educated* or the *standard* variety as opposed to its *non-standard* varieties. The educated or standard variety of Indian English will also allow variation, as does educated British English or American English. In this context let me present the sober words of a blue-blooded Englishman and a distinguished linguist, J. R. Firth. (Firth, 1930, reprint 1966:196)

> Educated English shows a wide range of permissible variation. Speakers of this kind of English do not necessarily submerge all signs of social or geographical origin. Their accent is often unmistakably local or characteristic of a class. Educated English is spoken by all classes of people all over the English-speaking world. This is the only kind of English that has the remotest chance of universality even in Great Britain itself.

And he also warns against cultivating ". . . a shameful negative English which effectually masks social and local origin and is a suppression of all that is vital in speech."

At present we have very little empirical evidence on the question of the intelligibility of non-native varieties of English. The results of a study completed in 1969 (Bansal, 1969) are summarized in Table 1 below. The table presents the results of tests for measuring intelligibility between, (i) Indian

TABLE 1. *The Intelligibility of Indian English (Test Results)*

	Participants in test	Highest %	Lowest %	Average
1.	Indian English & RP speakers (group)	73	67	70
2.	Indian English & RP speakers (cline of intelligibility)	95	53	—
3.	Indian English & American English speakers	81	72	74
4.	Indian English & German speakers	67	40	57
5.	Indian English speakers & Nigerians	66	34	53
6.	Indian English speakers with other Indian English speakers	88	54	74
7.	RP speakers with other RP speakers	100	95	97

English speakers and native speakers of English (both American English and RP speakers); (ii) between Indian English speakers and other non-native speakers of English (Germans and Nigerians); (iii) among the speakers of Indian English. Note that the highest figures and the average figures are of interest, and these do not support the subjective judgment of Prator.

In his third claim Prator is only partly correct; at least, that is what the above-mentioned survey shows. His claim is that *"An Afghan will probably be greatly pleased if you tell him he speaks English like an Englishman or an American; an Indian may be quite disconcerted by the same remark"* (460; emphasis added). Any educator working in the field of English studies in India could intuitively tell Prator that he is not completely correct in making such a statement.

In chapter 2 (p. 23 Table 3), I have presented the responses to the self-identification of the spoken variety of English by graduate students majoring in English. (See also Shaw, 1981).

Indian English in the Indian Sociolinguistic Context

After discussing Prator's attitudinal linguistic "sins" and "heresies," let me now turn to the question of Indian English in the Indian sociolinguistic context. In order to contextualize Indian English with reference to its participants in what may be termed "the Indian English speech community," two questions must be asked: First, *why* is Indian English (or, if one prefers, just English) used in India? Second, *how* is Indian English used by the Indian English speech community? The first question then relates to the *functions* of Indian English in typically Indian contexts, and the second to the *formal* aspects of Indian English. It seems to me that it is only after one relates the functions and form of Indian English that one can provide a pragmatic profile of this variety of English in Indian culture and society. It is only then that one can meaningfully explain the deviations of Indian English from the native varieties of English at different linguistic levels.

In the development of the distinct non-native varieties of English three types of grids have primarily determined their 'deviations' from the native varieties of English: *the cultural grid, the linguistic grid,* and *the pragmatic grid.*

The interaction of cultural and linguistic grids in a language contact situation, and their influence on languages at different linguistic levels, has formed part of linguistic studies from the neo-grammarian period to the recent studies of Black English and the non-native varieties of English (for a detailed bibliography see Kachru, ed. 1982 and 1983a). I shall, therefore, not discuss these here. By the term "pragmatic grid" I mean the use of language in contextually determined situations, the emphasis being on the appropriateness of an utterance in a well defined contextual unit. (See for discussion Kachru, 1983a). The appropriateness of an utterance may be judged by *contextual substitution* and *textual substitution* (Kachru, 1983a, chapters 3 and 4). The contextual unit is, of course, to be related to the wider "context of situation" peculiar to the speech community which is actually using the language under discussion.

A pragmatic profile of Indian English: A pragmatic profile of Indian English will not be complete without answering the following questions: Who are the members of the Indian English speech community? Who do the members of the Indian English speech community interact with outside their own speech community?

The membership of the Indian English speech community consists primarily of those bi- or multilingual Indians who use English as a second language mainly in Indian sociocultural, educational and administrative contexts. In all these contexts the interaction is basically among Indians who make use of English as a "link" language or as an "official" language. Only a minimal fraction of the English-using Indian literate population has any interaction with native speakers of English. In fact, it is interesting that out of the graduate faculty of English in the universities and colleges surveyed by me, 65.64 percent had only occasional interaction with native speakers and 11.79 percent had no interaction. Only 5.12 percent claim to have daily interaction with native speakers of English. Note that in this case we are talking of a highly specialized segment of the Indian educated population, professionally involved in the teaching of English at the higher level (see Table 2). Such interaction will be considerably less if we take a typical cross section of the users of English in India from all walks of life.

TABLE 2. *Interaction of Graduate Faculty of English with Native Speakers of English*

Frequency	%
Daily	5.12
Very frequently	15.38
Occasionally	65.64
Never	11.79

The varieties of Indian English: In the multilinguistic and culturally pluralistic context of India, the English language has naturally developed its regional, social and occupational varieties just as any living language is expected to do. The standard (or educated) variety of Indian English cuts across these regional varieties, in the same way as does standard American English in America, or Standard Scottish English in Scotland. It is interesting to note that the members of the Indian English speech community surveyed by me intuitively recognized from one to ten varieties of Indian English. (See Table 3).

The uses of English in India: Indian English has developed typically Indian registers of legal system, business, newspapers, and also a large body of Indian English creative writing (fiction, poetry, etc.). A detailed

TABLE 3. *Varieties of Indian English Intuitively
Recognized by Members of the Indian English
Speech Community*

Number of varieties	% of respondents
One	16.59
Two	17.68
Three	16.73
Four	12.92
Five	7.75
Six	4.08
Seven	5.03
Eight	1.76
Nine	.54
Ten	.95

treatment of these and other aspects of Indian English is available in Iyengar (1962), Kachru (1983a), Mukherjee, (1971), Naik, *et al.* (1968) and Narasimhaiah (1967). (For an extensive bibliography see Singh *et al.*, 1981).

In chapter 2 (p. 27), two tables have been included (nos. 9 and 10) to show, for example, the use of Engish in the reading of general literature and also in personal interaction (see also K. Sridhar, 1982a).

Third World Englishes: Two Premises

It seems to me that it is essential that the attitudes toward the major Third World varieties of English should not be those of Prator. There is a need to see the function of these varieties with reference to the country in which English is used, its roles in the sociocultural network and the dependency of the local variety on the native variety with special reference to interaction with native speakers. If looked at in this way, the cases of India and West Africa are different from those of Japan and Iran. Let me provide here a specific example with reference to Indian English. We must accept two premises concerning Indian English, as we should about any other Third World variety of English. First, that the users of Indian English form a distinct speech community who use a variety of English which is by and large formally distinct because it performs functions which are different from the other varieties of English. Second, that Indian English functions in the Indian socio-cultural context in order to perform those roles which are relevant and appropriate to the social, educational and administrative network of India.

It is evident that the position Prator adopts is based on a fundamentally different assumption, namely that the aim of the Indian English speech community is necessarily to interact with (and become part of) those speakers of English who use it as their first language. This assumption is only partly true. A fraction of Indian English speakers certainly have such goals in mind if they desire positions in the foreign service or international business, or if they desire interaction with the international scholarly community. The small group of such status seekers in India, as elsewhere, have to be proficient in a model which is very high on the cline of intelligibility. It does not necessarily have to be RP or standard American English. Let the model be *educated* Indian English. A little effort on the part of the native speakers to understand Indians is as important as a little effort on the part of Indians to make themselves understood by those who use English as their first language. The result will be a desirable variety of English with the distinctiveness of Kissingerian English, intelligible, acceptable and at the same time enjoyable. Let us not make over twenty-three million Indian English speakers sound like WASPS lost in the tropical terrain of India, nor should they sound, as Quirk notes, like the RP speakers sound to the Americans, "clipped, cold and rather effeminate." (Quirk, 1972:22)

The second premise is that the *appropriateness* of these varieties should be judged with reference to the socio-cultural context of the particular non-native speech community which is using the variety. It seems to me that in language use one has to consider three things, namely role appropriateness, intelligiblity between the participants in the role, and cultural appropriateness. In the case of Indian English, the Indian context of situation provides the parameters of appropriateness. In turn, it is these parameters which determine the deviations of Indian English. These deviations are naturally variety-restricted, register-restricted and genre-restricted. (For details see Kachru, 1983a). A large number of deviations result from the process of acculturation which has rightly made the non-native varieties of English culture-bound and created a *distance* between the various varieties. This is an inevitable process which is both linguistically and culturally justifiable. After all, language is a tool of communication, and Indian English is used as a tool of linguistic interaction by Indians to communicate mainly with other Indians.

In the context of English as a second language, it is, therefore, desirable to recognize an hierarchy in its use. On that hierarchy, as mentioned earlier, the needs for the study of English, e.g. in Japan and Iran on the one hand, and India and West Africa on the other hand, will rank differently. It is crucial that the sociolinguistic realities of each country and area be taken into consideration in any discussion of the teaching of English in the Third World.

Conclusion

It is obvious that in the Third World countries the choice of functions, uses and models of English has to be determined on a pragmatic basis, keeping in view the local conditions and needs. It will, therefore, be appropriate that the native speakers of English abandon the attitude of linguistic chauvinism and replace it with an attitude of linguistic tolerance. The strength of the English language is in presenting the *Americanness* in its

American variety, and the *Englishness* in its British variety. Let us, there-fore, appreciate and encourage the Third World varieties of English too. The individuality of the Third World varieties, such as the *Indianness* of its Indian variety, is contributing to the linguistic mosaic which the speakers of the English language have created in the English speaking world. The attitude toward these varieties ought to be one of appreciation and under-standing, and not the attitude of Prator whose call is to ". . . cry out for . . . denunciation." (463)

It is, however, reassuring to note that Prator's linguistic purism is not shared by all scholars, even on this side of the Atlantic. Lloyd's refreshing discussion of this problem applies as much to the non-native varieties of English as to native varieties. His comments on the attitude of the "snobs and slobs" of the English language is worth recapitulating (Lloyd, 1951 [1972]:124)

> If there is one thing which is of the essence of language, it is its drive to adapt. In an expanding culture like ours, which is invading whole new realms of thought and experi-ence, the inherited language is not wholly suited to what we have to say. We need more exact and expressive modes of utterance than we have; we are working toward finer tolerances. The fabric of our language is flexible, and it can meet our needs. Indeed, we cannot stop it from doing so. Therefore it would be well and wholesome for us to see, in the locutions of the educated which bring us up sharply as we read, not evidences of a rising tide of illiteracy (which they are not), but marks of a grand shift in modes of expression, a self-reliant regionalism, and a persistent groping toward finer distinctions and a more precise utterance.

In recent literature, both by linguists and scholars involved in TESL and TEFL, one notices an increasing tendency toward the attitude present in Firth and Lloyd. (See, for example, Gleason, 1960; Halliday *et al.*, 1964; Richards, 1972.) This tendency is encouraging, but as yet this attitude has not been accepted by the practicing TESL specialists in general either in Britain or in the U.S.A.

In the preceding sections I hope that I have not given the impression that this chapter is intended primarily as a defense of Indian English and as a rejoinder to an attitude shown toward this non-native variety of English.[5] That was only a partial aim. My main aim is to question the bases of the linguistic attitude which one encounters in the English speaking world toward the non-native varieties of English which have developed in Africa, South Asia and other parts of the world. I have made a plea for a new perspective, a realistic vision and, of course, an understanding toward the Third World varieties of English. In some sense such a change in attitudes is already noticeable—though still in restricted circles—toward Black English and Chicano English in the U.S.A., and toward Scottish and other varieties of British English in Britain. The next step in this slowly increasing linguistic tolerance may hopefully be an understanding of the pragmatics of the "new Englishes." It is important to understand the func-tions of these varieties of English in the perspective of their uses and users. A change in the current language attitude is, therefore, desirable for various cultural, linguistic, educational, and, what is more important, pragmatic reasons, some of which I have discussed in this chapter.

Notes

This chapter is a slightly modified version of "Models of English for the Third World: white man's linguistic burden or language pragmatics?" *TESOL Quarterly* 1975, 10.2:221–39. It has also appeared in *New Varieties of English: Issues and Approaches,* edited by Jack C. Richards. Occasional Paper no. 8. SEAMEO Regional Language Centre, Singapore, 1979:pp. 1–17. An earlier version of this chapter was presented at the Ninth Annual Convention of the Teachers of English to Speakers of Other Languages, Los Angeles, California on March 7, 1975.

1. One might say that Prator has been unfair in condemning the whole British nation for a linguistic tolerance which traditionally they have not extended even to the first varieties of English, say Australian English, American English, and Scottish English. A Scotsman speaking Scottish English was until recently made to blush for his "dialect" in the portals of the British Broadcasting Corporation and the Foreign Service Office. The RP speaking fraternity was dominant, and RP was considered the only model for the teaching and learning of English. It seems to me that even now the attitude present in the work of David Abercrombie, M. A. K Halliday and Peter Strevens does not represent the attitude of the majority of British educators and TESL specialists, but, then, that is another story.
2. This point has been well presented by Marckwardt (1958:6) with reference to American English:

   . . . [Language] is the product of the society which employs it, and as it is employed it is engaged in a continual process of re-creation. If this is the case we may reasonably expect a language to reflect the culture, the folkways, the characteristic psychology of the people who use it."

   There is no reason to believe that the same logic should not apply to a non-native variety of English which has been used as a second language in a linguistically and culturally pluralistic context for over two hundred years in India or in parts of Africa.
3. I have taken this term from Rudolph C. Troike (personal communication).
4. The pilot survey was originally undertaken by me as a consultant to the Ford Foundation during 1974. (See Kachru, 1975b.) I am thankful to the following for helping me in abstracting the relevant information from the questionnaires: Syed Mohd Syeed, Ahmad Hasan Siddiqui, and S. N. Sridhar.
5. My views on the formal and functional aspects of Indian English are presented in Kachru, 1983a. This volume includes Kachru, 1965 and 1966.

Chapter 7

New Englishes and Old Models

IN chapter 4 the issues concerning regional norms of English have been discussed in a broad sense. In this chapter I shall return to the controversial question of norms for English. This question has resulted in serious discussion both in the case of native and non-native varieties of English. I shall focus primarily on the non-native varieties. It is evident that this discussion is a timely one and is crucial to evaluating the roles of English in a pragmatic context. So far TESL operations in the Third World have been seen only from the point of view of the native speakers of English, mainly in a pedagogical framework. The question of the Third World varieties of English is not a purely pedagogical one; it has several sociolinguistic and glossopolitical implications which are peculiar to each English-using country. One might, therefore, question the validity of a didactic approach, and suggest a dynamic approach for the teaching of English around the world. A dynamic approach entails—to some extent—rejection of a native *monomodel* concept and acceptance of a *polymodel* concept. A reconsideration, naturally, means taking a fresh look at some already established non-native *varieties* and *styles* of English, their uses and users, and their range of interaction with the native speakers of English. A reconsideration of these questions will provide answers to theoretical questions, as well as to sociolinguistically relevant questions such as *appropriateness*, *acceptance*, and *intelligibility*.

Focus of the Controversy

The recent concern and controversy about the models of English is primarily addressed to those who have acquired English as their second or foreign language. This concern has further intensified as a reaction to the development in the non-native varieties of English of local varieties, distinct localized registers, and culture-bound styles. (See chapters 2 and 10).

English as an international language

One might say that this controversy is a consequence of the slow but definite growth of the use of English as an international or universal second language, especially after the failure of artificial international

s, as I have discussed in chapter 1 (see also chapter 8). In the last
ades no serious competing models for a universal language have
posed. The lack of enthusiasm in this area may be due to sheer
on, or to the failure of those earlier efforts. At present we find that,
because of practical necessity, English has already acquired such a
status in spite of there being no formal declaration of this new universal
role for English.

It is natural that with the end of the political colonization by the English-
speaking part of the West, a reassessment of the roles and functions of
English in the post-colonial period is taking place in some of the Third
World countries. On the one hand, one finds in these countries an upsurge
of nationalism, and a strong current of language identity. But at the same
time, the English language is not only tolerated now; it has also been reas-
signed important roles in the language planning of several countries which
were anti-British and anti-English during the colonial period. One could
not have earlier predicted that the post-colonial era would initiate a
distinctly pragmatic language attitude toward the English language in these
Asian and African countries. The result of this changed attitude, and a
practical need for an international language, is that on all the continents
there is a demand for learning and teaching English. We now have a situation when for the first time a natural language has been given an
unprecedented and enviable role as a universal language, though under-
standably with hesitation and some resistance.

There is no need to reiterate here that several historical and other
factors contributed toward the attainment of this enviable position by the
English language. The diffusion of bilingualism in English was a result of
the colonization of Africa, Asia, and several other areas. This diffusion
had direct and indirect support and encouragement from the affluent and
powerful English-speaking countries. Western English-medium education
cultivated native elite groups in these countries who in turn became supporters of English. These historical factors should not, however,
overshadow the more positive and practical strengths of English; for
example, its rich and varied literary tradition, its wide use in science and
technology, and its capacity for absorption and acculturation in varied
sociocultural and linguistic contexts.

Diversities in the speech community

An outcome of the acceptance of English in this new role is that there is a
fast expanding international English-knowing speech community. The
term *English-knowing speech community* is a very strong generalization. It
conceals various diversities that are crucial for understanding its particular
functions. In order to understand the situation in the world context, one
must categorize the users of English into various types of speech fellowships. I will not elaborate on this point here as I have discussed it in
detail in Kachru 1985.

The Concept "Model"

In pedagogical literature the term "model" entails a prescriptivism with reference to a specific variety of a language or a dialect; it is, therefore, a useful concept both for language acquisition and for language teaching. In a sense, then, a model implies a linguistic *ideal* which a teacher and a learner keep in mind in imparting instruction or in learning a language (see Kachru, 1982c). It is generally the case that the underlying reasons for advocating a particular model are based on language attitude, language identity, and prestige factors. In practical terms it means acquisition of a language at various linguistic levels (phonetic, phonological, grammatical, lexical) consistent with the model under focus. In order to acquire "native-like control," to use Bloomfield's (1933:56) terms one would also have to acquire cultural nuances with the language in order to qualify to be a "native-like" speaker. A non-native RP (Received Pronunciation) speaker will appear incongruent if he puts on this linguistic mask but does not combine it with the mannerisms and cultural traits of an RP speaker.

One might argue that a prescriptive *linguistic* standard is incomplete unless one imbibes the relevant cultural component with it. I shall come back to this point later, but let me mention here that the need to integrate linguistic and cultural components is questionable, at least in some parts of English-speaking world (see chapters 5 and 6).

The concept 'model' is directly related to language intelligibility. Since one acquires a language to communicate, intelligibility naturally plays a crucial role in language pedagogy. One cannot deny, therefore, that in the teaching of English the question of a model has importance both in the native contexts for dialect speakers, and the non-native context for learners of English as a second or foreign language. We are not considering those contexts in which a passive knowledge of English is acquired for reading specialized texts and where proficiency in the spoken language is not emphasized. However, the situation of English is not as simple as it is, for example, in the case of German, Russian, or Hindi. The case of English is complex for more than one reason. First, there is no academy for English with the specific tasks of overseeing the standards and suggesting policies for overall standardization, as there is, for example, the French. The existence of such an academy does not necessarily mean that it would be successful in its task of universal standardization. But it could, at least, provide a forum for the purists and some amusement for the non-purists. In earlier chapters I have discussed this, particularly the proposal of Jonathan Swift which was submitted in 1712 (see e.g., chapter 5; for a detailed discussion see also Baron, 1982).

Another reason for the complexity of the English situation is that the second-language varieties of English have acquired numerous roles over an extended period—in some cases almost two centuries—and as a result have been embedded in the native sociocultural and linguistic matrix of the area where they are used. The acculturation of these varieties has been so deep that now questions are raised as to whether a *native* model of

English is desirable and possible for such non-native varieties. This position has been adopted by several educators in South Asia, West Africa, and other parts of the world. In their view, a pragmatic attitude has to be adopted toward the functions of these varieties with reference to the particular educational, political, and cultural needs of the countries in question (see Kachru, 1981c).

Two Views on the Models of English for the Third World

The recent discussion on the question of the models for English are based on very little empirical research. The debate seems to be based on language attitudes and native speakers' perceptions of the problem. There are primarily two approaches that have been recommended or adopted in TESL circles termed 'integrative' and 'instrumental' approaches. These two approaches and their relevance to the institutionalized varieties of English are discussed in chapter 6 (see pp. 106–7). As indicated in that chapter, there are adherents to both these approaches, though Prator (1968) associates the "integrative approach" with America and the "instrumental approach" with Britain. It is certain that the approach of some Americans, such as Prator, is diametrically opposed to the more pragmatic approach of some British linguists. In both these countries, however, a majority of TESL specialists continue to see the teaching of English from a native speaker's point of view, and very little effort has been made to understand the Third World user's point of view.

The Parameters for a Model

It is generally thought that the goal for excellence in language teaching and learning is acquiring a "native-like" command, and, as a consequence, *acceptance* by a native speaker. This argument seems to be valid for a majority of language-learning situations. One would, however, be reluctant to accept it as a crucial criterion for TESL in all countries since the reasons for retaining English in their language planning are not identical. The variations in the functions of English in each country, the diversity of proficiency, and the goals for acquiring proficiency make it essential to consider each country separately. In suggesting a model for each (sub-) speech community, therefore, the criteria will be different, since the contexts are different. In terms of intelligibility we find that in some countries—for example, India or Nigeria—the need for intelligiblity with the native speakers applies only to a fraction of the Indian Engilsh or Nigerian English speech community. (For relevant references and discussion see Nelson, 1982 and 1984).

There is thus a diversity with reference to varieties, and then each variety, as is expected, is not homogeneous. (This point has been discussed with examples on pp. 36–7). In certain countries the uses of English encompass *native* African or Asian real-life situations. Thus the form of a *speech event* in English in a parallel *social event* is determined by the culture in which English is used. This interaction of an "alien" language in a "non-English" context results in the *newness* in the new varieties, styles, and registers of English (see Kachru, 1983b). The authenticity and functional appropriateness of such uses cannot be judged by American or British standards, since the adopted (or transplanted) language has been nativized in non-American and non-British situations. We must, therefore, use a thoretically and pragmatically dynamic approach to account for the deviations that we find in such *Englishes.* One way of explaining these deviations is in terms of various types of nativization which a Western language has undergone in non-Western contexts. It is in this area, as in several other areas of second language acquisition, that sociolinguistic insights may be useful.

One can think of various theoretical frameworks with reference to which a model may be suggested—for example, the Firthian concept of *Context of Situation* (see Kachru, 1966), or Hymes' concept of *Ethnography of Communication* (see Hymes, 1964, 1972b, and 1974; see also Saville-Troike, 1981) or, simply, one may use pragmatic considerations for each speech fellowship. A good starting point may be to use Ferguson's schema for a sociolinguistic profile (see Ferguson, 1966). It seems to me that whichever underlying theoretical framework is used, it will soon become clear that a monomodel approach for all the varieties of English is open to question. The following are some tentative parameters in terms of which a model may be determined for each speech fellowship.

I. Context of situation

The educational, linguistic, and glossopolitical settings which determine the use of English.

II. Participants in a speech event

At one end an Amerian or British model may be desirable for those who desire international communication. On the other hand, there may be another group whose aim is a native model for communication in local multilinguistic situations. An extreme case is that of pidginized varieties which are appropriate in certain situations in, for example, South Asia and Africa.

III. Cline of intelligibility

The cline of intelligibility is linked with the cline of participants. Intelligibility is to be determined with reference to participants in various types of interactions. In several countries the uses of English entail acquiring repertoires of various subvarieties which are determined by the repertoire of roles one performs in a sub-speech community. In the Indian English speech fellowship one sees a speaker switching from the regionally marked variety (for example, *Punjabi English, Kashmiri English*) to *educated* Indian English. Some speakers may even switch over to a variety that is a close approximation of American or British English. It is not uncommon to find that in certain contexts only a code-mixed variety of English is used (see Kachru, 1983a, chapter 7). Intelligibility, then, is not an absolute criterion but is participant- and context-dependent.

IV. Roles and types of linguistic interaction

It is crucial to see what social roles lectal switch and "mixing" play in a speech fellowship. In Singapore, India and Nigeria to name just three countries, one immediately notices the social value of the use of subvarieties within a localized variety of English.

It seems to me that sociolinguistic profiles for English in the Third World countries will make it clear that the concept of one English for all consumers is pragmatically unsound. It should also become clearer that the *native* models for use in *all* Third World countries, at *all* levels, for *all* the members of a speech fellowship in *all* roles, is a constraint imposed by attitudes against which natural languages normally rebel.

New Englishes without Old Models: Toward Nativization

If we study the development of the new Englishes such as Indian English, Nigerian English, or Singaporean English within the framework that I have suggested above, it should become apparent that those who recommended a local model of English for the non-normative varieties are not out to get even with the past colonizers by nativizing the language of the Raj, or to demonstrate a nationalistic pride, or exhibit a linguistic perversity without realizing its ultimate consequences. One or all these motives have been attributed to those who have espoused the cause of local models of English, either for the native varieties of English or for the non-native varieties of English. One can easily demonstrate that the linguistic and contextual reasons for declaring independence from Mother English (British English) are identical for American English, Australian English, and Canadian English, and also for the well-established non-native varieties such as Indian English or Singaporean English.

The non-native varieties function in societal, linguistic and cultural networks that are distinctly different from those of America and Britain. Since English is used for intercultural interaction across languages in South Asia and Africa, the result has been a slow process of acculturation; which one might label, for example, South Asianization or Africanization. This is an inevitable linguistic process, which has applied earlier to Latin, Sanskrit, and various other languages. It is a process that is impossible to stop, but perhaps difficult for purists to accept.

A realistic understanding of the sociolinguistic context of each English-using country is not possible without taking into consideration the cultural, linguistic and pragmatic reasons for the use of English in these countries. These three reasons explain the acculturation of English in, for instance South Asia, parts of African, and in the West Indies. The cultural and linguistic factors have been discussed in literature earlier (see, for example, Kachru, 1983a; see also chapter 10). I shall not enumerate those here. In a pragmatic sense one might ask two types of questions. The first type may include the following, among others: Why is English used in a particular country as opposed to one of the native languages? What deviations (or innovations) have resulted because of those uses in that particular area? Are those deviations (or innovations) culturally and linguistically determined with reference to a specific area? The other set of questions is: Who are the members of a particular non-native speech community? Do they use English primarily to interact with the native speakers of English, or within their own speech fellowships? In functional terms, then, the role of the Third World varieties has to be viewed with reference to the sociocultural network of a particular country. Generalizations from an American or British standpoint are dangerous, and to a large degree irrelevant. The uses have to be perceived from the consumer's vantage point, not that of the native speaker's linguistically secure perch.

If we analyze and explain the styles and other innovations with reference to the context of situation, they become meaningful. Even the deviations in pronunciation and insistence on the use of *local* English pronunciation in certain educational contexts can be understood. It is in such a context that the nativization of English has to be justified. An extreme case of such nativization is the development of the code-mixed varieties of English such as "Spanglish" (see Nash, 1977 and Kachru, 1983a, chapter 7). These code-mixed varieties are used in varied contexts by educated and uneducated speakers alike all over the English-using world. Once we look at these varieties from this perspective, I hope that it will become clearer why Indian English is as much culturebound as is any other Indian language. Therefore, the modifier *Indian* with English is both linguistically and culturally indicative of the unique role that it plays in the Indian context of situation. As its Indian *uses* increase, the chances of its getting further away from the British or American varieties are greater. A time may come when certain subvarieties of Indian English may not even be intelligible to the native speakers of English, as some English-based pidgins are not intelligible to them now. This is already true of the code-mixed varieties such as "Hinglish." But then, that is how language works; and if it happens to one type of Indian English, all it means is that linguistic history is repeating itself. This is not a cause for alarm, since Indian English maintains varying degrees of *Englishness* which is graded from pidgin to educated Indian English. In a sense, the steps in the gradation reveal the degree of nativization of a language.

The formal manifestations of the processes of nativization of English in Africa and South Asia have only recently begun to be studied. When I first initiated such a study, even the term "Indian English" was academically suspect and linguistically esoteric. However, during the last twenty years the situation has changed. This changed context and research paradigm is well reflected in, for example, studies such as the following: Chishimba, 1983, Kachru, ed. 1982 and 1983a, Lowenberg, 1984, Magura, 1984, Nelson, 1984 and Pride, ed. 1982. The purists may find it repulsive, but pragmatists feel that at least a linguistic reality has been recognized.

The English-speaking world has been more receptive and, lately, appreciative too, of the creative writing in non-native varieties of English. This body of writing provides a good example of both contextual and linguistic nativization of the English language. Labels such as *African* English literature, the *Philippine* English literature and *Indian* English literature do not mark these literatures separate only in a geographical sense, but also in terms of form and content. These literatures are *national* literatures as much as the literatures in the African or Indian languages. The English language has been used to add another dimension to these literatures: a dimension that cuts across linguistic and cultural pluralism (see, for example, for Indian English literature, Iyengar, 1962; Mukherjee, 1971; and Naik, *et al.*, 1968; and for West Indies English, Ramchand, 1970; for African literature see discussion and bibliographic references in Chishimba, 1983 and Magura, 1984; see also relevant chapters in Kachru, ed. 1982). The creative uses of the English language in such writing has naturally resulted in a style range. These styles are distinct from British or American creative styles. They have to be, since they function in an African or an Indian cultural context.

The question then is: is English still an "alien" language for these users? In what sense can they sue English "creatively" in an Indian or African context and still not deviate from the American or British model? These are pragmatic questions and not polemic ones.

Communicative Competence in English: Culture-Bound or Culture-Free?

On the basis of the preceding discussion, one might say that concepts such as "communicative competence" in English are conditioned by the context of situation of each English-speaking country. One cannot claim a pedagogical universality and communicative universality for such concepts for all the English-speaking countries. The totality of verbal repertoire which forms part of communicative competence entails *acceptability, appropriateness,* and *intelligibiltiy* in the context of culture. These notions are dependent on the participants in specific functions. A speech act that is appropriate and congruent for American English is not necessarily appropriate in *Indian* English, *Nigerian* English, or *Singaporean* English. A casual reading of fiction and journalistic writing in these three varieties of English will make this point clearer. Does this mean, then, that I am making a plea for rejecting prescriptivism? That interpretation would be an extreme and uncharitable one. My claim is that as an international language the functions of English vary with each country. The criteria for a model will vary from one country to another. In certain contexts the goal must be interaction with the native speakers. On the other hand, the peculiar contexts of South Asia, and West African cannot be ignored. In these areas, English functions both as an *international* link and a *national* link. In certain cases both these roles are performed by the same person. In other cases—that is, in a majority of cases—the uses are exclusively *national*. English is the only language that the user has known in such contexts. The uses are so varied, so deep, and so culture-bound that the nativization of the English language becomes an inevitable process.

Conclusion

In view of the universal uses of English, a didactic approach based on monomodel concept seems to be unrealistic. The pragmatics of the uses of the English language can be understood only if a dynamic polymodel approach is adopted. What we should recognize is that at one level we have an internationally understood English, in spite of its local characteristics. In addition, there are several types of *Englishes*, for example in South Asia or parts of Africa, which are not meant necessarily for the consumption of a *native* speaker of English. They have their national or regional functions. On the cline of *Englishness* these may be low, but functionally they serve the purpose of communication as does any other human language.

The universality of pedagogical models is suspect: it has to be sacrificed for local sociopolitical, educational, and communicative needs. An important question still remains, which is in the minds of many who propose a didactic approach for TESL: Is it possible now to fulfil the dream of Jonathan Swift and set up an international academy for universal standardization of English, say, in Los Angeles, London, or Edinburgh? I am very cynical about such an undertaking.

Note

This chapter is adapted from "New Englishes and Old Models," *English Language Forum*, July 1977, pp. 29–35

PART III
Impact and Change

Chapter 8

American English and other Englishes

THE total number of languages in the world is large: say between 4,000 and 4,500. But, considering the total world population of 4 billion and 19 million, this seems to be a small number. If we divide this number by 4,500 languages, we have approximately one language for every 893,111 people, but that is not exactly how human languages are distributed. There are only five languages that can claim a really large number of speakers: Chinese, English, Hindi-Urdu, Russian, and Spanish. Of these languages, only English can claim to have attained the enviable position of a more or less universal language. A universal language is one which, in its various forms and functions, is used by a large portion of the human population for easy communication between peoples of diverse cultural and language backgrounds. Attempts have been made toward developing a universal or international language since the 1880s. These attempts, however, have not been successful, though some artificial international languages have had partial success: for example, Esperanto. Other such attempts were much less successful, as was the case with Novial, Occidental, Interlingua, Volapük, Ido, etc. The reasons for their failure are many, but the fact is that they have less chance of general acceptance and survival than does a choice from among existing natural languages.

As I have mentioned in chapter 1, in the past, several natural languages have acquired widespread roles in ritual, diplomacy, literature, or fashion. One does not have to think hard to find examples: Latin for ritualistic uses and learned professions in Europe, French in diplomacy and fashion, and Sanskrit for ritualistic, religious, and literary functions in South Asia. However, in the last two centuries, the picture has completely changed. English, which was a minor language in the sixteenth century, has slowly but definitely gained an edge over other major languages as an international language. If we compare the present position of English with what the English Poet John Dryden had to say about it in 1693, we can understand the extent of its diffusion and gain in prestige in the last three hundred years. Dryden complained, "We have yet no prosodia, not so much as a tolerable dictionary, or a grammar, so that our language is in a manner barbarous" (cited in Baugh and Cable, 1978:255). The primary reasons for such development and expansion are not essentially linguistic, but political, social, and technological. After all, linguistically speaking, or in terms of the communicative potential of a language, any human language has the potential of becoming an international language.

Let us briefly discuss what contributed to the attainment of such status by English. The main reason was colonization, which brought major parts of Africa and Asia under the direct rule of English-speaking Britain. This initiated the diffusion of various types and degrees of bilingualism in English. The introduction of western English-medium education resulted in the emergence of native elite groups in the far-flung areas of the empire, who in turn became the supporters of English and of western models of education. The diffusion of English as the language of colonial masters need not overshadow many positive aspects for which English was accepted and even demanded by the colonized people. The positive aspects of English include its long and rich literary tradition in various forms, its widespread use as a language of science and technology, and its proven capacity to absorb from various languages and cultures.

Englishes of the World

When we talk of the English language as an international language or as a universal language, we are talking of an abstract concept. Actually, there are a number of *Englishes* present in the world. The all-embracing concept of the English-using speech community entails a strong generalization, since this speech community includes a number of subcommunities which may be divided in various ways. The first broad division may be in terms of the English-speaking nations of the world, for example, American English, Australian English, British English, Canadian English, Indian English, Jamaican English and so forth. If we use ethnic criteria, we have, among others, Chicano English and Anglo-Indian English. On the other hand, if we are fond of color categories, we may use labels such as Black English, Brown English, White English, and Yellow English. The ways to cut the cake are limitless, and one can use a number of linguistic or functional criteria to do so.

There is, however, one distinction among the users of English which is useful and important to our present discussion. We must divide this speech community into further sub-groups, as I did in chapter 2, pp. 19–20, in order to see the roles and functions of the world Englishes in a realistic international context. The first group comprises those who use English as their first language—their mother tongue—as do a large number of Americans, British, Australians, or English-speaking Canadians, South Africans or West Indians. These speakers may form culturally distinct groups, but they are *native* speakers of English. The second group uses English as their *second* language. In their case English is an acquired language which is learned after they have learned their mother tongue, which may be one of the languages of Africa or South or Southeast Asia. The second language speakers of English must further be separated from those who use it as a *foreign* language, as for example in Iran for science and technology, in Japan for international commerce and tourism, or in Sweden where it has become the most popular foreign language in the schools. English as a second language has a distinct status in the language planning of a number of countries. In India, for example, it is treated as one of two associate official languages in the Indian Constitution, the other being Hindi. However, this is not true of those countries where it is used basically as a foreign language. The members of the English-speaking community thus form a spectrum with reference to their competence in English: those who use English as their first language or mother tongue, as a second language—a medium of education, language of government, and the like—or simply as a foreign language. These distinctions are important since they separate these varieties in terms of their functions, the proficiency of their speakers, and the processes which are used to acquire each variety.

The relevant figures concerning the speakers of various varieties of English have been given in chapter 2 (p. 20).

American English and Other Colonial Englishes

The American variety of English has several special characteristics associated with its growth and development that offer an interesting linguistic case study for comparison with other varieties of English. On the one hand, it provides an example of linguistic pride and what may be termed a conscious effort toward establishing language identity. On the other hand, it has the unique characteristics of a transplanted language. In this respect, then, it can be related to other Englishes which have been transplanted in various parts of the world. Mathews (1931:9) was therefore correct when he said:

> The fact should be borne in mind that the treatment given the English language in this country does not differ in kind from that given to the language wherever English colonists have gone. In India, Canada, Australia, and Africa the English language has been modified in very much the same way that it has in this country.

Other terms have also been used for transplanted English. Turner (1966) used the term "English transported" for Australian and New Zealand English: later Ramson (1970) also used this term as the title of his book, *English Transported: Essays on Australasian English*. Indian English fiction has been termed by Mukherjee (1971) *The Twice Born Fiction*, since as she says, it is "the product of two parent traditions . . ."

The attitude of British English speakers toward American English was not much different from their attitude toward other varieties of English. As an example, it is useful to read what the Very Reverend Henry Alford, D. D., Dean of Canterbury, had to say in his "Plea for the Queen's English" in 1863: "Look at the process of deterioration which our Queen's English has undergone at the hands of the Americans. Look at those phrases which so amuse us in their speech and books; at their reckless exaggeration and contempt for congruity . . ." One way to show nationalistic pride against such an attitude of the "mother English" speakers was to proclaim American English distinct from the variety spoken by the cousins on the other side of the Atlantic. Therefore, initially some scholars preferred to call it the *American language* as opposed to *American English*. One might say that this was one way of getting even with the colonizers' linguistic superiority. This attitude is present in the well-known book by H. L. Mencken entitled *The American Language*. It was published in 1919 and embodies what Noah Webster (the "cracker-barrel lexicographer") had said over a century earlier about American English. The following words of Webster may not necessarily have proved correct, but they do demonstrate an attitude which cannot be ignored in understanding the genesis of American English.

> Several circumstances render a future separation of the American tongue from the English necessary and unavoidable. The vicinity of the European nations, with the uninterrupted communication in peace, and the changes of dominion in war, are gradually assimilating their respective languages. The English with others is suffering continual alterations. America, placed at a distance from those nations, will feel, in a much less degree, the influence of the assimilating causes; at the same time, numerous local causes, such as a new country, new associations of people, new combinations of ideas in arts and science, and some intercourse with tribes wholly unknown in Europe, will introduce new words into the American tongue. These causes will produce, in a course of time, a language in North America as different from the future language of England, as the modern Dutch, Danish and Swedish are from the German, or from one another . . . [Webster 1789:22].

We have introduced the term "transplanted language," and it is natural to ask what such a term implies and in what sense a language may be transplanted. A language may be considered transplanted if it is used by a significant number of speakers in social, cultural, and geographical contexts different from the contexts in which it was originally used. In this sense, then, there are several varieties of English which continue to be used as native languages by a majority of the people in Australia, Canada, the United States, and New Zealand which, as we know, were transplanted from the mother country, England. There are many other languages which have such transplanted varieties, for example, Spanish and Portuguese in Latin America; French in Canada and parts of Africa; Portuguese in Brazil, Sri Lanka, and Africa; Persian in India and Afghanistan; and Hindi in Fiji, South Africa, and the West Indies.

One might then say that a transplanted language is cut off from its traditional roots and begins to function in new surroundings, in new roles and new contexts. This newness initiates changes in language. It is these changes which eventually result in certain characteristic linguistic manifestations and are identified with labels such as the "Australianness" in one variety, the "Americanness" in another variety, or the "Indianness" in still another variety of English. These linguistic characteristics can be described with reference to the typical linguistically relevant "clue-marking" indicators such as those of social status, geographical origin, caste membership, or educational background, and in terms of the traditional linguistic levels. Phonological (and phonetic) clues show the differences in the way speakers pronounce words and use rhythmic or intonation patterns in a sentence. Syntactic (or grammatical) clues show how words are combined in larger units, clauses, or sentences. Morphological clues mark how words are formed from minimal meaningful terms. Lexical clues provide information about the vocabulary of language. Semantic clues are concerned with what is generally known as "meaning." Thus, the "Americanness" in American English lies in the way Americans pronounce words, combine smaller units into larger units, and use the vocabulary. The same can be said about the "Australianness" in Australian English and the "Indianness" in Indian English. It is therefore appropriate that the modifiers of nationality (e.g. American, Australian, Canadian, Caribbean, Indian) are used to mark each variety different from the other varieties.

At this point, it should be noted that the concept of difference must not be taken too far. There are more similarities than differences between the diverse varieties of English; that is how an underlying Englishness is maintained in all these Englishes spoken around the globe. If it were not so, there would be serious problems in intelligibility between the speakers of various types of Englishes. Imagine the situation if Americans could not understand Australians, and Australians could not understand the British; or for that matter, if the educated non-native speakers of English, such as Indians and Nigerians, could not be understood by native speakers. But as we know, that is not generally the case. Any native speaker of English may have value judgments about varieties of English other than his own, i.e. an American may intuitively recognize the speech of Englishmen as· "clipped, cold and rather effeminate"; an Englishman may speak of "the nasal twang" of an American, or the "sing-song" English of an Indian. However, in spite of these stereotypes of varieties of English, educated speakers of all these varieties generally understand each other. A native speaker of a language does not have to be a linguist to notice the individual, regional, or national speech characteristics of a person. After all, we often hear people say "he speaks a dialect," "he sounds like an Indian," "this person sounds Australian"; such judgments are based on associating some features of a person's speech with a dialect, Indian English, or Australian English. The professional describes the differences for which non-linguists use cover terms such as "nasal twang" or "sing-song English" in a much more precise and technical way, but the fact of variation is recognized by both. Differences in speech are characteristic of the subgroups in speech communities.

The distinction which I mentioned earlier between the mother English of Britain and transplanted Englishes will, I think, be useful to us now. Mother English had a development and growth typical of a natural language. It was a historical development with various phases. English has done substantial pick-pocketing from other languages, such as Arabic (e.g. *alcohol, algebra, cork*); Dutch (e.g. *brandy, gin, golf*); French (e.g. *cavalier, garage, rapport*); German (e.g. *hamburger, wiener, bum*); Italian (e.g. *balcony, granite, sonnet*); Persian (e.g. *divan, shawl, spinach*); Greek (e.g. *barometer, idiot, tactics*); Hindi (e.g. *shampoo, pajama, pandit*); Spanish (e.g. *alligator, mosquito, sherry*); American Indian languages (e.g. *choco-*

late, hominy, moose), thereby enriching its word stock. But that is a different story and has been well documented in most of the histories of the English language, for example Baugh (1935).

Let us now use the term "other Englishes" for those varieties of English which were spread and developed in areas other than the British Isles. As we noted, the speakers of mother English were not always tolerant and patient toward the growth and development of such varieties. On the contrary, they often had an attitude of arrogance and impatience toward transplanted varieties of English, since the speakers of such varieties did not conform to the patterns of Standard British English—what came to be called in the linguistics literature the received pronunciation (generally abbreviated RP). RP is a type of acquired British speech generally considered as standard; it is the language of the famous old "public" schools and the universities of Oxford and Cambridge.

We might say that there is a bond which connects all the transplanted varieties of English, among them American English. This is perhaps as it should be. There are many reasons for it, one being that the processes which the speakers of these languages had to go through to establish their language identities have been more or less the same. The process of establishing an identity for a language can be as painful and as arduous as the struggle for political emancipation. In fact, that is part of the reason why some people attach so much importance to language in a political system or in nation-building activities. This is also the reason why language and nationalism are related and sometimes result in violent language conflicts, as for example in Belgium, Canada, Sri Lanka, and India.

The kinship among the transplanted varieties is historical, cultural, and linguistic. In historical terms the other Englishes have developed in two ways. The most stable and powerful centers of the other Englishes are those countries which were settled in by the British and have proportionately high populations from the mother country, i.e. Australia, Canada, the United States, and New Zealand. These countries were for a long time closely dependent on the mother country economically, culturally, and otherwise. As Laird (1970:377) observes, "Until about the time of the 1914–18 war, the United States, well supplied with raw materials, imported almost everything else—human beings, religions, customs, education, science and technology, ideas, manufactured goods, books—in fact, most things that could bring language with them." If we add up the number of native speakers of English in the above-mentioned four countries, it is only 211.2 million; less than the number of speakers who use English as a non-native language around the world (see Strevens, 1982).

In addition to these transplanted varieties, the other Englishes that have significantly contributed to the diffusion of the English language are the result of Asian and African colonization which made Britain a world power of unparalleled strength and wealth for almost three hundred years. The contribution of colonialism to the countries in Asia and Africa has been a controversial and an ongoing topic since the loss of the colonies. There are those who have only a critical or nationalistic attitude toward

TABLE 1. *Enrollment in English in the top ten*
nations in which English functions as a second language

Country	Students (millions)
India	17.6
Philippines	9.8
Nigeria	3.9
Bangladesh	3.8
Republic of South Africa	3.5
Malaysia	2.4
Pakistan	1.8
Kenya	1.7
Ghana	1.6
Sri Lanka	1.2

Source; Statistics based on Gage and Ohannessian 1974.

the colonial period, emphasizing the oppressive aspects of empire. There are also those who consider the British benign colonizers who, among other things, left the unifying legacy of the English language behind them. In the newly independent and formerly colonized nations, when hectic efforts are being made to remove marks of the colonial past with an upsurge of nationalistic pride, the English language is not necessarily considered a mark of that past; after all, it has been Africanized, Indianized, Caribbeanized, and has become a part of the living national traditions.

Therefore, it is not surprising that the non-native Englishes show a wide spectrum of uses—English in the former British colonies continues in the form of an "official" or "complementary" language or as a "library" language. It has also been termed a "link" language, and rightly so.

How was bilingualism in English initiated in various parts of the world? In chapter 3 (pp. 33–6) there is a brief discussion of the introduction of English in South Asia. It is a fascinating study of language imposition and language acculturation, and in many respects, it is similar to the cases of other non-native World Englishes. The African case, for example, is not much different. However, on that continent the missionaries had a deeper and greater impact on education and were more successful in the conversion of local people than they were on the Indian subcontinent. Their initial impact on African education started in the seventeenth century and did not stop with the end of Western colonization in Africa. The results in spreading Christianity in Africa are, therefore, more visible than elsewhere. Mazrui (1975:12; see also Chishimba, 1983 and Magura, 1984) correctly observes that "The Christian nations of the world are either white nations or black nations—there are almost no Christian nations in the intermediate colours of Asia." The colonial administrators also approached education differently in Africa. There the missionaries seem to have controlled education even after the European administrators began to pay attention to education. Knappert (1965:99) notes:

European administrations began to think of education, they found that apart
Coranic schools, all the education in Africa was being carried out by the
ies. The government then gave the missionaries full responsibility for all edu-
to and including secondary level. That is how the number of languages
primary level rose to more than twenty in some countries and the govern-
uraged diversity rather than unity.

The Asian, African, and West Indian varieties of English therefore have a clear colonial past. There are people in these countries who associate the English language with the colonial period and consider the supporters of English in those countries "Indo-Saxons" or "Afro-Saxons." Others in the now independent countries of Africa and Asia have a strong desire to establish identity with Great Britain and remain loyal to the British Standard.

The colonial past of the not-so-colonial Englishes, such as American English or Australian English, cannot be equated with the colonial experiences of Asia and Africa. But in linguistic terms, these varieties demonstrate all the characteristics of a transplanted language. They also share an attitude of linguistic schizophrenia toward mother English, some wishing to be emancipated, others to remain loyal, considering British English the model and, therefore, an authority to be followed and imitated. "The standard writers of a language are, like the guardians of a well ordered state, its preservers from anarchy and revolution. They must be read—and as far as imitation is allowable must be copied . . ." (Beck, 1830:79).

Let us consider the earlier history of American English. At the beginning, the idea of a British model for American English was not actually relished by leaders of the American Independence movement. But there were some who felt a bond of "loyalty" toward it (see Heath, 1977; Kahane and Kahane, 1977). Those who supported the continuation of the linguistic bond felt a "language loyalty" toward Britain for cultural, humanistic, and literary reasons and, above all, to maintain "language solidarity." In opposition to this attitude of loyalty, there were those who wished to declare American English separate. Linguistic "emancipation" was, in the United States as in other post-colonial nations, a natural consequence of political strife. In the United States, this attitude was behind suggestions to eradicate all symbols of the colonial past, including the English language. Attitudes favoring linguistic emancipation or loyalty in every nation are, however, most often caused by factors which are not linguistic. Desires to separate from or unify with a group motivate language loyalties. Ethnicity and or nationalism may cause groups to promote or decry English as a first or second language. In no case, especially for the now independent countries of Africa and Asia, is it possible to ascribe loyalty to or renunciation of English to single or simple causes.

Nativization of Other Englishes

As I have mentioned, the other Englishes have more similarities to mother English than differences. Otherwise, it would be inappropriate to treat them as varieties of English. In *A Common Language: British and American English* by Marckwardt and Quirk (1964:5) an attempt has been made to show that "the two varieties of English . . . have never been so different as people have imagined, and the dominant tendency, for several decades now, has clearly been that of convergence and even greater similarity." A study of Australian, Caribbean, Indian, Nigerian, or Filipino English will also show that in all these varieties there is an underlying Englishness. There is no need to elaborate on this point further.

However, I would like to discuss some typical characteristics of these other Englishes, which mark their distinct "Americanness," "Caribbeanness," "Indianness," or "Africanness." We will also see that the typical national or regional characteristics in each variety are, by and large, the result of the particular contexts. It is these linguistic, cultural, and ethnic contexts which provide the sources for what are termed Americanisms, Indianisms, Africanisms, or Caribbeanisms. Thus, the sources which result in the distinctiveness of these other Englishes are results of typical language-contact situations. In the new contexts, two or more languages come into contact for political, geographical, historical, or educational reasons; and the natural outcome of such contacts is linguistic innovation. The innovations specific to each variety can be regarded as deviations with reference to a norm. It is the sum total of these *deviations* in pronunciation, grammar, vocabulary, style-range and discourse strategies which provides the framework for labeling various formations as Americanisms, Indianisms, Caribbeanisms, etc. Traditionally, the mother English of Britain has been considered the norm for marking the deviations; although in the case of certain second language varieties of English, as in the Philippines, Standard American English is treated as the norm.

Since we are focusing on the other Englishes primarily from a linguistic point of view, we should be able to account for the linguistic characteristics of each new variety, explained in terms of what the native context has contributed to it. The contribution of the native cultural and or linguistic contexts results in what is technically called interference or transfer.

A quick glance at the dictionaries of other Englishes will show us many examples of such transfer. If a variety of English already has its own dictionary or other lexical studies, as American English, Australian English, Caribbean English, and Indian English have, it shows that the process of Americanization, Australianization, Caribbeanization, or Indianization of the English language has already taken place. In a variety-oriented lexicon we find several types of deviations. These may include words or compounds which are the result of the culturally pluralistic contexts of the New World, or of Asian and African colonies in which the English language was introduced. Also, these might demonstrate the new specialized uses to which the English language has been put in new contexts in administration, education, and politics.

One hundred and fifty years ago, in 1828, Noah Webster (see Sledd and Ebbit, 1962:32–3) presented the following arguments for a distinctly American lexicon of the English language:

> It is not only important, but, in a degree necessary, that the people of this country, should have an *American Dictionary* of the English language; for, although the body of the language is the same as in England, and it is desirable to perpetuate that sameness, yet some differences must exist. . . . A great number of words in our language require to be defined in a phraseology accommodated to the condition and institutions of the people in these states, and the people of England must look to an American dictionary for a correct understanding of such terms.

Webster's point regarding definitions of words suited to local circumstances is similar to the observation of Wilson (1940:1) about the uniqueness of certain terms in Indian English:

> *Ryot* and *Ryotwar*, for instance, suggest more precise and positive notions in connection with the subject of the land revenue in the South of India, than would be conveyed by cultivator, or peasant or agriculturist, or by an agreement for rent or revenue with the individual members of the agricultural classes.

The Englishman's terms, *cultivator, peasant,* and *agriculturist,* have to be replaced by *ryot* and *ryotwar* in the South Indian context. In their monumental and entertaining work, *Hobson-Jobson,* Yule and Burnell (1886:xxi) have pointed to the typical Indian characteristic of Indian English:

> Within my own earliest memory Spanish dollars were current in England at a specified value if they bore a stamp from the English mint. And similarly there are certain English words, often obsolete in Europe, which have received in India currency with a special stamp of meaning; whilst in other cases our language has formed in India new compounds applicable to new objects or shades of meaning. To one or other of these classes belong *outcry, buggy, home, interloper, rogue(-elephant), tiffin, furlough, elk, roundel* ('an umbrella,' obsolete), *pish-pash, earth-oil, hog-deer, flying-fox, garden-house, musk-rat, nor-wester, iron-wood, long-drawers, barking-deer, custard-apple, grass-cutter,* etc.

It is due to the typically Caribbean uses of English that Allsopp (1972:5) has proposed "an authoritative lexicographical account of English *usage* in the Caribbean which must do more than give 'meanings' in isolation, but refer words and phrases to their areas and contexts of occurrence . . ." Such a Caribbean lexicon would account for the nativization of English in various forms; but it will also account for lexical variation (different names for the same item), for example, *golden apple* in Barbados has regional variants such as *pomme, cythere, jew plum, golden plum, box, meeting-turn, pardner, sousou, syndicate*; and it will explain the ethnic impact "in Caribbean culture from Trinidad and Guyana" and list Indic words such as *daru, holi, phagwa, anjuman, taja,* which were introduced by the East Indian to Caribbean English. In the global context of English, as Allsopp (1972:4) says, "Webster's or any other American dictionary, even when it calls itself 'International,' deals essentially with North American life, and fails, for Caribbean purposes . . ." Americanisms such as *bull-frog, razor-back, turkey-gobbler, egg-plant, jimson-weed, fox-grape,* and *apple-butter* listed by Mencken (1936:113–21) are context-bound in the same way as the Indianisms such as *twice-born, dining-leaf,* or *caste-mark* are in Indian

English. There is, as Spencer (1971:28) says, "certainly a sufficiency of terms and expressions" to justify the term West Africanisms in English. Consider, for example, *cutting-grass, chewing-stick, head-tie, market-mammy, mammy-wagon,* and *fetish-priest.*

The best example of the influence of the multilingual settings of the new Englishes is provided by the process of hybridization. This process results in a number of formations which comprise lexical items from two or more languages and, in a sense, contextualize an item in a particular variety of English. Consider, for example, the following hybridized Indianisms listed in Kachru (1975a): *lathi-charge, tiffin-carrier, tonga-driver, ahimsa-soldier.* Such formations may further be divided into those which have and those which do not have grammatical constraints in the selection of the members of a hybridized item; for example, the four illustrations provided above, as opposed to others which have certain grammatical constraints. In such items we have a prefix from one language, as in *non-Brahmin,* and the noun from another language. On the other hand, we may have a suffix from one language and the preceding noun from another language as *-wala* in *policewala,* *-hood* in *Brahminhood,* *-dom* in *cooliedom,* and *-ism* in *goondaism.*

The nativization of English manifests itself in a much deeper form than merely in pronunciation and vocabulary. These two aspects are, of course, very obvious to any observant speaker of any variety of English. The aspect which has been least studied is the acculturation of English in various non-Western contexts. One can think of a number of contexts which have resulted in such acculturation. For instance, the caste system, in the typical Indian sense, is absent in those countries where English is used as the first language. Therefore, when the English language is used in typically non-English contexts, as in referring to the caste system or non-Western social roles, various linguistic devices are used to represent such contexts. These devices may include lexical borrowing from the local languages, extension of the semantic range of the English lexical items, or translation of native situation-dependent formations into English. The use of *forehead-marking* for the crimson caste mark which Hindus put on their forehead, or *nine-stranded thread* for the ritualistic thread worn after initiation called *yagnopvīt* by the Hindus, have semantic relevance only if viewed in the context of the Indian caste system.

It is the use of English in non-Western social roles or speech functions in Africa or Asia which brings out its Africanization or Asianization. Let us consider the following examples which are used in the speech functions of greetings or personal interaction in Asian or African English and are translated from their native languages into English for certain stylistic effect and local color. Such formations are not part of day-to-day linguistic interaction. That, however, is not an important point. What is interesting is the underlying motivation for such transcreations. A large number of such examples from Africa are given in Chishimba, 1983 and Magura, 1984, from South Asia in Kachru, 1983a and from Southeast Asia in Lowenberg, 1984. A number of such innovations are discussed in chapters 2, 4 and 10.

(1) May we live to see ourselves tomorrow
(2) He has no chest
(3) He has no shadow
(4) Where does your wealth reside?
(5) What honorable noun does you honour bear?

If we consider these five examples from an American English speaker's point of view, they are contextually deviant and also deviant in the selection of words. One might say this is not the company which these words keep in such contexts in American English. In linguistic terms the Indian or African use of these words places them in a deviant collocation.

If seen from another point of view, we might say that their functional and formal appropriateness is doubtful, since they do not form part of the communicative repertoire of an American English speaker. On the other hand, let us consider (1) and (3) above from the point of view of an African English user whose first language is Ijaw, and for him, *May we live to see ourselves tomorrow* is roughly the equivalent of *Good night* in Western societies. Sentences (2) and (3) are the equivalent of *He is timid*, and as Okara (1963:15) says, "Now a person without a chest in the physical sense can only mean a human that does not exist. The idea becomes clearer in the second translation. A person who does not cast a shadow of course does not exist . . ."

Sentences (4) and (5) are translations from Punjabi, an Indian language, and have been used in Indian English fiction by Khushwant Singh in his *Train to Pakistan*. These are culturally dependent polite forms for what would be equivalent to American English *Where do you live?* and *What is your name?* Many Indian English speakers will use these in normal speech only for comic effect, but in written English they are used by Singh for developing a character type in a plot, in which such use of English does not sound incongruous.

The device of translation is generally adopted by creative writers in English in Africa (e.g., Amos Tutuola, Chinua Achebe), in India (e.g., Mulk Raj Anand, Khushwant Singh), and in Singapore (e.g., Arthur Yap, Catherine Lim). The response to the use of this device is not always enthusiastic: It has been termed 'linguistic exhibitionism'.

As such formations gain wider currency, they become more acceptable—there is nothing intrinsically non-English about them. If we compare the idioms *a crocodile in a loin cloth* and *pin drop silence*, we notice that the first is more deviant in Indian English than is the second, the reason being that *pin drop silence* is heard and read more often than is *a crocodile in a loin cloth*. The device of translation is also used for creating local color. Consider, for example, the comparative constructions *lean as an areca-nut tree, helpless as a calf, as good as kitchen ashes,* and *as honest as an elephant* (Kachru, 1976a). In Australian English (Ramson, 1970:52) what may be termed "local color" is similarly conveyed by formations such as *fit as a Malee bull, looking like a consumptive kangaroo, mean as a dishwasher, awkward as a pig with a serviette,* and *handy as a cow with a musket.*

In the preceding paragraphs we have seen that each variety of English undergoes a process of acculturation in its new sociocultural context. In its new surroundings the transplanted English naturally becomes culture-bound. In order to make clearer what is meant by culture-bound, I shall present below two texts which can be properly understood and appreciated only if they are related to the cultural context of each variety. In *No Longer at Ease* (1960), Chinua Achebe, a West African English novelist, presents a blend of pidgin and educated English and provides a good example from West African speech of the functional use of code switching, i.e. the switching from one language or language variety to another in the stream of discourse.

The text by Achebe has already been cited in chapter 4 (p. 63), I will, therefore, not repeat it here. It begins with "Good! See you later." It is interspersed with sentences from another code, a pidgin. Achebe is consciously code switching here to introduce linguistic realism in an interaction between the African participants. The 'switch' provides an authenticity to the text, and Africanizes the context. It also shows the range of varieties within which switches are possible. In this particular text, out of the two varieties, one variety is generally intelligible to educated English speakers across cultures, and the other variety is highly localized—and functionally restricted. But given the appropriate context and participants both varieties are appropriate and pragmatically useful.

Another way of contextualizing a text is to use the device of code-mixing, i.e. the use of elements such as lexical items or larger units from another language or language variety in the stream of discourse (Kachru, 1978a). In discussing South Asian music, to give one example, English lexical items are inadequate to present the technical concepts of Indian traditions of music. Consider the following example.

> He set the pace for the recital with a briskly rendered Pranamamayakam in Gowlai a composition of Mysore Vasudevachar. One liked the manner in which he and his accompanying vidwan built up the kriti embellishing it with little flourishes here and there ... Then came Kamboji Alapana for Pallavi ... with Vedanayagam Pillai's Nane Unnic Nambinane in Hamsanandi the recital came to a glorious end. (*The Statesman*, December 14, 1969).

This excerpt is from a standard national newspaper.

Labels such as "West African" English, "Indian" English, and "American" English are useful to show that these varieties are not marked separately only in a geographical sense, but also in terms of their cultural component and language features. In order to adapt his discourse to a specific cultural context, an author may use a spectrum of Englishes—as does Achebe in the passage on page 63—which vary from pidgin, regional, and national to international.

The national Englishes have essentially local uses in culturally and linguistically pluralistic societies. In turn, they have subvarieties which have varying degrees of intelligibility with the English of native speakers or with that of educated speakers of particular national varieties. Allsopp (1972) proposes several subvarieties of Caribbean English, namely "free vernacular," "vernaculars of subcultures," "elevated vernacular," "creolized English," and "formal Caribbean English." One might say that Indian English, too, has various subvarieties, ranging from almost complete intelligibility with native speakers of English to very limited intelligibility. These subvarieties are "educated Indian English," "Babu English," "Chee Chee English," "Butler English," and "Bazār English" (see Kachru, 1981c).

It is, however, the pronunciation of a speaker which provides an index to the variety of his speech, or to a variety within a variety. As we know, one does not have to be initiated in phonetics or linguistics to identify, for example, a speaker of the American, British, or Indian varieties of English. Pronunciation seems to provide crucial clues toward marking a person as being within a particular group or outside it. By pronunciation we mean the use of segments, termed vowels and consonants, and equally if not more importantly, the way a person arranges syllables for the rhythm of language. It is well known now that rhythm plays an important role in intelligibility. We see that in English, as in other natural languages, some forms of pronunciation acquire prestige or become more acceptable. In chapter 5, we have seen that the two well-documented and generally acceptable forms of the native varieties of English are Received Pronunciation (RP), and General American (GA). There is no legal or official acceptance for these forms since, as mentioned earlier, English has no academy to regularize language use or prescribe language "etiquette." These standard forms develop by general acceptance or judgment, by looking up to some group, caste, or class for providing a language model, by accepting a model because it is spoken in a particular area, or by considering dictionaries, manuals, or certain types of educated people as "models" for linguistic etiquette. RP or GA are not necessarily "correct," but are more widely known. The radio has contributed to their acceptance.

It is generally true that a standard variety of language is well documented and described by phoneticians, linguists, and language pedagogues. English has pronouncing dictionaries for both RP and GA. That was not, for example, true for Indian English or West African English until recently. Therefore, it was not uncommon to hear questions such as: What is Indian English? What is its "standard" or "educated" form? By form, of course, was meant description, as this term is understood by linguists.

There is no doubt that the users of non-native Englishes found it more convenient to use RP, or a close approximation to it, as a pedagogical model. RP was well documented and teaching aids and materials were readily available. The well known British phonetician Daniel Jones had by 1918 made the job of teachers easier by his classic work *An Outline of English Phonetics* (OEP). It is not surprising that by 1956 it had already run into eight editions. Then appeared his *Everyman's English Pronouncing Dictionary* (*EPD*). What was more important, Jones stimulated a number of other young phoneticians to supplement his work. It was not long after Jones' *OEP* that John S. Kenyon published *American Pronunciation* (1924), followed by *A Pronouncing Dictionary of American English* (*PDAE*) (1944). Kenyon (1924:3) was unhappy to see that

> there are few subjects on which educated Americans are so ready to pass judgment and give advice on the basis of so little sound knowledge as the pronunciation of the English we use. Influenced by certain types of teaching in the schools, by the undiscriminating use of textbooks on grammar and rhetoric, by unintelligent use of the dictionary, by manuals of "correct English", each with its favorite (and different) shibboleth, and, it would seem, by anybody or anything that has an air of cocksureness about it, we accept rules of pronunciation as authoritative without inquiry into either the validity of the rules or the fitness of their authors to promulgate them.

These works on either side of the Atlantic opened the flood gates for such manuals. But it would be erroneous to say that Jones and Kenyon were the first to make such attempts. Since there is always demand for such books on language "etiquette," we find, for example, that in 1687 a phonetician named Christopher Cooper published *The English Teacher, or The Discovery of the Art of Teaching and Learning the English Tongue.* The aim of this book was to present rules of English pronunciation for "Gentlemen, Ladies, Merchants, Tradesmen, Schools and Strangers ..." We see here an attempt to produce an all-purpose manual for English. Over a century before Cooper, prescriptive statements about a standard variety were made. John Hart, another phonetician, wrote in 1569 that "the flower of English tongue is used" in the Court and London region. There are various attitudes which encourage prescriptivism in pronunciation and contribute toward a "standard" form. Pronunciation manuals or dictionaries are only the instruments which are used to fulfill such functions. After all, one function of a dictionary is to provide "standard" pronunciation and the variants. And when the users of other Englishes— Indian, West Indian, or West African—compile these dictionaries, they are aiming to show that they do recognize a standard pronunciation for the educated form of their variety, which may be different from RP or GA.

Pronunciation differences may be minor, and thus scarcely contribute to the problem of intelligibility, or they may create substantial problems. It may also be that the "educated" varieties of an English may be intelligible, but not some other varieties. It is possible that a speaker of GA might find educated Indian English more intelligible than, say, Cockney English.

But, small or large, the differences between RP and GA are such that the cousins on the two sides of the sea can be marked as separate. Some of the more obvious speech differences may be given as illustration. Americans tend to pronounce an *r*-sound in words if it follows a vowel; thus the vowel is "*r*-coloured." In British English this *r* is not pronounced. Consider the following sets of words which the RP speaker will pronounce in an identical way: *law, lore*; *paw, pore, pour*; *saw, sore, soar*; *maw, more*; *bawd, bored, board.* To a speaker of RP, GA speakers seem to pronounce the following words in the same way: *writer–rider*; *petal–pedal*; *catty–caddy*; *latter–ladder*; *utter–udder.* It is, however, the difference in the pronunciation of vowels that is a distinctive feature of GA, labeled by others "the drawl of Americans." The GA speaker tends to lengthen the vowels in strongly stressed syllables, while in RP these are "slightly lengthened." This "extra length" may be "drawl" to an RP speaker, but his reduced length is "clipped" for an American speaker. This would apply to, for example, first syllables of *after, daughter, terrible,* and the second syllables of *before, improve, control.* There are other differences, or what Daniel Jones called "mispronunciations" in Indian English, but we shall not discuss these here (see Kachru, 1969, 1976a). But for intelligibility, it seems rhythm is more important than is pronunciation of individual speech sounds.

The grammatical differences between the educated *native* varieties of English are not significant. But there are some differences which may result in ambiguities. One of these, as Strevens (1977:150) puts it, is "the have–have got–get–gotten complex." The American use of *have* results in speech situations such as the following, when the other participant is British. American: "Do you have many children?" English woman: "No, only one a year" (see also Marckwardt and Quirk, 1964; Foster, 1976).

The Search for a Model: a Dilemma in Prescriptivism

In chapter 5 it has been shown that the users of other Englishes who speak it as their second language generally tend to have as a model one of the native varieties of English. Why certain models are preferred, as opposed to others, depends on historical, cultural, geographical, and attitudinal considerations. Languages which have academies for standardization, as is the case with French, may offer a clearer choice of a model seeker. English seems to have lost the opportunity of creating such an academy in the second decade of the eighteenth century as I have discussed in chapter 5; but according to some, it really was not such a serious loss. However, the debate on this topic continues both in Britain and the U.S.A. (see, e.g., Baron, 1982, Greenbaum, ed. 1985).

My aim in this chapter is not to discuss this debate in detail, but to draw certain conclusions from the two rather similar cases of Britain and America. In the absence of an official academy, other factors contributed toward providing a model of English to those who acquired it as a second or foreign language. A particular model was selected because of colonization, economic dependence, geographical proximity, or cultural impact. Why people prefer a certain model is difficult to ascertain. It involves attitudes which researchers find elusive. One does not always know how to separate people's attitude toward a model from their actual performance. The area is difficult to probe because one's perception of a norm and one's actual behavior do not necessarily correlate. In studies on attitudes toward models, one notices what may be called "linguistic schizophrenia." In India, for example, the preferred model is British English, but in actual performance, Indians speak Indian English with various degrees of competence—this is a difference between the norm (the attitude toward a preferred model) and the behavior of speakers.

As we will see in the following section, American English is slowly becoming today's world language, and its impact is all-pervasive on the English-speaking world. This new trend may therefore influence the choice of a model.

The Growing Impact of American English

Two hundred years ago on September 23, 1780, John Adams wrote in a casual way to a fellow American, prophesying that "English will be the most respectable language in the world and the most universally read and spoken in the next century, if not before the close of this." Adams further proclaimed that English

> is destined to be in the next and succeeding centuries more generally the language of the world than Latin was in the last or French is in the present age. The reason of this is obvious, because the increasing population in America, and their universal connection and correspondence with all nations will, . . . force their language into general use . . . [cited in Mathews, 1931:42]

In these observations, although Adams uses the term "English," what he actually meant was "American English." At that time, naturally, Adams could not foresee all the reasons which later caused the diffusion and spread of American English, but, by and large, his prophecy has come true in our lifetime.

We must ask then: What is it that changed the picture? And why is American English no longer regarded as "a quaint, barbarous or amusing appendage to the British original" (Foster, 1976:18)? The reasons for this change in the position of American English are essentially non-linguistic, though there are some who belive that there is something intrinsic about the English language or the American variety of English which entitles it to this unique position. One has to make it clear at the outset that there is no validity in arguments that are based on ethnocentrism and linguistic ignorance. Consider, for example, Laird's speculation (1970:480) that "the English language is spreading through the world partly because it is a good language with a simple grammar and a vast and highly flexible vocabulary . . ." An even more startling observation is found in Barnett (1964:9) who smugly proclaims that:

> . . . contrary to popular supposition, languages evolve in the direction of simplicity. English, being a highly evolved, cosmopolitan, sophisticated language, has been refined and revised, planed down and polished through centuries of use, so that today it is far less complicated than any primitive tongue.

Then Barnett has a dig at "primitive" people and adds: "Some of the most difficult languages in the world are spoken by some of the world's most backward people—e.g. the Australian aborigines, the Eskimos, the Hottentots, and the Yahgan Indians of Tierra del Fuego." One might ask:

difficult for whom? The hypothesis that English is accepted abroad on the basis of its simplicity or its sophistication is not acceptable. It is therefore surprising that such a view was held even by a distinguished linguist, Jespersen (1905). In his view:

> ... the English language is a methodical, energetic businesslike and sober language, that does not care much for finery and elegance, but does care for logical consistency and is opposed to any attempt to narrow-in life by police regulation and strict rules either of grammar or lexicon. As the language is, so also is the nation ... One need not be a great prophet to predict that in the near future the number of English-speaking people will increase considerably. It must be a source of gratification to mankind that the tongue spoken by two of the greatest powers of the world is so noble, so rich, so pliant, so expressive and so interesting. (Cited in Fishman 1977f: epigraph)

This shows that Anglophile linguists can get as much carried away as do nonlinguists who know little about how language works.

What actually happens is that language and power go together. American English is accepted for the power and superiority which America as a nation has acquired in the areas of science, technology, commerce, military affairs, and politics since Adams wrote those prophetic words. After all, in the 1950s people started to learn Russian. This seemed a natural reaction after the phenomenal success of Sputnik I and the sudden evidence of the technological advance of the Russians. The U.S.A. has become the center of Western political, economic, and technological innovations and activities. Therefore, as we will see below, it is not surprising that even the speakers of mother English in Britain have become tolerant of the encroachment of American English into their English, as have the Australians who earlier took mother English as the model. One notices this slow but definite encroachment in several semantic areas in British English. Let us consider the areas of film, television, theater, and advertising as typical examples. Foster (1976:20) gives "pride of place ... to film as a vehicle of American linguistic influence ... (which) have brought transatlantic speech to the British domestic hearth itself." Film, television, and theater have resulted in use of the language with American shades of meaning, for example, "when a film is said to *feature* an actor who has been *built up* by his company" (Foster, 1976:20). The theater has provided words such as *stooge* and *double-talk*. In advertising and salesmanship, Americans certainly excel and demonstrate "the transatlantic love of grandiloquence." American techniques are followed, and words which were exclusively American (e.g. *sales talk* or *sales resistance*) may be heard in Piccadilly Circus or Bond Street.

The British press is opening up to American innovations. The style of typically American news magazines like *Time* and *Newsweek* shows up in British newspapers; for example, the name of a town in the genitive is no more a typically American stylistic feature (e.g. *Newcastle's Central Station, London's Victoria Coach Station*). The same tendency is seen in the use of verbs such as *ban* "prohibit", *crash* "collide", *cut* "reduce", *probe* and *quiz* "investigate", and *sue* "prosecute".

It is not only in the use of single words that one notices this change; the conversation of the British is also spiced with set phrases which are considered to be of "American provenance," for example, *I wouldn't know, let's face it, simple as that, by and large, right now, way over (-down, -back), consult with, baby-sitter, round-trip.* There are idioms such as *to have a chip on one's shoulder, to scrape the bottom of the barrel,* and *out on a limb.*

This intrusion of American English into British English, or for that matter into Australian English, is slow but perceptible. One can correlate generational differences with the use of the American variety. John Wain, the British novelist, has very aptly captured this linguistic difference between two generations in his *Hurry on Down* (1959). In this novel a young man and his father are linguistically very dissimilar. The young man

> talked a different language for one thing; it was demotic English of the mid-twentieth century, rapid, slurred, essentially a city dialect and, in origin, essentially American. By contrast it was a pleasure to hear his father whose speech had been formed, along with all his other habits, before 1914 . . .

The difference in speech and use of "American" is associated with a linguistic attitude toward American English in the new generation. In their minds American speech "is the hall-mark of the tough guy and the he-man" (Foster, 1976:14). The changing British attitude and its acceptance of Americanisms is, of course, interesting for historical reasons. The linguistic wheel has turned full circle, and now the users of mother English are recognizing the legitimacy of the offspring.

In France, Spain, and Germany—in spite of puristic resistance to the American influence on French, Spanish, and German—one notices an intrusion of Americanisms in the press, at social gatherings, and on the radio and television. In a number of countries in Asia and Africa, the Englishization (or shall we say Americanization?) of the native languages has become a symbol of elitism and Westernization, and for the vocal new generations, Westernization represents modernization. In the last fifty years, America has become a phenomenon of envy and emulation for the new and emerging nations, for it combines technology, scientific progress, and, above all, power. The ubiquitous American tourist has contributed toward the spread of American English as much as Hollywood movies and student and faculty training programs. Even in the erstwhile British colonies, American English is having its impact. One can notice it in the newspapers from Ibadan, New Delhi, or Singapore.

Worldly success and elitism continue to be associated with Westernization, and specifically with a knowledge of English. The refrain of a Ghanaian song succinctly sums it up. A person is successful if he has *been-to, Jaguar, fridgeful.* The term *been-to* (feminine, *beentress*) refers to a person who has been to England, indicating a status symbol; the possession of a *Jaguar* car shows prestige; and *fridgeful* marks class and affluence, indicating a refrigerator filled with food. In recent years *been-to* (or *beentress*) includes America too, and competence in American

English. The Indianism *England-returned* is parallel to the Ghanaian *been-to*, but now it has less currency. The term *America-returned* is heard more often, conveying the same prestige, class, and status as did *England-returned* during the colonial days. Matrimonial advertisements also seem to prefer *America-returned* bridegrooms. And a person who is *America-returned* naturally comes with "Americanized" English.

It should not be inferred from the preceding discussion that an American traveling in the world will find, on various continents, American English used with the Midwestern or East Coast accent; far from it—the English language, American or British, will continue to be nativized and undergo changes in new contexts and new uses. Its uses will vary, as they do now, from an internationally understood "educated English," to several types of Englishes which are not necessarily meant for native speakers of English. These varieties have national and regional uses, developed because of the specific linguistically and culturally heterogeneous contexts of these societies: functionally, these "national varieties" are an essential tool of human communication. A monolithic universal English, therefore, is rather difficult to imagine. It would also be uninteresting to live in a society which used a universal English without any variation.

Note

This chapter is a revised version of "American English and Other Englishes" in *Language in the U.S.A.*, edited by Charles A. Ferguson and Shirley Brice Heath. Cambridge and New York: Cambridge University Press, 1981, pp. 21–43.

Chapter 9

Englishization and Language Change

In the linguistic history of South Asia there are several cases of language contact which have resulted in a two-way linguistic impact, and like Janus both the faces of the impact are crucial in order to understand the mutual interaction and influence.[1]

Two well known such cases are those of Persian and English. These two languages have deeply influenced the South Asian languages, and in return these languages have undergone a process of Indianization both linguistically and contextually (Bahri, 1960; Kachru, 1983a; Rao, 1954). The Dravidization of the Indo-Aryan languages, and the counter influence of the Indo-Aryan languages on the Dravidian languages is another case of such linguistic give and take (see, Gumperz and Wilson, 1971).

There are, however, very few detailed linguistically oriented studies of the interaction between the South Asian languages and what may be termed "imposed" languages. I am particularly thinking of those imposed languages which rank high in the language hierarchy in terms of their prestige and their varied and prolonged functions in multicultural and multilinguistic South Asian societies, for example, Persian in Islamic India and English in the period of the British Raj.[2]

It is generally recognized that South Asia presents a unique case of language contact, language convergence (*Sprachbund*) and linguistic assimilation. This chapter discusses a specific case of language contact in which language rivalry and linguistic borrowing co-exist, and a linguistic love-hate relationship has developed between two languages: English and Hindi. One linguistic manifestation of this relationship is the Englishization of Hindi (Bhatia, 1967; Mishra, 1963) and the other manifestation is the Indianization of English (Kachru, 1983a; see also chapter 3).

It is worth noting that, in spite of the linguistic interaction between Hindi and English, there is a large body of literature in these languages which demonstrates the linguistic rivalry, bordering on antagonism, between the supporters of these languages (see for details Desai, 1964; Das Gupta, 1970; John, 1969; Kachru, 1969:663–67; Lohia, 1965; and Shah, ed. 1968). This linguistic rivalry has developed basically because both languages continue to be possible candidates for recognition as a pan-Indian language in India's prolonged and tortuous period of language planning. The attitude of rivalry has developed various loyalty groups, and has resulted in competition for acquiring those linguistic roles for Hindi which it has not been able to acquire for various linguistic, attitudinal or political reasons. The confrontation between the Hindi loyalists, primarily

147

from what is termed the *madhya deśa* (the Hindi belt of northern and central India), and the English loyalists came to the forefront after the forties. Before that period, the *madhya deśa*, and parts of the non-Hindi area too, were confidently working toward the goal of assigning to Hindi the linguistic roles which English had acquired earlier due to the patronage of the British and the Indian supporters of English. (See for details Kachru, 1983a). In this chapter I am only indirectly concerned with the controversy of the role-acquiring tensions between Hindi and English (Das Gupta, 1970). However, as mentioned earlier, attitudinally the Hindi area considers English as the main linguistic rival. This attitude naturally reflects itself when linguistically relevant decisions have to be made concerning borrowing in general, in the choice of technical terminology, and the extension of style and register[3] ranges for Hindi. (See Raghuvira, 1973:85–89; Sharma, 1968:116–33).

The process of Englishization of Hindi has taken place in spite of an attitude of resistance to such linguistic borrowing. In a sense this attitude toward English is not identical to the earlier attitude of the *madhya deśa* toward Persian when the Muslim rulers introduced that language in that vast area as the language of the elite, of administration, and of law (Bahri, 1960, especially 1–21).

In the following sections there is a brief discussion of some selected aspects of the Englishization of Hindi and the linguistic motivations of the well known Hindi-English rivalry. The term "Englishization" refers to some selected, formally definable linguistic influences on the Hindi language. I have not discussed the all-pervading influence of English on various genres of Hindi literature (for a detailed discussion of that aspect see Mishra, 1963).

Language Rivalry, Linguistic Roles and Language Change

In terms of the linguistic roles assigned to various Indian languages a hierarchy of languages has emerged in which each language has a specific role or roles at particular administrative, social and/or educational levels. There is thus a competition between various languages in which each competing language is eager to extend the range of its total functional roles on what may be termed the multilingual spectrum of India. The main competing languages are Indian English, Standard Hindi (also termed *śuddha* Hindi, High Hindi and *ṭhēṭh* Hindi), bazār Hindi (or Hindustani), and the regional languages. The result of this competition is a continuing language rivalry and language conflict.

In this competition for acquiring linguistic roles, English has been a serious candidate, especially in the post-Independence period, when several unsuccessful attempts were made toward implementing various language planning policies in India. The English language has therefore been seen as an imposed language usurping the roles of its rivals and hence as the main source of linguistic antagonism (Lohia, 1965).

It is generally true that the "imposed" languages usually rank high in the language hierarchy in linguistically pluralistic societies. The position of English in India has not been an exception, and even now, after the end of the British rule in India, it continues to be a serious candidate in India's language planning. One might ask: Why does English continue to hold such a position in terms of its functions and prestige? The answer is that English has acquired important functional roles in the Indian sociological context and has provided appropriate registers for those contexts. Once the decision concerning the substitution or reranking of languages is made, the language which ascends on the scale has to be functionally (more or less) equal to English. In the context of language planning what does the concept of functional equivalence mean? The linguistic method of evaluating the degree of functional equivalence between two competing languages is to compare among other things the range of their registers, the range of styles, and the stability of registers. In such a comparison with English, the Hindi language has several disadvantages.

The question then is: In spite of continuous competition and rivalry, why has Hindi been open to the process of Englishization? It seems to me that one reason for the linguistic "openness" toward English on the part of the Hindi enthusiasts is that the process of Englishization unconsciously operates as a linguistic device to "equip" the Hindi language with the functional range of English, which, consequently, might lead toward an "upward" move of Hindi in the hierarchy of linguistic roles. This would mean that the range of the functional uses of Hindi would be extended. Such a move might lead even to the eventual replacement of English by Hindi in the roles which the former has occupied.

One can think of several other equally important reasons for the Englishization of Hindi. Consider, for example, the following reasons which motivate such a language change:

(a) Concept of modernization

By the term "modernization" is meant the effort to equip a language in linguistic terms for functioning in those educational and administrative contexts, which are associated with modern technological societies. It primarily means developing productive processes for generating technical terminology and extending the register-range of the language. In the case of Hindi there still is no agreement on the processes to be adopted toward producing the technical terminology, and the language sources to be used for such formations. Consider, for example, the following excerpts from what may be termed "the medical register" in Hindi. The lexical items in parenthesis have been added.[4]

   (i) *āpreśan* (operation) *thiyeṭar* (theatre) mẽ *sarjan* (surgeon) tathā *enasthetiṣt* (anessthetist) kī *ṭīm* (team) bilkul sahaj tathā tanāv rahit rahne kī kośiś kartī hai (*SH*, 27.5.73).

   (ii) *hārṭ* (heart) ke *čembar* (chamber) se dūsrī taraph ek *kamyūnikeśan* (communication) *čenal* (channel) hotā hai (*SH*, 27.5.73).

(See for details on various points of view Raghuvira, 1973:85–89; Sharma, 1968:116–33; and Tiwari and Chaturvedi, eds. 1973:15–22).

(b) Linguistic pull

In the last hundred years all the educational, administrative and politically and socially important language roles were assigned to English. The members of the elite group in the so called Hindi area, even the Hindi loyalists, largely received their education through the medium of English. The influence of English education was transferred to several fields, especially in developing literary genres, in journalism and in literary criticism.

(c) Realism in creative writing

The growth of fiction and the short story as literary genres is a rather recent development in modern Indian languages, including Hindi; this development has been traced to the direct influence of English (Mishra, 1963:289–320). In these genres, various types of code-mixing (see below) have been experimented with for a linguistic representation of character types. The code-mixing therefore included the use of Hindi and English. Consider, for example, the following excerpts.

> 'ab bekār mẽ bŏr mat karō', kah kar shēkhar ne apne donŏ hathŏ sē mujhē kas kar pakar liyā . . .
> Rinā darling, (don't be silly) pāgal mat banō.' (*Sarita*, Aug. 1974).

(d) Newspaper register

The influence of English is evident in direct lexical borrowings, hybridization and loan translations. A number of syntactic patterns which are transferred from English have a high frequency in the newspaper register such as in sports news, reporting of international news and in headings and captions. There are several reasons for the direct influence on this particular register of Hindi. One reason is that until recently English was used as the main source for translating news items into Hindi, since facilities for direct communication of news in Hindi (say, teleprinters in Hindi) were not available. Second, a large number of successful English newspapers started sister publications in Hindi; therefore, there was significant interaction between the two sister publications, usually English providing the source for translation into Hindi (e.g. *The Hindustan Times* and *Hindustan* (New Delhi); *Amrita Bazar Patrika* and *Amrit Patrika* (Allahabad); *The Times of India* and *Nav Bharat Times* (Delhi)). The following headings and captions from some Hindi newspapers are illustrative; the lexical items given in parentheses have been added.

(i) *bajaṭ* (budget) sīmā kā nayā *rikārḍ (record) (NBT,* 1, 3, '75)
(ii) viśwa *kap* (cup) hockey *ṭūrnāmenṭ* (tournament) (*NBT,* 2, 3, '75)
(iii) vipakśa dvārā *wāk-āoṭ* (walkout) (*NBT,* 7, 3, '75)
(iv) *ḍilars* (dealers) tathā kamiśan (commission) *ejenṭs* (agents) kī āvaśyaktā hai (*NBT,* 7, 3, '75)
(v) *ṭank* (tank) va *rāḍār* (radar) prāpt karnē kī yōjanā (*NBT,* 8, 3, '75)

The Exponents of the Englishization of Hindi

I shall discuss below a few selected linguistic processes of the Englishization of Hindi.

PHONOLOGY: In a detailed study Bhatia (1967) has presented the range of English lexical borrowing in Hindi, and the process of the assimilation of such borrowed items into the phonological system of the language.

The lexical borrowings from English have resulted in additions to the phonological system, especially, for example, in the extension of clusters (e.g. *st-, sk-, sl-*). The distribution of these clusters is restricted in Hindi since these clusters do not occur in initial position. However, in High Hindi (Sanskritized variety) these clusters are possible in words such as *sthān* "place"; *sparsha* "touch"; *star* "breast". The influence of English is also shown in the additions to the vowel and consonant inventories of Hindi (e.g. /ɔ/ and /f/ and /z/).[5]

SYNTAX: It is generally claimed that the syntactic level of a language is less prone to change. In the case of Hindi the following syntactic characteristics are attributed to the influence of English.

Impersonal constructions: By an impersonal construction I mean structures such as *it is said*, or *it has been learnt*. In Hindi traditionally the active forms such as *kehte haĩ, sunā hai* are used. In the newspaper register of Hindi, it is not uncommon to come across constructions such as *kahā jātā hai (it is said), dekhā gayā hai (it has been seen),* or *sunā gayā hai (it has been learned).*

Change in word order: The surface word order of Hindi is SOV as opposed to the SVO order of English. The SVO construction is used in Hindi for stylistic effects (Mishra, 1963:175–77).

Indirect speech: The introduction of indirect speech as a feature of Hindi discourse is also attributed to the influence of English syntax.

Passivization with "dvārā": In Hindi, as in other Indo-Aryan languages, the agent is deleted in passive constructions. The *dvārā (by)* construction is considered a transfer from English (e.g. *hemlet nāṭak śekspiyar dvārā likhā gayā hai* "The play Hamlet was written by Shakespeare").

Post-head modifier "jo": The use of *"jo"* constructions in the post-head position (e.g. *var laṛkā jo jā rahā hai merā bhāī hai,* "that" "boy" "who" "going" "is" "my" "brother" "is", "The boy who is going is my brother") is attributed to the influence of English.

There are other syntactic constructions such as parenthetical clauses, which have been attributed to the English influence. There is, however, evidence that parenthetical clauses are present in Lāllujī Lal's (1763–1835) prose and may not necessarily have developed due to the influence of English (see also chapter 4, pp. 73–6).

LEXIS: At the lexical level the impact of English is very evident, and manifests itself in several ways.

The lexicon of Hindi has developed three types of parallel lexical ranges which mark three types of styles: Sanskritized, Persianized (Bahri, 1960) and Englishized (Mishra, 1963, especially 134–203). The style of a discourse in Hindi is thus marked by a lexical choice which results in a new style. Consider, for example, the following pairs of lexical items which have identical semantic ranges and may be used to form compound verbs with *karnā* "to do"; *ārambh, śurū* "begin"; *adhikār, kabzā* "control"; *bhūl, galatī* "mistake"; *čintā, fikr* "worry"; *dayā, raham* "pity"; *ghriṇā, nafrat* "hate"; *kripā, meharbānī* "favor"; *prayōg, istēmāl* "use"; *praśamsā, tārīf* "praise"; *pratīkṣā, intizār* "wait"; *smaran, yād* "remember". The first members in the above pairs are from Sanskrit and the second members from Perso-Arabic sources.

In the choice of a lexical item there is not necessarily complete free variation. The total range of lexical items is also dependent upon the particular register. A number of registers have a predominance of lexical items from a particular source. For example, the Sanskritized style is by and large associated with literary criticism, philosophical writing, and Hindi news broadcasts of the All India Radio. The Persianized style is a feature of the legal register. The Englishized style, as stated earlier, is associated with the newspaper register, the technical register and the portrayal of certain character types in prose.

Collocations and Idioms

The English language also provides a source for transfer of various types of collocations[6] and idioms into Hindi. First, loan translations to mark repetitive speech events (e.g. *greetings*) which are associated with British culture, e.g. *suprabhāt* "good morning", *śubhrātrī* "good evening". Second, loan-translations of register-determined items of English. Consider, for example, *āgyānusār* "according to order", *niyamānusar* "according to rules", *khabar dī jātī hai* (or *sūčit kiyā jātā hai*) "it is informed". Third, transfer of fixed collocations (idioms) of English e.g. *ā̃khõ sē dūr man se dūr* "out of sight out of mind".

Code Mixing and the Emergence of "Hinglish"

The language contact between Hindi and English, and the resultant language change shows itself in another form too, namely code-mixing. In code-mixing the co-existence of at least two codes is a necessary prerequisite. The codes involved in code-mixing should be formally patterned in such a way that functionally they may be assigned to well-defined contexts.

It is, therefore, appropriate to consider code-mixing a feature of a discourse or of a register. The following excerpt from the register of economics illustrates the point. I have italicized the lexical items from English.

Economics ek aisā *subject* hai jiskī *utility day to day life* mē̃ *realize* kī jā saktī hai (Bhatia, 1967:57).

The lexical spread in the above is clearly register-restricted. In selecting the lexical items the author could have selected either English source items or Sanskrit source items. But, the register of social sciences, as mentioned earlier, is more dependent on English source items, as opposed to literary criticism which draws on Sanskrit lexical items. (For further discussion and illustrations see chapter 4 (pp. 69–71); see also Kachru, 1983a, chapter 7).

Productive Hybridization

In Hindi several devices are used to hybridize lexical items. I shall discuss some of the more productive processes below. First, a large number of compound verbs (Y. Kachru 1968) with a verb and operator structure take the verb from English and the operator from Hindi, e.g. *feel karnā* "to feel"; *try karnā* "to try"; *satisfy karnā* "to satisfy"; *work karnā* "to work"; *bore karnā* "to bore"; *fit karnā* "to fit"; *survey karnā* "to survey". Second, in conjunct verbs (Y. Kachru, 1968) the nominal item is from English and the verbal item from Hindi e.g. *permission denā* "to grant permission"; *help denā* "to give help"; *holiday lēnā* "to take a vacation". Third, a large number of compounds with various grammatical structures are produced with hybridized lexical items. The following are illustrative. Note, however, that all these compounds are register restricted, *aibstrekt čitr* (*D*, 26.3.72) "an abstract painting"; *aithletik pratiyōgitā* (*D*, 13.2.72) "athletic competition"; *dyūtī čhuttī* (*D*, 13.2.72) "duty leave"; *grajvēt satr* (*D*, 13.2.72) "graduate level"; *kriket maidān* (*D*, 13.2.72) "cricket field"; *oubjektiv type prašn* (*D*, 13.2.72) "objective type questions"; *semestar paddhati* (*D*, 13.2.72) "semester system"; *šēyar bāzār* (*NBT*, 2.3.75) "share market"; *skūtar čālak* (*NBT*, 1,3,75) "scooter-driver"; *višva čempiyan* (*D*, 7.11.71) "world champion"; *višāl sṭāk* (*NBT*, 2.3.75) "large stock".

In several South Asian languages reduplication is used as a process of indefinitization. This process is extended to hybridization too. Consider, e.g. *court-kačharī* (*D*, 26.3.72) as in *mãi zarā kort kačharī se ghabrātā hũ* (*D*, 26.3.72) "I am frightened of the court". In *court-kačharī* both the items have roughly the same meaning; the difference is that one is from English and the other from Hindi.

The Two Manifestations of Lingusitic Pragmatics: Hinglish and Indian English

The linguistic melting pot of India, and its unique context of language contact has resulted in several acculturized functional languages, for example, Indian Persian, Indian English and Hinglish.

I shall now discuss the pragmatic reasons for the development of Indian English and its continued use in India, and the growth of Hinglish. There are several pragmatic reasons why Indian English is considered vital to India's language planning. These reasons, as discussed in chapters 1 and 2, have to be viewed in terms of the preeminence of (Indian) English in linguistic roles in Indian society.

The English language provides an expansion of an individual's roles. In the multilinguistic hierarchy of India, English thus ranks highest in terms of its functional utility. The higher a language ranks on the multilingual hierarchy, the greater role mobility it provides to its user. In attitudinal terms, English has prestige and provides an in-group membership in the Indian English speech community whose members use English as a second language. The English-using Indians thus form an elite group, who, whether one likes it or not, are considered attitudinally more 'prestigious' than users of 'prestige' varieties of Indian languages (e.g. Kharībolī). However, a person may conveniently function in both speech communit- ies, and switch or mix languages with the change of roles. In spite of the language-switching and role-switching potential of an Indian bilingual, there is a tendency to identify with a specific speech community (Kachru, 1977b). In the present sociolinguistic context of India, therefore, English is crucial since linguistically it has the widest range of functional registers, it has acquired a stability of registers, it has the potential for providing role extension to a user, and, in addition, it provides linguistic mobility.

The code-mixing which has developed in Hinglish is the result of language contact, language appropriateness and linguistic pragmatics. The variety termed "Hinglish" is tolerated by Hindi purists more than Indian English. The following two excerpts are illustrations of the use of Hinglish in the personal letters of a writer of *śuddha* (pure) Hindi and a distin- guished Hindi poet, Sumitranandan Pant (Bachchan, 1970).

(a) kuch sambhav na hō tō *monthly contract* par 250/ *as staff assistant* unhẽ kām denā unhī kē hāth mẽ hai—*womens section* me *compare* yā *script writer and announcer* kā kām kar saktī hãi—*record keeper* kā bhi kām kar saktī hãi (45).

(b) shāntā bīmar hai—*medical leave* mẽ parī hai. mere bād *flu* usī kō hō gayā. kyā kiyā jāyē—ab *servant* bhī khãs rahā hai (33).

(c) din ki *radio news* sunne ke bād ek *phonogram condolence* kā mẽne bhi karnā učit samjha (28).

(d) . . . *sugar* ke kāran koī *serious work* bhī *take up* nahi kar saktā (50).

In functional terms Hinglish is performing the same roles in modern India at one level of society that bazār Hindustani has performed for a long time in metropolitan towns in India. The users of these two varieties are not necessarily mutually exclusive. However, these two varieties do not perform identical roles in the sense that the areas of their function are not overlapping. There is great need of sociolinguistic research on the roles of Hinglish and bazār Hindustani in modern India.

Conclusion

The Indianization of the English language and the pragmatics of its uses in India have already been discussed in several studies (see bibliography in Kachru, 1983a; also see Aggarwal, 1982). The continued use of English in India has also motivated an evaluation of the whole process of the English- ization of Hindi. In literature on language planning in Hindi, linguistically relevant questions such as the following are being asked now: What do terms such as "efficiency"; "intellectualization"; and "register stabilization" mean? What are the linguistic implications of linguistic roles and social roles and how are these interrelated? What linguistic factors determine the acceptability of a language in language planning in linguistically and culturally pluralistic societies?

At present there are two main language pressure groups in India: one represented by the supporters of English who attempt to extend (or protect) the function of English in various roles and, second, the supporters of Hindi, and other regional languages, who are enthusiastically trying to displace English from the linguistic roles assigned to it. The displacement of English is considered an achievement but carries further responsibility. For example, if English is replaced by Hindi in the teaching of technology, that implies that Hindi must extend the range of its registers to include the register of technology. The addition of such a register to the overall range of registers in Hindi naturally involves the selection of appropriate lexical sets functional in such a register. The extension of a register and its stabilization is not an artificial process—language use and register extension cannot be separated. Register stabilization is in a sense related to language standardization.

This chapter illustrates that in code-mixing and in the development of Indian English and Hinglish we again find linguistic manifestation of the traditional power of linguistic assimilation in the pluralistic culture of India. In the case of Hindi, appropriation of the lexical, collocational and syntactic resources of English is the natural first step.

Notes

This chapter was published with the title "The Englishization of Hindi: Language Rivalry and Language Change" in *Linguistic Method: Papers in Honor of H. Penzl,* edited by Irmengard Rauch and Gerald F. Carr, The Hague: Mouton, 1979, pp. 199–211.

1. These notes present a first report on a research project initiated in the Department of Linguistics, University of Illinois at Urbana on the Englishization of Hindi and some other Indian languages. I am aware that some readers might raise their eyebrows at my use of the term "Englishization"? I prefer this term to alternatives such as "Anglicization". I think the use of the term "Englishization" can be linguistically and contextually explained. The term "Anglicization" has special connotations in India, I have, therefore, chosen a neutral term.
2. For a discussion of what are termed "imposed" languages see Brosnahan, 1963:7–24. Also in Bailey and Robinson, eds. 1973:40–54.
3. The term "register" is used in the sense of a functionally determined variety of language. See Halliday *et al.,* 1964:87–98.
4. I have used the following abbreviations for the sources of the illustrations. *D. Dharmayug.* Bombay; *NBT, Nav Bharat Times,* New Delhi, *SH, Saptahik Hindustan,* New Delhi.
5. Note also that /f/ and /z/ have also been traced to the influence of Persian. (See Bahri, 1960:57–59.) Perhaps it should be mentioned here that in modern Hindi all the punctuation marks of English have been borrowed. Traditionally the Hindi writing system had only two marks: *purna virām* indicated by two vertical lines (i.e. I I) and *ardha virām* indicated by one vertical line (i.e. I). The impact of these punctuation marks on rhythm in reading written Hindi has yet to be investigated.
6. For discussion of "collocation" see Firth, 1957:190–215.

PART IV

Contact, Creativity and Discourse Strategies

Chapter 10

The Bilingual's Creativity and Contact Literatures

THE bilingual's creativity[1] in English on a global scale, and the issues concerning nativization of discourse patterns, discourse strategies and speech acts, are a natural consequence of the unprecedented world-wide uses of English, mainly since the early 1920s. The phenomenon of a language with fast increasing diaspora varieties—and significantly more non-native users than native speakers[2]—has naturally resulted in the pluricentricity[3] of English. The sociolinguistic import of this pluricentricity is that the non-native users of English can choose to acquire a variety of English which may be distinct from the native varieties. As a result, as discussed in earlier chapters, two types of models of English have developed: native and institutionalized non-native (see Chapter 5). It is with reference to these models that the innovations, creativity and emerging literary traditions in English must be seen.[4] Each model has its own linguistic and literary norms—or a tendency to develop such norms. This is the linguistic reality of English in its world context. Attitudinally, however, the way people react to this situation opens up an entirely different can of worms, not directly related to discussing in this chapter.[5]

The concept "pluricentricity" of English is a useful beginning point for this chapter: I will address certain issues which, it seems to me, are related to both Western and non-Western pluricentricity of the English language. I will first raise a theoretical question concerning linguists' common perception of a speech community, particularly their understanding of the linguistic behavior of the members of a speech community which alternately uses two, three or more languages depending on the situation and function. One might ask: How valid is a theory of grammar which treats monolingualism as the norm for description and analysis of the linguistic interaction of traditional multilingual societies? Yet in linguistic description—save a few exceptions—the dominant paradigms have considered monolingualism as the norm (i.e., judgments based on the ideal hearer-speaker).[6] My second concern—not unrelated to the first point—is with description and methodology: Are the models proposed for discourse and text-analysis of monolinguals' linguistic interaction observationally, descriptively, and explanatorily adequate for the analysis of bilinguals' language use? My third aim is to discuss some underlying processes of nativization and innovations which characterize *literariness*[7] (both formal and contextual) of selected texts manifesting the bilinguals' creativity. The examples have been taken primarily from what has earlier been termed "contact literature".[8] Finally, I shall refer to the issue of relationship between this creativity and underlying thought-patterns of bilinguals.

I believe that the theoretical and methodological tracks followed to date in the study of contact literatures in English fail on several counts.[9] The foremost limitation one detects in a majority of studies is that of using almost identical approaches for the description of the bilingual's and monolingual's creativity. Literary creativity in English has until now been studied within the Western Judaic-Christian heritage and its implications for understanding English literature. True, the English language shows typical characteristics of a "mixed" language development in its layer after layer of borrowings, adaptations, and various levels of language contact.[10] But even there, the earlier main intrusion has been essentially European and more or less consistent with the Hellenistic and Roman traditions.

However, the prolonged colonial period substantially changed that situation in the linguistic fabric of the English language, and extended its uses as a medium for ethnic and regional literatures in the non-Western world (e.g., Indian English, West African English; see Kachru, 1980c). The extreme results of this extension can be observed in the "Sanskritization" and "Kannadaization" of Raja Rao's English,[11] and in the "Yorubaization" and "Igboization" of Amos Tutuola and Chinua Achebe. The labels indicate that these authors have exploited two or more linguistic—and cultural—resources which do not fit into the paradigms of what Kaplan (1966) terms "the Platonic-Aristotelian sequence"[12] and the dominant Anglo-Saxon thought patterns of the native speakers of English. Recognition of this "mixing" of Western and non-Western resources has implications for our use of terms such as *cohesion* or *coherence*[13] and even *communicative competence.* We should also be cautious in suggesting typologies of culture-specific speech acts in various varieties of English (see Chishimba, 1983 and Magura, 1984).

In contact literature, the bilingual's creativity introduces a nativized thought-process (e.g., Sanskritic, Yoruba, Malaysian) which does not conform to the recognized canons of discourse types, text design, stylistic conventions and traditional thematic range of the English language, as viewed from the major Judaic-Christian traditions of literary and linguistic creativity.

The linguistic realization of the underlying traditions and thought processes for a bilingual may then entail a *transfer* of discoursal patterns from one's other (perhaps more dominant) linguistic code(s) and cultural and literary traditions. That such organization of discourse strategies—conscious or unconscious—arise in different ways in different cultures has been shown in several studies on non-Western languages.[14]

"Contact" in contact literatures

What does the term "contact literatures" imply? The term refers to the literatures in English written by the users of English as a second language to delineate contexts which generally do not form part of what may be labeled the traditions of English literature (African, Malaysian, and Indian and so on). Such literatures, as I have stated elsewhere, are "a product of multicultural and multilingual speech communities" (1982b: 330). Contact literatures, like languages in contact, have two faces: their own face and the face they acquire by linguistic contact with another language and society. The degree of contact with other language(s) determines the degree of impact at various linguistic levels. There are several examples of such literatures in English (e.g. in India, West Africa), in French (e.g. in Francophone Africa), in Persian (e.g. in India), and in Hindi (e.g. in Fiji, Trinidad and South India).

It has already been shown that contact literatures have both a national identity and a linguistic distinctiveness (e.g., *Indianness, Africanness)*. The "linguistic realization" of such identities is achieved in several ways: the text may have both a surface and an underlying identity with the native varieties of English; it may show only partial identity with the native norms; or it may entail a culture-specific (e.g., African, Asian) identity both at the surface and the underlying levels and share nothing with the native variety. Thus contact literatures have several linguistic and cultural faces: they reveal a blend of two or more linguistic textures and literary traditions, and they provide the English language with extended contexts of situation within which such literatures may be interpreted and understood. In such literatures there is a range of discourse devices and cultural assumptions distinct from the ones associated with the native varieties of English. One must extend the scope of the historical dimension and cultural traditions from that of Judaic-Christian traditions to the different heritages of African and Asia. This kind of historical and cultural expansion results in a special type of linguistic and literary phenomenon: such texts demand a new literary sensibility and extended cultural awareness from a reader who is outside of the speech fellowship which identifies with the variety.

It is in this sense that English writing has become, to give an example, "our national literature", and English "our national language" in Nigeria as claimed by Nnamdi Azikiwe, the first president of Nigeria, (quoted in Thumboo, 1976:vii). The same is, of course, true of most of the former British and American colonies or areas of influence, such as India, Singapore, and the Philippines.

Thumboo (1976:ix) is making the same point in connection with Commonwealth writers in English when he says that "language must serve, not overwhelm, if the Commonwealth writer is to succeed. Mastering it involves holding down and breaching a body of habitual English associations to secure that condition of verbal freedom cardinal to energetic, resourceful writing. In a sense the language is remade, where necessary, by adjusting the interior landscape of words in order to explore and meditate the permutations of another culture and environment."

And discussing the problems of such writers, Thumboo adds (xxxiv):

> The experience of peoples crossing over into a second language is not new, though the formalization of the move acts as a powerful rider. What amounts to the re-location of a sensibility nurtured by, and instructed in one culture, within another significantly different culture, is complicated in the outcome.

Discoursal Thought Pattern and Language Design

The relationship between underlying thought patterns and language design has been illustrated by Achebe in his discussion of the style of *Arrow of God*, Achebe provides two short texts as an illustration, one nativized (Africanized) and the other Englishized, and then gives reasons for choosing to use the former. In explaining his choice, he says that it will ". . . give some idea of how I approach the use of English." In the passage, the Chief Priest is telling one of his sons why it is necessary to send him to church. Achebe (1966:20) first gives the Africanized version:

> I want one of my sons to join these people and be my eyes there. If there is nothing in it you will come back. But if there is something then you will bring back my share. The world is like a mask, dancing. If you want to see it well, you do not stand in one place. My spirit tells me that those who do not befriend the white man today will be saying, "had we known", tomorrow.

Achebe, then asks, "supposing I had put it another way. Like this for instance":

> I am sending you as my representative among these people—just to be on the safe side in case the new religion develops. One has to move with the times or else one is left behind. I have a hunch that those who fail to come to terms with the white man may well regret their lack of foresight.

And he rightly conludes: "The material is the same. But the form of the one is in character and the other is not. It is largely a matter of instinct but judgment comes into it too."

It is thus a combination of creative *instinct* and formal *judgment* which makes a text language—or culture-specific within a context of situation (e.g., Yoruba speech, Chicano English, Kannada influence, Punjabi English).[15]

Furthermore, if we accept Kaplan's claim that the preferred dominant "thought patterns" of English are essentially out of "the Anglo-European cultural patterns" based on "a Platonic-Aristotelian sequence", the logical next step is to recognize that in the case of, for example, Raja Rao or Mulk Raj Anand, the underlying thought patterns reflect the traditions of Sanskrit and the regional or national oral lore. And in the case of Amos Tutuola and Chinua Achebe, they stem from Yoruba and Igbo traditions, respectively.

Raja Rao makes it clear that such transfer or tradition is part of his creativity.

There is no village in India, however mean, that has not a rich *sthala-purana* or legendary history, of its own . . . The *Puranas* are endless and innumerable. We have neither punctuation nor the treacherous "ats" and "ons" to bother us—we tell one interminable tale. Episode follows episode, and when our thoughts stop our breath stops, and we move on to another thought. This was and still is the ordinary style of our story telling. I have tried to follow it myself in this story [*Kanthapura*] (1963:vii–viii).

Raja Rao's narration of an "interminable tale" results in breaking the Western norms of punctuation and prose rhythm, and he shares it, for example, with the writers on another continent, West Africa. Tutuola has a "peculiar use of punctuation, resulting in an unending combination of sentences," which he "owes to his Yoruba speech" (Taiwo, 1976:76).

When he tried all his power for several times and failed and again at that moment the smell of the gun-powder of the enemies' guns which were shooting repeatedly was rushing to our noses by the breeze and this made us fear more, so my brother lifted me again a very short distance, but when I saw that he was falling several times, then I told him to leave me on the road and run away for his life perhaps he might be safe so that he would be taking care of our mother as she had no other sons more than both of us and I told him that if God saves my life too then we should meet again, but if God does not save my life we should meet in Heaven (*Bush of Ghosts*, p. 20; quoted in Taiwo 1976:76)

In addition to this characteristic, Taiwo (1976:111) argues that Tutuola and his compatriot Achebe ". . . exhibit in their writings features which may be described as uniquely Nigerian." Taiwo further explains (1976:75) that Tutuola "has carried Yoruba speech habits into English and writes in English as he would speak in Yoruba . . . He is basically speaking Yoruba but using English words." And, "the peculiar rhythms of his English are the rhythms of Yoruba speech" (1976:85). With regard to Achebe, Taiwo (1976:116–117) observes that in the following scene which he quotes from *Things Fall Apart,* Achebe "has had to rely heavily on the resources of Igbo language and culture to dramatise the interrelation between environment and character":

"Umuofia kwenu!" shouted the leading *egwugwu*, pushing the air with his raffia arms. The elders of the clan replied, "Yaa!"

"Umuofia kwenu!"
"Yaa!"
"Umuofia kwenu!"
"Yaa!"
Evil Forest then thrust the pointed end of his rattling staff into the earth. And it began to shake and rattle, like something agitating with a metallic life. He took the first of the empty stools and the eight other *egwugwu* began to sit in order of seniority after him.

The Bilingual's Grammar: Some Hypotheses

It seems to me that for understanding the bilingual's creativity one must begin with a distinct set of hypotheses for what has been termed "the bilingual's grammar" (or multilingual's grammar). I am, of course, not using the term "grammar" in a restricted sense: It refers to the productive linguistic processes at different linguistic levels (including that of discourse and style) which a bilingual uses for various linguistic functions.

The bilingual's grammar has to be captured in terms of what sociolinguists term "verbal repertoire" or "code repertoire", with specific reference to a speech community or a speech fellowship.[16] Such speech communities have a formally and functionally determined range of languages and or dialects as part of their competence for linguistic interaction as shown in chapter 4.

A characteristic of such competence is the faculty and ease of mixing and switching, and the adoption of stylistic and discoursal strategies from the total verbal repertoire available to a bilingual.[17] One has to consider not only the blend of the formal features, but also the assumptions derived from various cultural norms, and the blending of these norms into a new linguistic configuration with a culture-specific meaning system. There are several salient characteristics of the creativity of such a person. I shall discuss some of these below.

First, the processes used in such creativity are based on multinorms of styles and strategies. We cannot judge such devices on the basis of one norm derived from one literary or cultural tradition (see Parthasarathy, 1983). Second, nativization and acculturation of text presupposes an altered context of situation for the language. Traditionally accepted literary norms with reference to a particular code (say, Hindi or English) seem to fail here. A description based on an approach which emphasizes the monolingual "speaker-hearer" is naturally weak in terms of its descriptive and explanatory power. Third, the bilingual's creativity results in the configuration of two or more codes. The resultant code therefore has to be contextualized in terms of the new uses of language. Finally, such creativity is not to be seen merely as a formal combination of two or more underlying language designs, but also as a creation of cultural, aesthetic, societal and literary norms. In fact, such creativity has a distinct context of situation.

It is this distinctive characteristic which one might say on the one hand formally *limits* the text and on the other hand *extends* it, depending on how one looks at linguistic innovations. The creative processes used in such texts have a limiting effect because the conventional "meaning systems" of the code under use is altered, lexically, grammatically, or in terms of cohesion (see Y. Kachru, 1983a and 1983b). A reader-hearer "outside" the shared or recreated meaning system has to familiarize himself or herself with the processes of the design and formal reorganization, the motivation for innovations, and the formal and contextual implications of such language use. In other words, to borrow Hallidayan terms (1973:43) one has to see what a multilingual "can say" and "can mean". The *range in saying* and the *levels of meaning* are distinct and one has to establish "renewal of connection" with the context of situation.[18]

What is, then, inhibiting (limiting or unintelligible) in one sense may also be interpreted as an extension of the codes in terms of the new linguistic innovations, formal experimentation, cultural nuances, and addition of a new cultural perspective to the language.[19] If the linguistic and cultural "extension" of the code is missed, one also misses the interpretation at the linguistic, literary, sociolinguistic and cultural levels. One misses the relationship between *saying* and *meaning,* the core of literary creativity.

What does it take from a reader to interpret such creativity? It demands a lot: it almost demands an identification with the literary sensibility of the bilingual in tune with the ways of *saying* and the levels of new *meaning.*

Linguistic Realization of Distinctiveness

This altered "meaning system" of such English texts is the result of various linguistic processes, including nativization of context, of cohesion and cohesiveness, and of rhetorical strategies.

Nativization of Context: One first thinks of the most obvious and most elusive process which might be called *contextual* nativization of texts, in which cultural presuppositions overload a text and demand a serious cultural interpretation. In Raja Rao's *Kanthapura,* to take a not so extreme example, such contextualization of the following exemplary passage involves several levels.

> "Today", he says, "it will be the story of Siva and Parvati." And Parvati in penance becomes the country and Siva becomes heaven knows what! "Siva is the three-eyed", he says' "and Swaraj too is three-eyed: Self-purification, Hindu-Moslem unity, Khaddar." And then he talks of Damayanthi and Sakunthala and Yasodha and everywhere there is something about our country and something about Swaraj. Never had we heard *Harikathas* like this. And he can sing too, can Jayaramachar. He can keep us in tears for hours together. But the *Harikatha* he did, which I can never forget in this life and in all lives to come, is about the birth of Gandhiji. "What a title for a *Harikatha?*" cried out old Venkatalakshamma, the mother of the Postmaster. "It is neither about Rama nor Krishna."—"But," said her son, who too has been to the city, "but, Mother, the Mahatma is a saint, a holy man."—"Holy man or lover of a widow, what does it matter to me? When I go to the temple I want to hear about Rama and Krishna and Mahadeva and not all this city nonsense," said she. And being an obedient son, he was silent. But the old women came along that evening. She could never stay away from a *Harikatha.* And sitting beside us, how she wept! . . . [1963:10]

In this passage, it is not so much that the underlying narrative technique is different or collocational relationships are different, but the historical and cultural presuppositions are different than what has been traditionally the "expected" historical and cultural milieu for English literature. One has to explain Siva and Parvati with reference to the multitude of the pantheon of Hindu gods, and in that context then *three-eyed* (Sanskrit *trinetra*) makes sense: it refers to Lord Siva's particular manifestations when he opens his "third eye", located on his forehead, spitting fire and destroying the creation. Damayanthi [Damayantī], Sakunthala [Sakuntalā], and Yasodha [Yasodā] brings forth the epic tradition of Indian classics: Damayanthi, the wife of Nala; Sakunthala, who was later immortalized in Kalidasa's [Kālīdāsa : fifth cent A.D.?] play of the same name; and Yasodha, the mother of Krishna, the major character of the epic *Mahābhārata.* The contemporariness of the passage is in reference to Gandhi

(1869–1948), and the political implications of Hindu-Muslim unity and *khaddar* (handspun cloth). The *Harikatha* man is the traditional religious storyteller, usually in a temple, who has woven all this in a fabric of story.

Now, this is not unique: this is in fact characterisitic of context-specific texts in general.[20] But that argument does not lessen the *interpretive* difficulties of such texts. Here the presupposition of discourse interpretation is at a level which is not grammatical. It is of a special lexical and contextual nature. It extends the cultural load of English lexis from conventional Greek and Roman allusions to Asian and African myths, folklore, and traditions. It univeralizes English, and one might say "de-Englishizes" it in terms of the accepted literary and cultural norms of the language.

Nativization of cohesion and cohesiveness

The second process involves the alteration of the native users concept of cohesion and cohesiveness: these concepts are to be redefined in each institutionalized variety within the appropriate universe of discourse (see Y. Kachru, 1983a and 1983b). This is particularly true of types of lexicalization, collocational extension and the use or frequency of grammatical forms. A number of such examples are given in my earlier studies.[21]

The lexical *shift*, if I might use that term, is used for various stylistic and attitudinal reasons.[22] The lexicalization involves not only direct lexical transfer but also entails other devices, too, such as hybridization and loan translation. Such English lexical items have more than one interpretive context: they have a surface "meaning" of the second language (English) and an underlying "meaning" of the first (or dominant) language. The discoursal interpretation of such lexicalization depends on the meaning of the underlying language, say Yoruba, Kannada, Punjabi, Malay, etc.

Nativization of rhetorical strategies

The third process is the nativization of rhetorical strategies in close approximation to the devices a bilingual uses in his or her other codes(s). These include consciously or unconsciously devised strategies according to the patterns of interaction in the native culture, which are transferred to English.

A number of such strategies are enumerated below. First, one has to choose a style with reference to the stylistic norms appropriate to the concepts of "high culture" and "popular culture". In India, traditionally, high culture entails Sanskritization, and in certain contexts in the north, Persianization. We see such transfer in the much discussed and controversial work of Raja Rao, *The Serpent and the Rope*. On the other hand, in *Kanthapura*, Rao uses what may be called a "vernacular style" of English. His other work, *The Cat and Shakespeare*, introduces an entirely new style.[23] In devising these three styles for Indian English, Rao has certainly demonstrated a delicate sense for appropriate style, but such experimentation has its limitations, too. These innovations make his style linguistically "deviant" from a native speaker's perspective, and culturally it introduces into English a dimension alien to the canons of English literature.[24]

In the expansion of the style range, the African situation is not different from the South Asian. In Achebe, we find that "he has developed not one prose style but several, and in each novel he is careful to select the style or styles that will best suit his subject" (Lindfors, 1973:74). It is for this reason that, as Lindfors says, "Achebe has devised an African vernacular style" (74).[25]

Once the choice of the style is made, the next step is to provide authenticity (e.g., *Africanness, Indianness)* to the speech acts, or to the discourse types. How is this accomplished? It is achieved by linguistic realization of the following types:

1. The use of native similes and metaphors (e.g., Yoruba, Kannada, Malay) which linguistically result in collocational deviation;
2. The transfer of rhetorical devices for "personalizing" speech interaction;
3. The translation ("transcreation") of proverbs, and idioms;
4. The use of culturally-dependent speech styles; and
5. The use of syntactic devices.

Let me now illustrate these five points one by one. First, the use of native similes and metaphors: It is through such similes that Achebe, for example, is able to evoke the cultural milieu in which the action takes place (Lindfors, 1973:75). Examples of such similes are: *like a bush-fire in the harmattan, like a yam tendril in the rainy season, like a lizard fallen from an iroko tree, like pouring grains of corn into a bag full of holes* (also see Kachru, 1965 (1983a:131ff)).

Second, the transfer of rhetorical devices for contextualizing and authenticating speech interaction. Such devices provide, as it were, the "ancestral sanction" to the interaction, a very important strategy in some African and Asian societies. It is one way of giving "cultural roots" to English in African and Asian contexts, particularly to its "vernacular style". One might say it is a device to link the past with the present. Onuora Nzekwu (*Wand of Noble Wood*) accomplishes this by use of what may be called "speech initiators" which appear "empty" to one who does not share the cultural and linguistic presuppositions. But for contextualizing the text, these are essential. Consider among others the following: *our people have a saying; as our people say; it was our fathers who said; the elders have said.* Stylistically this also preserves the "orality" of the discourse.

A third strategy is that of "transcreating" proverbs and idioms from an African or Asian language into English. The culture-embeddedness of such linguistic items is well recognized and as Achebe says, they are "the palm-oil" with which words are eaten" (1964:viii). The function of such expressions is to universalize a specific incident and to reduce the harshness of an utterance. Achebe's use of proverbs, in Lindfors' view (1973:77), sharpens characterization, clarifies conflict, and focuses on the values of the society. In other words, to use Herskovits' term, (1958) the use of such a device provides a "grammar of values". Consider for example, the use of the following proverbs by Achebe: *I cannot live on the bank of the river and wash my hand with the spittle; if a child washed his hands he could eat with kings,* and *a person who chased two rats at a time would lose one.* It is through the proverbs and word play that the wit and wisdom of the ancestors is passed on to new generations. I have shown earlier (1965 and 1966) how this device is used to nativize speech functions such as abuses, curses, blessings and flattery.

A fourth characteristic is to give the narrative and the discourse a "naive tall-tale style" typical of the earthy folk style (Lindfors, 1975:57). This is typical of Tutuola, or of Raja Rao's *Kanthapura.* This, as Jolaoso observes (quoted by Lindfors, 1973:57), "reminds one very forcibly of the rambling old grandmother telling her tale of spirits in the ghostly light of the moon." (See also Afolayan, 1971 and Abrahams, 1983:21–59).

The fifth strategy is the use of particular syntactic devices. An example is the enhancement of the above folk style by using the device of a traditional native village storyteller and occasionally putting questions to the audience for participation: This assures a reader's involvement. Tutuola makes frequent use of asking direct questions, or asking rhetorical questions in the narration. In Raja Rao's case, the Harikathaman or the grandmother uses the same devices, very effective indeed for passing on the cultural tradition to new generations and for entertaining other age groups.

One might ask here: Is there evidence that the discourse of Indians reflects features which according to Lannoy represent a "culture of sound" (1971:275)? Would one agree with him that one consequence of belonging to such a culture is "the widespread tendency of Indians to use language as a form of incantation and exuberant rhetorical flourish on public occasions? Orators rend the air with verbose declamations more for the pleasure of the sound than for the ideas and facts they may more vaguely desire to express" (176). One wonders, is Babu English (see Widdowson, 1979:202–211) a manifestation of such "culture of sound" in the written mode?

Linguistic Realization of Thought Patterns

The above discussed characteristics are essentially related to what may be called the texture of discourse or the nativized cohesive characteristics of various Englishes. The question of linguistic realization of the underlying thought pattern in the bilingual's creativity still remains. I shall now return to that aspect and briefly explore it with reference to South Asia.

Let me begin with two recent studies, both on Indo-Aryan languages of South Asia: Hindi and Marathi. In Hindi discourse, according to Y. Kachru (1983b:58), there is a "spiral-like structure", and there is a greater degree of tolerance for digressions in an orthographic paragraph in Hindi as compared with English, provided the digressions link various episodes in discourse paragraphs in a spiral-like structure.

The paragraph structure of Marathi has been labelled "circular" (from the point of view of an English speaker) by Pandharipande (1983:128). Contrasting what Kaplan calls the "linear" paragraph structure of English with the "circular" structure of Marathi, Pandharipande further points out that (a) ". . . a paragraph in English begins with a general statement of its content, and then carefully develops that statement by specific illustrations; (b) while it is discursive, a paragraph is never digressive; (c) the flow of ideas occurs in English in a straight line from the opening sentence to the last sentence. In contrast to this, the paragraph structure in Maranthi is full of digressions. The paragraph opens with a hypothesis and proceeds with arguments to either support or to oppose the hypothesis. Finally, the validity of the hypothesis is confirmed. Thus a paragraph in an expository discourse in Marathi begins and ends roughly at the same point."

We find an identical position in Heimann, who believes that an Indian "thinks" in "a circle or a spiral of continuously developing potentialities and not on the straight line of progressive stages" (quoted in Lannoy 1971:278). In Lannoy's view, a characteristic trait of Indian minds is ". . . indifference to the logical procedure defined in Aristotle's law of the excluded middle" (277). The Indian preference then is for "non-sequential logic" (279). However, Lannoy assures us that "this is not to suggest that India is unconcerned with logic, but that it employs a different system of logic from the West" (277; also see Nakamura, 1964).

Here the difference between the two systems, the Aristotelian and Indian, should interest us. This important difference between the two has clearly been brought out by Basham (1954:501–2); I cannot resist the temptation to quote the relevant passage here.

A correct inference was established by syllogism, of which the Indian form (pañcāvay-ava) was somewhat more cumbrous than the Aristotelian. Its five members were known as proposition (pratijñā), reason (hetu), example (udāharaṇa), application (upanaya), and conclusion (nigamana). The classical Indian example may be paraphrased as follows:

1. There is fire on the mountain
2. because there is smoke above it,
3. and where there is smoke there is fire, as, for instance, in a kitchen;
4. such is the case with the mountain,
5. and therefore there is fire on it.

The third term of the Indian syllogism corresponds to the major premise of that of Aristotle, the second to Aristotle's minor premise, and the first to his conclusion. Thus the Indian syllogism reversed the order of that of classical logic, the argument being stated in the first and second clauses, established by the general rule and example in the third, and finally clinched by the virtual repetition of the first two clauses.[26]

On the basis of the above illustrations one can argue that distinct African, Indian, Chinese, or Thai thought-processes manifest themselves in distinct English types.[27] Before one comes to that conclusion, a word of warning is in order here: I am not claiming that such "transfer in contact" is limited to literary texts or that such "creativity" appears in literature only. Rather these apply to all linguistic interactions in which multilinguals participate.[28] It is, in fact, part of being an India, an African, or a Singaporean.

It is, of course, evident that for understanding such texts, the barriers to intelligibility have to be broken at a minimum of two levels: at the surface level of structural relationships which provide culture-specific text-design or cohesion to the text, e.g., collocational, lexical, or grammatical, and in the reinterpretation of a text within the extended (or altered) sociosemantic and pragmatic system. The structural relationships are just the visible part of such a discoursal iceberg. There is more to it which is beyond the monolingual interpreter's ken—especially for a monolingual who has made no effort to cross the barriers created by monoculturalism and monolingualism.

This then takes us to a related research area, that of contrastive discourse (or contrastive stylistics): But this research must venture beyond its present concerns into contrastive pragmatics, relating linguistic realization to the cultural norms and the "meaning systems" of a society which uses English.[29] The discourse strategies in contact literatures should be seen as linguistic realizations of a new sociosemiotic and linguistic phenomenon which is being added to the canons of literatures of English.

Conclusion

The study of the bilingual's creativity has serious implications for linguistic theory, and for our understanding of culture-specific communicative competence. It is of special interest for the study and analysis of the expanding body of the non-native literatures in English and of the uses of English in different cultures.

The universalization of English may be a blessing in that it provides a tool for cross-cultural communication. But it is a double-edged tool and makes several types of demands: a new theoretical perspective is essential for describing the functions of English across cultures. In other words, the use of English is to be seen as an integral part of the sociocultural reality of those societies which have begun using it during the colonial period, and more important, have retained it and increased its use in various functions in the post-colonial era.

In recent years many such proposals for a theoretical reorientation have been made, not necessarily with reference to international uses of English, by Gumperz, Halliday, Hymes and Labov, among others. And in 1956, when Firth suggested (in Palmer, 1968:96–97) that "in view of the almost universal use of English, an Englishman must de-anglicize himself" he was, of course, referring to the implications of such universalization of the language. In his view, this de-anglicization was much more than a matter of the readjustment of linguistic attitudes by the Englishmen; it entailed linguistic pragmatism in the use of English across cultures.

The diaspora varieties of English are initiating various types of changes in the English language. More important is the decannonization of the traditionally recognized literary conventions and genres of English. This change further extends to the introduction of new Asian and African cultural dimensions to the underlying cultural assumptions traditionally associated with the social, cultural, and literary history of English. The shared conventions and literary milieu between the creator of the text and the reader of English can no more be taken for granted. A text thus has a unique context. English is unique in another sense too: it has developed both national English literatures, which are specific and *context-bound*, and certain types of *context-free* international varieties. The national varieties show more localized organisational schemes in their texture, which may be "alien" for those who do not share the canons of literary creativity and the traditions of underlying culture which are manifest in such varieties.

The national English literatures are excellent resources for culture learning through literature, a topic which has attracted considerable attention in recent years.[30] However, for such use of these texts one has to acquire the appropriate interpretive methodology and framework for identifying and contextualising the literary creativity in English, especially that of its non-native bilingual users. It is only by incorporating such pragmatic contexts, as has been recently shown, for example in Chishimba (1983),[31] that the functional meaning and communicative appropriateness of the new discourse strategies and discourse patterns will be understood and appreciated.[32]

Notes

This chapter is based on a talk given at the Conference on English as an International Language: Discourse Patterns Across Cultures, East-West Culture Learning Institute, East-West Center, Honolulu, Hawaii, June 1–7, 1983. A somewhat revised and enlarged version with the title "The Bilingual's Creativity: Discoursal and Stylistic Strategies in Contact Literatures in English" appeared in *Studies in the Linguistic Sciences*. 1983, 13.2. pp. 37–55.

1. In this chapter I have used the term "bilingualism" to include "trilingualism", "multilingualism", and "pluralingualism". The "bilingual's creativity" refers to linguistic creativity exhibited by non-monolinguals in all these situations.
2. Strevens (1982:419) claims that English has 400 million non-native speakers and 300 million native speakers.
3. This term was suggested to me by Michael G. Clyne. It was, however, first used by Heinz Kloss. I have earlier used the term "polymodel" in roughly the same sense. See also chapter 7.
4. The issues related to the models and norms of English and the implications of these issues have been discussed in chapters 6 and 7.
5. For discussion of this topic see, e.g., Prator, 1968, and my response to Prator in Kachru, 1976a reproduced with minor changes in chapter 6. Also see relevant studies in Smith, 1983.
6. Ferguson, 1978 raises several interesting questions concerning "multilingual grammars", and summarizes several attempts for describing multilinguals' linguisitic interaction. Also see Hymes, 1972b.
7. See, e.g., Jakobson (quoted in Erlich, 1965:172) "The subject of literary scholarship is not literature in its totality, but literariness (*literaturnost'*), i.e., that which makes of a

given work a work of literature". For the relationship of *context* and *text* see also Seung, 1982.

8. See Kachru, 1982b:330 and 341.
9. However, there are some exceptions to this. An excellent study is Chishimba, 1983. See also Lowenberg, 1984 and Magura, 1984 regarding contact literatures in Southeast Asia and Africa, respectively. For further references see B. Kachru, 1983a, Pride, 1982, ed. and 1983, and Sridhar, 1982.
10. For lexical evidence see Serjeantsen, 1935 [1961].
11. For further discussion see Parthasarathy, 1983.
12. I am grateful to Wimal Dissanayake for pointing out to me that the Platonic and Aristotelian sequences are not identical and that Kaplan's coupling of these two together is misleading.
13. A discussion of the bilingual's discourse strategies in educated English and specific illustrations of some cohesive characteristics of educated Indian English are given in Y. Kachru, 1983a, and 1983b.
14. See the following for discussion and illustrations of contrastive discourse: for Hindi, Y. Kachru, 1983a and 1983b; for Japanese, Hinds, 1983; for Korean, Chang, 1983; for Mandarin, Tsao, 1983; and for Marathi, Pandharipande, 1983.
15. See Kachru, 1983a, Pride, 1983, and Sanchez, 1983.
16. In this context one might mention the insightful work of John Gumperz, Dell Hymes and several other scholars. For references and further discussion see Chishimba, 1983 and Kachru, 1982b.
17. See Kachru, 1978a for references, illustrations, and further discussion. Also see Sridhar and Sridhar, 1980.
18. The relationship of sociolinguistic context and the "meaning potential" of non-native Englishes, with specific reference to African varieties of English, has been discussed extremely well by Chishimba, 1983 and Magura, 1984. Also see Kachru, 1982b and 1983a and Lowenberg, 1984.
19. Nelson, 1982 and 1984 discusses several issues related to intelligibility of non-native Englishes. Also see Smith, ed. 1983.
20. One also finds this in James Joyce, Walter Scott or Thomas Hardy, to give just three examples. But all these were still experimenting within the Western cultural and literary traditions.
21. See Kachru, 1965 and later, reproduced with an extensive bibliography in Kachru, 1983a.
22. For example, consider Yorubaization in Amos Tutuola, Sanskritization in Raja Rao and Hindiization and Punjabiization in Mulk Raj Anand. For references and discussion, see Kachru, 1983a.
23. See Parthasarathy, 1983.
24. A recent example of such stylistic experimentation is provided by another acclaimed South Asian writer, Salman Rushde, in his novels *Midnight's Children,* which won the Brooker Prize, and *Shame.*
25. Also see Chinweizu, Jemie and Madubuike, 1983; Moore, 1962; Mphahlele, 1964; and Sridhar, 1982.
26. For discussion of this topic see also a very insightful discussion in Nakamura, 1964.
27. For Chinese see Cheng, 1982, and for Thai see studies by Mayuri Sukwiwat, especially 1983.
28. See, e.g., Gumperz, 1964, and later; Kachru, 1981a; Sridhar and Sridhar, 1980; Pandharipande, 1982 and later.
29. The term "meaning system" is used here in a wider sense, more or less as used by Halliday.
30. See e.g., Amirthanayagam, 1976, and Sharrad, 1982. Sharrad provides a useful list of relevant references.
31. See also relevant chapters in Kachru, ed. 1982; Lowenberg, 1984; Magura, 1984; and Pride, 1983.

32. As an important afterword, I should point out that the issues raised here have several parallels in situations of bi-/or multidialectism (for example, Scottish, Welsh, and Irish literatures, or what are termed "dialect" literatures in other languages). A reader who does not share the linguistic and cultural norms of such writers is therefore at a disadvantage. True, a text does provide its own context, but it does not necessarily provide its culture-specific or language-specific interpretive context.

Bibliography

The bibliography includes references cited in the text or notes and also selected studies relevant to aspects of the English language in the world context, specifically to South Asia and Southeast Asia.

Abercrombie, David (1951) "R.P. and local accent." *The listener* 6, September, 1951. [Reprinted in D. Abercrombie, *Studies in phonetics and linguistics*. London: Oxford University Press, 1965.]

Abeysinghe A. and I. Abeysinghe (1970) "Some thoughts on the contemporary Ceylonese literature in English". *New Ceylon Writing*. pp. 4–7.

Abrahams, Roger D. (1983) *The man-of-words in the West Indies: Performance and the emergence of creole culture*. Baltimore: Johns Hopkins University Press.

Abrahams, Roger D. and Rudolph C. Troike (eds.) (1972) *Language and cultural diversity in American education*. Englewood Cliffs. NJ: Prentice-Hall.

Achebe, Chinua (1964) "Foreword". In Wilfred Howell Whiteley, (ed.), *A selection of African prose*. Oxford: Clarendon Press.

Achebe, Chinua (1965) "English and the African writer." *Transition* 4(18):27–30. Also in Mazrui, 1975.

Achebe, Chinua (1966) *Things fall apart*. London: Heinemann.

Adams, John (1856) *Life and works of John Adams*. 10 vols. Boston: Little, Brown.

Afolayan, A. (1971) "Language and sources of Amos Tutuola." In Christopher Heywood (ed.), 1971. pp. 49–63.

Aggarwal, Narindar K. (1982) *English in South Asia: A bibliographical survey of resources*. Gurgaon and Delhi: Indian Documentation Service.

Alatis, James E. (ed.) (1970) *Report of the 20th annual roundtable meeting on linguistics and language studies*. Monograph series on languages and linguistics. Washington, D.C.: Georgetown University Press.

Alatis, James E. (ed.). 1978. *International dimensions of bilingual education*. Monograph series on language and linguistics. Washington, D.C.: Georgetown University Press.

Ali, Ahmed (1966) *Twilight in Delhi*. London: Oxford University Press.

Allen, Harold B. and G. N. Underwood (1971) *Readings in American dialectology*. New York: Appleton-Century Crofts.

Allen, W. S. (1953) *Phonetics in ancient India*. London: Oxford University Press.

Allsopp, Richard (1972) *Why a dictionary of Caribbean English usage?* Circular "A" of the Caribbean Lexicography Project. Barbados: The University of the West Indies.

Amirthanayagam, Guy (1976) *Culture learning through literature*. Honolulu: East-West Center.

Anand, Mulk Raj (1935) *Untouchable: a novel*. London: Wishart Books.

Anand, Mulk Raj (1948) *The king-emperor's English*. Bombay: Hind Kitabs.

Annamalai, E. (1971) "Lexical insertions in a mixed language." *Papers from the seventh regional meeting*. Chicago: Chicago Linguistic Society. pp. 20–27.

Annamalai, E. (1978) "The Anglicized Indian languages: a case of code-mixing." *International Journal of Dravidian Linguistics* 7(2):239–47.

Ansre, Gilbert (1971a) "The influence of English on West African languages." In John Spencer (ed.), 1971. pp. 145–164.

Ansre, Gilbert (1971b) "Language standardization in sub-Saharan Africa." In T. O. Beidelman (ed.), 1971. pp. 680–698.

Ansre, Gilbert (1979) "Four rationalizations for maintaining European languages in Africa." *African Languages/Languages Africaines* 5(2):10–17.

Apte, M. L. (1974) "Pidginization of a lingua franca: a linguistic analysis of Hindi-Urdu spoken in Bombay." *International Journal of Dravidian Linguistics* 3(1):21–41.

Apte, M. L. (1976) "Language controversies in the Indian Parliament (Lok Sabha); 1952–1960." In William M. O'Barr and J. F. O'Barr (eds.), *Language and Politics*. The Hague: Mouton. pp. 213–234.

Babbitt, E. H. (1896) "The English of the lower classes of New York City and vicinity." *Dialect notes* **1**, pp. 457–64.

Bachchan, Harivansh Rai (ed.) (1970) *One hundred letters of Pant addressed to Bachchan* (in Hindi). Delhi: Rajpal and Sons.

Bahri, Hardev (1960) *Persian influence on Hindi.* Allahabad: Bharati Press Publications.

Bailey, Richard W. and M. Görlach (eds.), (1982) *English as a world language.* Ann Arbor: University of Michigan Press.

Bailey, Richard W. and J. L. Robinson (eds.) (1973) *Varieties of present-day English.* New York: Macmillan and Co.

Baker, O. R. (1980) "Categories of code-switching in Hispanic communities: untangling the terminology." *Sociolinguistic Working Paper* No. 76. Austin, TX: Southwest Educational Development Laboratory.

Baker, Sidney J. (1945) *The Australian language.* Sidney: Currawong Publishing.

Bamgbose, Ayo (1971) "The English language in Nigeria." In John Spencer (ed.), 1971. pp. 35–48.

Bamgbose, Ayo (1982) "Standard Nigerian English: issues of identification." In Braj B. Kachru (ed.), 1982. pp. 99–111.

Bansal, R. K. (1969) *The intelligibility of Indian English.* Monograph 4. Hyderabad: Central Institute of English and Foreign Languages.

Barnes, Sir Edward (1932) *The history of Royal College.* Colombo.

Barnett, Lincoln (1964) *The treasure of our tongue: the story of English from its obscure beginnings to its present eminence as the most widely spoken language.* New York: Alfred A. Knopf.

Baron, Dennis (1982) *Grammar and good taste: reforming the American language.* New Haven: Yale University Press.

Basham, A. L. (1954) *The wonder that was India.* London: Sidgwick and Jackson.

Baugh, Albert C. (1935 [1978]) *A history of the English language.* New York: Appleton Century Crofts. [Revised edition (with Thomas Cable), 1978. Englewood Cliffs, NJ: Prentice-Hall.]

Bautista, Ma Laurdes S. (1975) "A model of bilingual competence based on an analysis of Tagalog-English code switching." *Philippine Journal of Linguistics* **6**:51–89.

Bautista, Ma Laurdes S. (1977) "The noun-phrase in Tagalog-English code-switching." *Studies in Philippine Linguistics* **1**(2):1–16.

Bazell, C. E., J. C. Catford, M. A. K. Halliday, and R. H. Robins (eds.) (1966) *In memory of J. R. Firth.* London: Longman.

Beck, Theodoric Romeyn (1830) "Notes on Mr. Pickering's vocabulary of words and phrases, which have been supposed to be peculiar to the United States." In M. M. Mathews, (ed.), 1931. pp. 78–85.

Beebe, James and Maria Beebe (1981) "The Filipinos: a special case." In Charles A. Ferguson and Shirley B. Heath, (eds.), 1981. pp. 322–338.

Beidelman, T. O. (ed.) (1971) *The translation of culture.* London: Tavistock.

Bernstein, Basil (1965) "A sociolinguistic approach to social learning." In J. Gould (ed.), 1965. pp. 144–168.

Bernstein, Basil (1971–75) *Theoretical studies toward a sociology of language.* Vol. 1 in *Class, codes and control* (3 vols.). London: Routledge and Kegan Paul.

Bhatia, Kailash Chandra (1967) *A linguistic study of English loan words in Hindi* (in Hindi). Allahabad: Hindustani Academy.

Bills, G. A. (ed.) (1974) *Southwest areal linguistics.* San Diego: Institute for Cultural Pluralism.

Bloomfield, Leonard (1933) *Language.* New York: Holt, Rinehart and Winston.

Bokamba, Eyamba (1982) "The Africanization of English." In Braj B. Kachru (ed.), 1982. pp. 77–98.

Bose, Amalendu (1968) "Some poets of the writers' workshop." In M. K. Naik, S. K. Desai and G. S. Amur (eds.), 1968. pp. 31–50.

Brass, Paul R. (1974) *Language, religion and politics in North India.* London: Cambridge University Press.

Bright, Williams (1960) "Linguistic change in some Indian caste dialects." In Charles A, Ferguson and John J. Gumperz (eds.), 1960. pp. 19–26.

Bright, William (ed.) (1966) *Sociolinguistics: proceedings of the UCLA sociolinguistics conference, 1964.* The Hague: Mouton.

Brosnahan, L. F. (1963) "Some historical cases of language imposition." In John Spencer (ed.), 1963. pp. 7–24. [Also in Richard W. Bailey and J. L. Robinson (eds.), 1973. pp. 40–54.]

Brown, Charles Phillip (1852) *The Zillah dictionary in the Roman character. Explaining the various words used in business in India.* Madras: Printed by D. P. L. C. Cooner Society's Press.

Brown, Penelope and Stephen Levinson. (1979) "Social structure, groups and interaction." In Klaus R. Scherer and Howard Giles (eds.), 1979. pp. 33–62.

Buck, Harry M. and G. E. Yocum (eds.) (1974) *Structural approaches to South Indian Studies.* Chembersburg, PA: Wilson Books.

Bughwan, D. (1970) "An investigation into the use of English by Indians in South Africa with special reference to Natal." Unpublished doctoral dissertation, University of South Africa.

Burling, Robbins (1973) *English in black and white.* New York: Holt, Rhinehart and Winston.

Candlin, C. N. (1981) "Discoursal patterning and the equalizing of integrative opportunity." In Larry E. Smith (ed.), 1981. pp. 166–199.

Carnegy, P. (1877) *Kachahari technicalities, or a glossary of terms, rural, official, and general, in daily use in the courts of law, and in illustration of the tenures, customs, arts and manufacturers of Hindustan.* 2nd. ed. Allahabad: Allahabad Mission Press.

Catford, J. C. (1950) "Intelligibility." *English Language teaching* (1):7–15.

Catford, J. C. (1959) "The teaching of English as a foreign language." In Randolph Quirk and A. H. Smith (eds.), 1959. [Reprinted, London: Oxford University Press, 1964.]

Cazden, Courtney B., Vera P. John, and Dell Hymes (eds.), (1972) *Functions of language in the classroom.* New York and London: Teachers College Press.

Central Institute of English and Foreign Languages (1972) *A bibliography of Indian English.* Hyderabad: Central Institute of English and Foreign Languages (CIEFL).

Chang, Suk-Jan (1983) "Linguistics and written discourse in English and Korean." *Annual Review of Applied Linguistics, 1982.* pp. 85–98.

Chaudhuri, Nirad C. (1976) "The English language in India—past, present and future." In Alistair Niven (ed.), 1976. pp. 89–106.

Cheng, Chin-Chuan (1982) "Chinese varieties of English." In Braj B. Kachru (ed.), 1982. pp. 125–140.

Chinweizu, Onwuchekwa Jemie, and Ihechukwu Madubuike (1983) *Toward the decolonization of African literature.* Washington, D.C.: Howard University Press.

Chutisilp, Ponpimol (1984) A Sociolinguistic study of an additional language English in Thailand. Unpublished doctoral dissertion, University of Illinois, Urbana.

Chishimba, Maurice M. (1983) "African varieties of English: text in context." Unpublished doctoral dissertation, University of Illinois, Urbana.

Circourel, A. V., *et al.* (1974) *Language use and school performance.* New York: Academic Press.

Clyne, Michael (1972) *Perspectives on language contact: based on a study of German in Australia.* Melbourne: Hawthorn Press.

Coballes-Vega, Carmen (1979) "A comparison of the form and function of code-switching of Chicano and Puerto Rican children." Unpublished doctoral dissertation, University of Illinois, Urbana.

Cooper, Robert L. (1985) "Fantasti! Israeli attitudes toward English." In Sidney Greenbaum (ed.), 1985.

Currie, Haver C. (1952) "A projection of sociolinguistics: the relationship of speech to social status." In Juanita V. Williamson and V. M. Burke (eds.), 1971. pp. 39–47.

Daniels, Harvey A. (1982) *Famous last words: the American language crisis reconsidered.* Carbondale: Southern Illinois University Press.

Das, Kamala (1973) *The old playhouse and other poems*. Delhi: Orient Longman.
Das Gupta, Jyotirindra (1969) "Official language problems and policies in South Asia." In T. A. Sebeok (ed.), 1969. pp. 578–596.
Das Gupta, Jyotirindra (1970) *Language conflict and national development: group politics and national language policy in India*. Berkeley: University of California Press.
Day, Lal Behari (1913) *Bengal peasant life*. 2nd edition. London: Macmillan and Co.
Denison, N. (1968) "Sauris: a trilingual community in diatypic perspective." *Man* **3**:578–592.
Desai, M(aganbhai) P. (1964) *The problem of English*. Ahmedabad: Navajivan Publishing House.
Dil, Afia (1972) "The Hindu and Muslim dialects of Bengali." Unpublished doctoral dissertation, Stanford University.
Dil, Anwar S. (1966) "The position and teaching of English in Pakistan." In Anwar S. Dil (ed.), 1966. pp. 185–242.
Dil, Anwar S. (ed.) (1966) *Pakistani linguistics: Shahidullah presentation volume*. Lahore: Linguistic Research Group of Pakistan.
Dil, Anwar S. (ed.) (1971) *Language in social groups*. Stanford: Stanford University Press.
Dillard, J. L. (1972) *Black English: its history and usage in the United States*. New York: Random House.
Dustoor, Phiroz E. (1968) *The world of words*. Bombay and New York: Asia Publishing House.
Elias-Olivares, Lucia (1976) "Ways of speaking in a Chicano community: a sociolinguistic approach." Unpublished doctoral dissertion, University of Texas, Austin.
Emeneau, Murray B. (1956) "India as a linguistic area." *Language* **32**:3–16.
Erlich, Victor (1965) *Russian formalism: history:doctine*. The Hague: Mouton.
Ervin-Tripp, S. (1972) "On sociolinguistic rules: alteration and co-occurrence." In John J. Gumperz and Dell Hymes (eds.), 1972. pp. 213–250.
Fennel, C. A. M. (1982) *The Stanford dictionary of Anglicized words and phrases*. London: Cambridge University Press.
Ferguson, Charles A. (1966) "National sociolinguistic profile formulas." In William O. Bright (ed.), 1966. pp. 309–315.
Ferguson, Charles A. (1978) "Multilingualism as object of linguistic description." In Braj B. Kachru (ed.), 1978. pp. 97–105.
Ferguson, Charles A. (1982a) "Foreword." In Braj B. Kachru (ed.), 1982 pp. vii–xi.
Ferguson, Charles A. (1982b) "Religious factors in language spread." In R. L. Cooper (ed.), *Language spread: studies in diffusion and language change*. Bloomington, Indiana: Indiana University Press. pp. 95–106.
Ferguson, Charles A. and John J. Gumperz (eds.) (1960) "Linguistic diversity in South Asia." *IJAL* **26**[3] part IV. Bloomington, IN: Indiana University Press.
Ferguson, Charles A. and Shirley B. Heath (eds.) (1981) *Language in the USA*. London: Cambridge University Press.
Fernando, Chitra (1977) "English and Sinhala bilingualism in Sri Lanka." *Language in Society* **6**:341–360.
Finegan, Edward (1980) *Attitudes toward English usage: the history of a war of words*. New York: Teachers College Press.
Firth, John R. (1930) *Speech*. London: Ernest Benn. [Reprinted, London: Oxford University Press, 1966.]
Firth, John R. (1956) "Descriptive linguistics and the study of English." In F. R. Palmer (ed.), 1968. pp. 96–113.
Firth, John R. (1957) "Modes of Meaning." In *Papers in linguistics 1935–1954*. London: Oxford University Press. pp. 190–215.
Fishman, Joshua A. (1977) *Language and nationalism*. Rowley MA: Newbury House
Fishman, Joshua A. (ed.) (1968) *Readings in the sociology of language*. The Hague: Mouton.
Fishman, Joshua A. (ed.) (1978) *Advances in the study of societal multilingualism*. The Hague: Mouton.

Fishman, Joshua A., Charles A. Ferguson, and Jyotirinda Das Gupta (eds.) (1968) *Language problems in developing nations*. New York: John Wiley and Sons, Inc.

Fishman, Joshua A., Robert L. Cooper and Andrew W. Conrad. (1977) *The spread of English: the sociology of English as an additional language*. Rowley, MA: Newbury House.

Forster, E. M. (1924) *A Passage to India*. New York: Harcourt Brace and World. (Reprinted in 1952).

Foster, Brian (1976) *The changing English language*. Harmondsworth: Penguin Books. [First published, Macmillan and Co., 1968].

Fox, Melvin J. (ed.) (1975) *Language and development: a retrospective survey of Ford Foundation langauge projects 1952–1974*. New York: Ford Foundation.

Freed, B. F. (1978) *From the community to the classroom: gathering second language speech samples*. Arlington, VA: Center for Applied Linguistics.

Fremantle, Ann. (1974) *A primer of linguistics*. New York: St. Martin's Press.

Fried, V. (ed.). (1972) *The Prague School of Linguistics and language teaching*. London: Oxford University Press.

Gage, William W. and S. Ohannessian (1974) "ESOL enrollments throughout the world." *Linguistic Reporter* **16**(9):13–16.

Gilbert, Glenn (ed. and trans.) (1980) *Pidgin and creole languages: selected essays by Hugo Schuchardt*. London: Cambridge University Press.

Giles, Howard (1979) "Ethnicity markers in speech." In Klaus R. Scherer and Howard Giles (eds.), 1979. pp. 251–289.

Gimson, A. C. (1962) *An introduction to the pronunciation of English*. London: Edward Arnold.

Gingras, Rosario (1974) "Problems in the description of Spanish-English inter-sentential code-switching." In G. A. Bills (ed.), 1974. pp. 167–214.

Gladwin T. and W. Sturtevant (eds.) (1962) *Anthropology and human behaviour*. Washington, D. C.: Anthropological Society of Washington.

Gleason, Henry A. Jr. (1960) "Language variation." *Linguistics and English grammar*. Garden City, NY: Doubleday.

Goffin, R. C. (1934) *Some notes on Indian English*. Society for Pure English Tract, no. 41. Oxford: Society for Pure English.

Gokak, V. K. (1964) *English in India: its present and its future*. Bombay and New York: Asia Publishing House.

Gokak, V. K. (1970) *The golden treasury of Indo-Anglian poetry*. Delhi: Sahitya Akademi.

Goodwin, K. L. (ed.) (1970) *National identity*. Papers delivered at the Commonwealth Literature Conference, University of Queensland, Brisbane, 9th–15th August, 1968. London and Melbourne: Heinemann.

Goonewardene, James (1970) "Ceylonese writing in English and British literary traditions." In K. L. Goodwin (ed.), 1970. pp. 148–152.

Gould, J. (1965) *Penguin survey of social sciences*. Harmondsworth: Penguin Books.

Grant, Charles (1912–13) "Observations on the state of society among the Asiatic subjects of Great Britain, particularly with respect to morals, and on the means of improving it." [written chiefly in 1792. Ordered by the House of Commons to be printed, 15 June 1813.] London: *General appendix to Parliamentary papers* 1812–13. Vol. 10. No. 282

Greenbaum, Sidney (ed.) (1985) *The English language today*. Oxford: Pergamon Press.

Grierson, George A. (1911) *A manual of the Kashmiri language*. Oxford: Clarendon Press (two parts).

Gumperz, John J. (1964) "Linguistic and social interaction in two communities." In John J. Gumperz and Dell Hymes (eds.), pp. 137–153.

Gumperz, John J. (1968) "The speech community." *International encyclopedia of the social sciences*. Vol. 9. pp. 381–386.

Gumperz, John J. (1970) "Verbal strategies in multilingual communication." In Roger D. Abrahams and Rudolph C. Troike (eds.), 1970. pp. 184–197.

Gumperz, John J. (1972) "Introduction." In John J. Gumperz and Dell Hymes (eds.), 1972. pp. 1–25.

Gumperz, John J. and Eduardo Hernandez-Charez (1972) "Bilingualism, bidialectism and classroom interaction." In Courtney B. Cazden, Vera P. John. and Dell Hymes (eds.), 1972.

Gumperz, John J. and Dell Hymes (eds.) (1964) *The ethnography of communication*. Special publication of American Anthropologist, part 2, vol. 66, no. 6.

Gumperz, John J. and Dell Hymes (eds.) 1972) *Directions in sociolinguistics: the ethnography of communication*. New York: Holt, Rhinehart and Winston.

Gumperz, John J. and Robert Wilson (1971) "Convergence and creolization: a case from the Indo-Aryan/Dravidian border." In Dell Hymes (ed.), 1971. pp. 151–167.

Guru, Kamtaprasad (1962) *Hindi grammar*. (in Hindi). Benares: Nagari Pracharani Sabha.

Halliday, Michael A. K. (1970) "Language structure and language function." In J. Lyons (ed.), 1970. pp. 140–165.

Halliday, Michael A. K. (1973) *Explorations in the functions of language*. London: Edward Arnold.

Halliday, Michael A. K. (1974) *Learning how to mean: explorations in the development of language*. London: Edward Arnold.

Halliday, Michael A. K. (1978) "Antilanguages." In *Language as social semiotic*. Baltimore: Univeristy Park Press. pp. 164–182.

Halliday, Michael A. K., Angus McIntosh, and Peter Strevens. (1964) *The linguistic sciences and language teaching*. London: Longman.

Halverson, J. (1966) "Prolegomena to the study of Ceylon English." *University of Ceylon Review* 24:61–75.

Hartford, B., A. Valdman and C. Foster (eds.). 1982. *Issues in bilingual education: the role of the vernacular*. New York: Plenum.

Heath, Shirley B. (1977a) "Language and politics in the United States." In M. Saville-Troike (ed.), 1977. pp. 267–296.

Heath, Shirley B. (1977b) "A national language academy? Debate in the nation." *Linguistics* 189:9–43.

Heath, Shirley B. (1978) "Bilingual education and a national language policy." In James E. Alatis (ed.), 1978. pp. 53–64.

Heath, Shirley B. (1980) "Standard English: biography of symbol." In T. Shopen and J. M. Williams (eds.), 1980. pp. 3–32

Herbert, R. K. (ed.) (1979) *Metatheory III: applications of linguistic theory in the human sciences*. East Lansing: Department of Linguistics, Michigan State University.

Herskovits, M. J. (1958) *Dahomean narrative*. Evanston: Northwestern University Press.

Heywood, Christopher (ed.) (1971) *Perspectives on African literature: selections from the proceedings of the Conference on African Literature held at the University of Ife, 1968*. London, Ibadan, Nairobi: Heinemann Educational Books, Ltd. in Association with University of Ife Press.

Hinds, John (1983) "Linguistics and written discourse in English and Japanese." *Annual Review of Applied Linguistics, 1982*. pp. 78–84.

Hymes, Dell (1962) "The ethnography of speaking." In T. Gladwin and W. Sturtevant (eds.), 1962. pp. 15–53. [A revised version in Joshua A. Fishman (ed.), 1968. pp. 99–138.]

Hymes, Dell (1964) "Introduction: toward ethnographies of communication." In John J. Gumperz and Dell Hymes (Eds.), 1964). pp. 1–34.

Hymes, Dell (1972a) "Introduction." In Courtney B. Cazden, Vera P. John, and Dell Hymes (eds.), 1972. pp. xi–lvii.

Hymes, Dell (1972b) "Models of the interaction of language and social life." In John J. Gumperz and Dell Hymes (eds.), 1972. pp. 35–71.

Hymes, Dell (1974) *Foundations in sociolinguistics: an ethnographic approach*. Philadelphia: University of Pennsylvania Press.

Hymes, Dell (ed.) (1971) *Pidginization and creolization of languages*. London: Cambridge University Press.

Iyengar, K. R. Srinivasa (1962) *Indian writing in English*. Bombay and New York: Asia Publishing House.

Jacobson, Rodolfo (1978) "The social implications of intra-sentential code-switching." In Ricardo Romo and Raymond Paredes (eds.), 1978. pp. 227–256.

Jernudd, Björn H. (1981) "Planning language treatment: linguistics for the Third World." *Language in Society* **10**:43–52.

Jespersen, Otto (1905) *Growth and structure of the English language.* Garden City, NY: Doubleday.

John, V. V. (1969) *Education and language policy.* Bombay: Nachiketa Publications.

Jones, Daniel (1918) *An outline of English phonetics.* [Revised edition, 1956.] Cambridge: Heffer.

Jones, Daniel (1956) *Everyman's English pronouncing dictionary.* London: Dent.

Kachru, Braj B. (1962) "An analysis of some features of Indian English: a study in linguistic method." Unpublished doctoral dissertation, University of Edinburgh.

Kachru, Braj B. (1965) "The *Indianness* in Indian English." *Word.* **21**:391–410. [A revised version in Braj B. Kachru, 1983a. pp. 128–144.]

Kachru, Braj B. (1966) "Indian English: a study in contextualization." In C. E. Bazell, J. C. Catford, M. A. K. Halliday, and R. H. Robins (eds.), 1966. pp. 255–287. [A revised version in Braj B. Kachru, 1983a. pp. 99–127.]

Kachru, Braj B. (1969) "English in South Asia." In T. Sebeok (ed.), 1969. pp. 627–678. [A revised version in Joshua A. Fishman (ed.), 1978. pp. 477–551. A further updated version in Braj B. Kachru, 1983a. pp. 17–65.]

Kachru, Braj B. (1970) "Some style features of South Asian English." In K. L. Goodwin (ed.), 1970. pp. 122–137.

Kachru, Braj B. (1973a) "General linguistic studies in Hindi: a review of resources. In papers on South Asian linguistics." Special issue of *Studies in the Linguistic Sciences* **3**, (2):59–86. [Revised version in *Lingua* 1976(38):335–355].

Kachru, Braj B. (1973b) *An introduction to spoken Kashmiri. A basic course and reference manual for learning and teaching Kashmiri as a second language.* Urbana: Department of Linguistics, University of Illinois.

Kachru, Braj B. (1973c) "Toward a lexicon of Indian English." In Braj B. Kachru, R. B. Lees, Y. Malkiel, A. Pietrangeli, S. Saporta (eds.), 1973. pp. 352–376. [A revised version in Kachru, 1983a. pp. 165–189.]

Kachru, Braj B. (1975a) "Lexical innovations in South Asian English." *International Journal of the Sociology of Language* **4**:55–74. [A revised version in Braj B. Kachru. 1983a. pp. 147–164.]

Kachru, Braj B. (1975b) "A retrospective study of the Central Institute of English and Foreign Languages and its relation to Indian universities." In Melvin J. Fox (ed.), 1975. pp. 27–94.

Kachru, Braj B. (1976a) "Indian English: a sociolinguistic profile of a transplanted language." In Braj B. Kachru (ed.), 1976. pp. 139–189. [A revised version in Braj B. Kachru, 1983a. pp. 66–95.]

Kachru, Braj B. (1976b) "Models of English for the Third World: White man's linguistic burden or language pragmatics?" *TESOL Quarterly* **10**:221–239. (A revised version in this volume; see chapter 6).

Kachru, Braj B. (ed.) (1976) *Dimensions of bilingualism: theory and case studies.* Special issue of Studies in Language Learning. Volume 1, Number 2, Spring 1976. Urbana: Unit for Foreign Language Study and Research, University of Illinois.

Kachru, Braj B. (1977a) "The new Englishes and old models." *English Teaching Forum* **15**(3):29–35. (A revised version in this volume, see chapter 7).

Kachru, Braj B. (1977b) "Linguistic schizophrenia and language census: a note on the Indian situation." *Linguistics* **186**:17–32.

Kachru, Braj B. (1978a) "Code-mixing as a communicative strategy in India." In James E. Alatis (ed.), 1978. pp. 107–124. [A revised version in Braj B. Kachru, 1983a pp. 193–207.]

Kachru, Braj B. (1978b) "English in South Asia." In Joshua A. Fishman (ed.), 1978. pp. 477–551. (A revised version of Kachru, 1969).

Kachru, Braj B. (1978c) "Toward structuring code-mixing: an Indian perspective." In Braj

B. Kachru and S. N. Sridhar (eds.), 1978. pp. 27–46. [An earlier version in *Studies in the Linguistic Sciences* 5(1):73–92.]

Kachru, Braj B. (ed.) (1978) *Linguistics in the seventies: directions and prospects.* Special issue of *Studies in the Linguistic Sciences* 8(2), Fall 1978. Urbana: Department of Linguistics, University of Illinois.

Kachru, Braj B. (1979) "The Englishization of Hindi: language rivalry and language change." In Irmengard Rauch and Gerald F. Carr (eds.), (1979) pp. 199–211. (A revised version in this volume; see chapter 9).

Kachru, Braj B. (1980a) *Kashmiri literature.* Wiesbaden: Otto Harassowitz.

Kachru, Braj B. (1980b) "Models for new Englishes.' *TESL Studies.* 3:117–150.

Kachru, Braj B. (1980c) "The new Englishes and old dictionaries: directions in lexicographical research on non-native varieties of English." In L. Zgusta (ed), 1980. pp. 71–101.

Kachru, Braj B. (1980d) "Socially-realistic linguistics: the Firthian tradition." *Studies in the Linguistic Sciences* 10(1):85–111. [A revised version in *International Journal of the Sociology of Language* 1981. 31:65–89.]

Kachru, Braj B. (1981a) "American English and other Englishes." In Charles A. Ferguson and Shirley B. Heath (eds.), 1981. pp. 21–43. (A revised version in this volume; see chapter 8).

Kachru, Braj B. (1981b) "Bilingualism." *Annual Review of Applied Linguistics, 1981.* pp. 2–24.

Kachru, Braj B. (1981c) "The pragmatics of non-native varieties of English." In Larry E. Smith (ed.), 1981. pp. 15–39. [A revised version in Braj B. Kachru, 1983a. pp. 211–240.]

Kachru, Braj B. (1982a) "The bilingual's linguistic repertoire." In B. Hartford, A. Valdman, and C. Foster (eds.), 1982. pp. 25–52. (A revised version in this volume; see chapter 4).

Kachru, Braj B. (1982b) "Meaning in deviation: toward understanding non-native English texts." In Braj B. Kachru (ed.), 1982. pp. 325–350.

Kachru, Braj B. (1982c) "Models for non-native Englishes." In Braj B. Kachru (ed.), 1982 pp. 31–57.

Kachru, Braj B. (1982d) "South Asian English." In Richard W. Bailey and M. Görlach (eds.), 1982. pp. 353–383. (A revised version in this volume; see chapter 3).

Kachru, Braj B. (ed.) (1982) *The other tongue: English across cultures.* Urbana: University of Illinois Press. (Paperback edition, Pergamon Press, Oxford, 1983).

Kachru, Braj B. (1983a) *The Indianization of English: the English Language in India.* Delhi: Oxford University Press.

Kachru, Braj B. (1983b) "The bilingual's creativity: discoursal and stylistic strategies in contact literatures in English." *Studies in the Linguistic Sciences.* 13(2):37. (A revised version in this volume; see chapter 10).

Kachru, Braj B. (1984a) "Institutionalized second language varieties." In Sidney Greenbaum (ed.), 1985. (A revised version in this volume; see chapter 2).

Kachru, Braj B. (1984b) "The alchemy of English: Social and functional power of non-native varieties." In Cheris Kramarae, Muriel Schulz, William O'Barr (eds.), Beverley Hills, CA: Sage Publications, Inc. pp. 176–193. (A revised version in this volume; see chapter 1).

Kachru, Braj B. (1984c) "Regional Norms for English." In Sandra Savignon and M. Berns (eds). 1984. pp. 55–78. (A revised version in this volume; see chapter 5).

Kachru, Braj B. (1985) "Standards, codification, and sociolinguistic realism: the English language in the outer circle." In Randolph Quirk and Henry Widdowson (eds.) *English in the World: teaching and learning the language and literatures.* Cambridge: Cambridge University Press, pp. 11–30.

Kachru, Braj B. and Yamuna Kachru (eds.) (1968) *Proceedings of Conference on Hindi.* New Delhi: American Institute of Indian Studies. (Mimeographed).

Kachru, Braj B., R. B. Lees, Y. Malkiel, A. Pietrangeli, S. Saporta (eds.) (1973) *Issues in linguistics: papers in honor of Henry and Renée Kahane.* Urbana: University of Illinois Press.

Kachru, Braj B. and Randolph Quirk (1981) "Introduction." In Larry E. Smith (ed.), 1981. pp. 13–20.

Kachru, Braj B. and S. N. Sridhar (eds.) (1978) *Aspects of sociolinguistics in South Asia.* Special issue of *International Journal of the Sociology of Language.* **16**. The Hague: Mouton.

Kachru, Yamuna (1968) *An introduction to Hindi syntax.* Urbana: Department of Linguistics, University of Illinois.

Kachru, Yamuna (1979) "The quotative in South Asian languages." In *South Asian Languages Analysis* **1**:63–77. Urbana: Department of Linguistics, University of Illinois.

Kachru, Yamuna (1983a) "Cross-cultural texts, discourse strategies and discourse interpretation." Paper presented at the Conference on English as an International Language: Discourse Patterns Across Cultures. Honolulu: East-West Center. June 1–7. (manuscript).

Kachru, Yamuna (1983b) "Linguistics and written discourse in particular languages: English and Hindi." *Annual Review of Applied Linguistics, 1982.* pp. 50–77.

Kachru, Yamuna and T. K. Bhatia (1978a) "The emerging 'dialect' conflict in Hindi: a case of glottopolitics." In Braj B. Kachru and S. N. Sridhar (eds.), 1978. pp. 47–58.

Kahane, Henry and Renée Kahane (1977) "Virtues and vices in the American language: a history of attitudes." *TESOL Quarterly* **11**(2):185–202.

Kandiah, Thiru (1964) "The teaching of English as a second language in Ceylon." *Transactions of the University of Ceylon Linguistic Society.* pp. 61–75.

Kandiah, Thiru (1971) "Writing in new Ceylon English." *New Ceylon Writing.* pp. 90–94.

Kandiah. Thiru (1981) "Lankan English schizoglossia." *English World-Wide: a Journal of Varieties of English* **2**(1):63–81.

Kansakar, Tej K. (1977) "The teaching of spoken English in Nepal." In *Report of the second national convention of the teachers of English.* Kathmandu: Tribhuvan University. pp. 85–102.

Kaplan, Robert B. (1966) "Cultural thought patterns in intercultural education." *Language Learning* **16**:1–20.

Kenyon, John Samuel (1924) *American pronunciation.* Ann Arbor: George Wahr.

Kenyon, John Samuel (1944) *A pronouncing dictionary of American English.* Springfield, MA: Merriam.

Kenyon, John Samuel and T. A. Knott (1953) *A pronouncing dictionary of American English.* Springfield, MA: Merriam.

King, Bruce (1980) *The new English literatures: cultural nationalism in the changing world.* New York: St. Martin's Press.

Kirk-Green, Anthony (1971) "The influence of West African languages on English." In John Spencer (ed.), 1971. pp. 123–144.

Knappert, Jan (1965) "Language problems of the new nations in Africa." *African Quarterly* **5**:95–105.

Kramarae, Cheris (1981) "Language and power: a bibliography." Urbana: Department of Speech Communication, University of Illinois. (manuscript).

Kramarae, Cheris, Muriel Schulz, and William O'Barr. (eds.) (1984) *Language and power.* Beverley Hills, CA: Sage Publication.

Krapp, George Philip (1919) *Pronunciation of standard English in America.* London: Oxford University Press.

Krishnamurti, Bh. (1978) "Spelling pronunciation in Indian English." In Ramesh Mohan (ed.), 1978. pp. 129–139.

Labov, William (1966) *The social stratification of English in New York City.* Washington, D. C.: Center for Applied Linguistics.

Labov, William (1970) "The logic of non-standard English." In J. Alatis (ed.), 1970. pp. 1–43.

Labov, William (1972a) *Language in the inner city: studies in the Black English vernacular.* Philadelphia: University of Pennsylvania Press.

Labov, William (1972b) *Sociolinguistic patterns.* Philadelphia: University of Pennsylvania Press.

Laird, Charlton (1970) *Language in America*. Englewood Cliffs, NJ: Prentice-Hall.

Lal, P. (1969) *Modern Indian poetry in English: an anthology and a credo*. Calcutta: Writers Workshop.

Lanham, L.W. (1978) "An outline history of the languages of Southern Africa." In L. W. Lanham (ed.), 1978. pp. xiii–xx.

Lanham, L. W. (ed.) (1978) *Language and communication studies in South Africa*. Cape Town: Oxford University Press.

Lannoy, Richard (1971) *The speaking tree: a study of Indian culture and society*. New York: Oxford University Press.

Lawton, D. (1980). "Language attitude, discreteness, and code-switching in Jamaican creole." *English World-wide: a journal of varieties of English* 2: 211: 226.

Leap, W. (1973) "Language pluralism in a south-western Pueblo: some comments on Isletan English." In P. R. Turner (ed.), 1973. pp. 275–293.

Lindfors, Bernth (1973) *Folklore in Nigerian literature*. New York: Africana.

Lindholm, K. J. and A. M. Padilla (1978) "Language mixing in bilingual children." *Journal of Child Language* 5(23): 327–378.

Lipski, John M. (1978) "Code-switching and the problems of bilingual competence." In Michel Paradis (ed.), 1978. pp. 250–264.

Llamzon, Teodoro A. (1969) *Standard Filipino English*. Manila: Ataneo University Press.

Llamzon. Teodoro A. (1983) "Essential features of new varieties of English." In R. B. Noss (ed.), 1983. pp. 92–109.

Lloyd, Donald J. (1951) "Snobs, slobs, and the English language." *The American Scholar* (Summer) 20(3): 279–288. [Also in Roger D. Abrahams and Rudolph C. Troike (eds.), 1972].

Lohia, Rammanohar (1965) *Langauge*. (in Hindi). Hyderabad: Nav Hind Prakashan.

Lowenberg, Peter H. (1984) "English in the Malay Archipelago: nativization and its functions in a sociolinguistic area." Unpublished doctoral dissertation, University of Illinois, Urbana.

Lyons, J. (ed.) (1970) *New Horizons in Linguistics*. Harmondsworth: Penguin Books.

Magura, Benjamin J. (1984) "Style and meaning in Southern African English: a sociolinguistic study." Unpublished doctoral dissertation, University of Illinois, Urbana.

Makkai, A., V. B. Makkai, and L. Heilmann (eds.) (1977) *Linguistics at the crossroads*. Lake Bluff: Jupiter Press.

Malla, Kamal P. (1977) *English in Nepalese education*. Kathmandu: Ratna Pustak Bhandar.

Marasigan, Elizabeth (1981) "Creolized English in the Philippines." Paper presented at the Sixteenth Regional Seminar: Varieties of English and their Implications for English Langauge Teaching in Southeast Asia. SEAMEO Regional Language Centre, Singapore. April 20–24, 1981.

Marasigan, Elizabeth (1983) Code-switching and code-mixing in multilingual societies. Singapore: Singapore Univesity Press.

Marckwardt, Albert H. (1958) *American English*, New York: Oxford University Press.

Marckwardt, Albert H. and Randolph Quirk. (1964) *A common language: British and American English*. London: British Broadcasting Corporation.

Masica, Colin P. (1976) *Defining a linguistic area: South Asia*. Chicago: University of Chicago Press.

Masica, Colin P. and P. B. Dave (1972) *The sound system of Indian English*. [Monograph 7.] Hyderabad: Central Institute of English and Foreign Languages.

Mathews, M. M. (ed.) (1931) *The beginnings of American English: essays and comments*. Chicago: University of Chicago Press.

Mazrui, Ali A. (Ed.) (1975) *The political sociology of the English language: an African perspective*. The Hague: Mouton.

McClure, Erica (1977) "Aspects of code-switching in the discourse of bilingual Mexican-American children." In Saville-Troike (ed.), 1977. pp. 93–115.

McClure, Erica and James Wentz (1976) "Functions of code-switching among Mexican American Children." *Papers from the parasession on functionalism*. Chicago: Chicago Linguistic Society. pp. 421–432.

McDavid, Raven I. Jr. (1948) "Postvocalic r in South Carolina: a social analysis." *American Speech* 23:194–203.

Mehrotra, R. R. (1975) "Some registral features of matrimonial advertisements in Indian English." *English Language Teaching Journal* 30(1):9–12.

Mehrotra, R. R. (1977) "English in India: the current scene." *English Language Teaching* 21:163–170.

Mencken, H. L. (1919) *The American language.* New York: Alfred A. Knopf.

Miranda, Rockey V. (1978) "Caste, religion and dialect differentiation in the Konkani area." In Braj. B. Kachru and S. N. Sridhar (eds.), 1978. pp. 77–91.

Mishra, Vishwanath. (1963) *The influence of English on Hindi language and literature 1870–1920* (in Hindi). Dehradun: Sahitya Sadan.

Mitchell, T. F. (1978) "Meaning is what you do—and how he and I interpret it: a Firthian view of pragmatics." *Die Neueren Sprachan.* Heft 3/4. Frankfurt and Main: Verlag Moritz Diesterweg. pp. 224–253.

Moag, Rodney F. (1982) "The life cycle of non-native Englishes: a case study." In Braj B. Kachru (ed.), 1982. pp. 270–288.

Mohan, Ramesh (ed.) (1978) *Indian English.* Delhi: Orient Longman.

Moore, Gerald (1962) *Seven African writers.* London: Oxford University Press.

Mphahlele, Ezekiel (1964) "The language of African literature". *Harvard Educational Review* (Spring) 34:90–101.

Mukherjee, Meenakshi (1971) *The twice-born fiction: themes and techniques of the Indian novel in English.* Delhi and London: Heinemann.

Munby, J. (1978) *Communicative syllabus design.* London: Cambridge University Press.

Nadkarni, M. V. (1975) "Bilingualism and syntactic change in Konkani." *Language* 51(3):672–683.

Naik, M. K. and S. Mokashi-Punekar (1977) *Perspectives on Indian drama in English.* Madras: Oxford University Press.

Naik, M. K., S. K. Desai and G. S. Amur (eds.) (1968) *Critical essays on Indian writing in English presented to Armando Menezes.* Dharwar: Karnatak University.

Naipaul, V. S. (1973) *The overcrowded barracoon.* New York: Alfred A. Knopf.

Nakamura, Hajime (1964) *Ways of thinking of Eastern peoples.* Edited by Philip P. Weiner. Honolulu: University of Hawaii Press.

Narasimhaiah, C. D. (1967) *Fiction and the reading public in India.* Mysore: Mysore University Press.

Narasimhaiah, C. D. (ed.) (1976) *Commonwealth literature: a handbook of select reading lists.* Madras: Oxford University Press.

Narasimhaiah, C. D. (ed.) (1978) *Awakened conscience: studies in commonwealth literature.* Delhi: Sterling Publishers.

Nash, Rose (1977) "Aspects of Spanish-English bilingualism and language mixture in Puerto Rico." In A. Makkai, V. B. Makkai and L. Heilman (eds.), 1977. pp. 205–225.

Nelson, Cecil L. (1982) "Intelligibility and non-native varieties of English." In Braj B. Kachru (ed.), 1982. pp. 58–73.

Nelson, Cecil L. (1983) "Syntactic creativity and intelligibility." Terra Haute. IN: Department of English, Indiana State University.

Nelson, Cecil L. (1984) "Intelligibility: the case of non-native varieties of English" Unpublished doctoral dissertation, University of Illinois, Urbana.

Newman, Edwin (1974 and 1976) *Edwin Newman on language: strictly speaking* and *a civil tongue.* New York: Warner Books, Inc. [Paperback edition, 1980].

Nihalani, Paroo, R. K. Tongue, and P. Hosali (1978) *Indian and British English: a handbook of usage and pronunciation.* Delhi: Oxford University Press.

Niven, Alastair (ed.) (1976) *The commonwealth writer overseas: themes of exile and expatriation.* Bruxelles: Librairie Marcel Didier S. A.

Noss, R. B. (ed.) (1983) *Varieties of English in Southeast Asia.* Singapore: SEAMEO Regional Language Centre.

Obeyesekere, Ranjani and Chitra Fernando (eds.) (1981) *An anthology of modern writing from Sri Lanka.* Tucson: University of Arizona Press.

Okara, Gabriel (1963) "African speech . . . English words". *Transition* **10**:13–18.
Palmer, F. R. (ed.) (1968) *Selected papers of J. R. Firth, 1952–59*. Bloomington, IN: Indiana University Press.
Pandharipande, Rajeshwari (1980) "Language contact and language variation: Nāgpurī-Marathi and Hindi." Urbana: Department of Linguistics, University of Illinois. (mimeographed).
Pandharipande, Rajeshwari (1981) "On the nativization of lexicon: the case of Marathi." *Linguistics: An international Review* **19**: 987–1011.
Pandharipande, Rajeshwari (1982) "Dimensions of multilingualism: language pluralism in India." (manuscript).
Pandharipande, Rajeshwari (1983) "Linguistics and written discourse in English and Marathi." *Annual Review of Applied Linguistics, 1982*. pp. 118–136.
Pandit, P. B. (1972) *India as a socio-linguistic area*. Poona: Poona University Press.
Pandit, P. B. (1977) *Language in a plural society: the case of India*. Delhi: Devraj Channa Memorial Committee.
Paradis, Michel (ed.) (1978) *Aspects of bilingualism*. Columbia, SC: Hornbeam Press.
Paradis, Michel (1979) "Contributions of neurolinguistics to the theory of bilingualism." In R. K. Herbert (ed.), 1979. pp. 180–211.
Parameswaran, Uma (1976) *A study of representative Indo-English novelists*. Delhi: Vikas Publishers.
Parthasarathy, R. (1983) "Tradition and creativity: stylistic innovation in Raja Rao." Paper presented at the conference on English as an International Language: Discourse Patterns Across Cultures. Honolulu: East-West Center. June 1–7. (manuscript).
Parthasarathy, E. (ed.) (1976) *Ten twentieth century Indian poets*. Delhi: Oxford University Press.
Passé, H. A. (1947) "The English language in Ceylon." Unpublished doctoral dissertation, University of London.
Pattanayak, Debi Prasanna. (1971) *Distribution of languages in India, in states and union territories*. Mysore: Central Institute of Indian Languages.
Paulston, C. (1971) "Linguistic and communicative competence." *TESOL Quarterly* **8**(4):347–362.
Pfaff, C. W. (1976) "Functional and structural constraints on syntactic variation in code-switching." *Papers from the parasession on diachronic syntax*. Chicago: Chicago Linguistic Society. pp. 248–259.
Pfaff, C. W. (1979) "Constraints on language mixing: intrasentential code-switching and borrowing in Spanish/English." *Language* **55**(2):291–318.
Pickering, John (1816) *A vocabulary, or collections of words and phrases which have been supposed to be peculiar to the United States of America*. In M. M. Mathews. (ed.), 1931).
Pillai, Shanmugam (1974) "Code-switching in the Tamil novel." In Harry M. Buck and G.E. Yocum (eds.), 1974. pp. 81–95.
Platt, John and Heidi Weber (1980) *English in Singapore and Malaysia: status: features: functions*. Kuala Lumpur: Oxford University Press.
Poplack, Shana (1981) "Sometimes I'll start a sentence in Spanish. Y TERMINO EN ESPANOL: toward a typology of code-switching." *Working Paper No. 4*. New York: Langauge Policy Task Force, Centro de Estudios Puertorrinquenos, City University of New York.
Prator, Clifford (1968) "The British Heresy in TESL." In Joshua A. Fishman, Charles A. Ferguson, and Jyotirindra Das Gupta (eds.), 1968. pp. 459–476.
Press, John (ed.) (1965) *Commonwealth literature: unity and diversity in a common culture*. London: Heinemann.
Pride, John B. (ed) (1982) *New Englishes*. Rowley, MA: Newbury House.
Pride, John B. (1983) "Linguistic competence and the expression of cultural identity." In R. B. Noss (ed.), 1983. pp. 50–91.
Quirk, Randolph (1960) "The survey of English usage." *Transactions of the Philological Society*. pp. 70–78. [Also in Randolph Quirk, 1968.]

Quirk, Randolph (1968) *Essays on the English language.* Bloomington, IN: Indiana University Press.

Quirk, Randolph (1972) "Linguistic bonds across the Atlantic." *The English language and images of matter.* London: Oxford University Press. pp. 14–31.

Quirk, Randolph, Sidney Greenbaum, Geoffrey Leech and Jan Svartvik (1972) *A grammar of contemporary English.* London: Longman.

Quirk, Randolph and A. H. Smith (eds.) (1959) *The teaching of English.* London: Martin, Secker, and Warburg. [Reprinted 1964].

Raghuvira (1973) "Why an Indian terminology"? In Bholanath Tiwari and M. Chaturvedi (eds.), 1973. pp. 85–89.

Ramakrishna, D. (ed.) (1980) *Indian English Prose: and anthology.* Delhi: Heinemann.

Ramanujan, Attipat Krishnaswami (1968) "The structure of variation: a study in caste dialects." In Milton Singer and Bernard S. Cohn (eds.), 1968. pp. 461–474.

Ramchand, Kenneth (1970) "The language of the master"? In Richard W. Bailey and J. L. Robinson (eds.), 1973. pp. 115–146.

Ramson, W. S. (ed.) (1970) *English transported: essays on Australasian English.* Canberra: Australia.

Rao, G. Subba (1954) *Indian words in English: a study in Indo-British cultural and linguistic relations.* Oxford: Clarendon Press.

Rao, Raja (1938) *Kanthapura.* London: G. Allen and Unwin. [Reprinted, New York: New Directions, 1963.]

Rao, Raja (1978a) "The caste of English." In C. D. Narasimhaiah (ed.), pp. 420–422.

Rao, Raja (1978b) *The policeman and the rose.* Delhi: Oxford University Press.

Rauch, Irmengard and Gerald F. Carr. (eds.). (1979) *Linguistic method: essays in honor of Herbert Penzl.* The Hague: Mouton.

Read, Allen Walker (1933) "British recognition of American speech in the eighteenth century." *Dialect Notes* **6**: 313–352.

Read, Allen Walker (1935) "Amphi-Atlantic English." *English Studies* **17**: 161–178.

Read, Allen Walker (1936) "American projects for an academy to regulate speech." *Publications of the Modern Language Association of America.* **51**(2): 1141–1179.

Read, Allen Walker (1938) "Suggestions for an academy in England in the latter half of the eighteenth century." *Modern Philology* **36**: 145–156.

Richards, Jack C. (1972) "Social factors, interlanguage and language learning." *Language Learning* **22**(2): 159–188.

Richards, Jack C. (ed.) (1974) *Error analysis: Perspectives on second language acquisition.* London: Longman.

Richards, Jack C. (1979) "Rhetorical and communicative styles in the new varieties of English." *Language Learning* **29**(1): 1–25.

Richards, Jack C. (1982) "Singapore English: Rhetorical and communicative styles." In Braj B. Kachru (ed.), 1982. pp. 154–167.

Roberts, T. T. (1800) *An Indian glossary, consisting of some thousand words and forms commonly used in the East Indies . . . extremely serviceable in assisting strangers to acquire with ease and quickness the language of that country.* London: Murray and Highley.

Robinson, P. (1978) *Language management in education: the Australian context.* London: Allen and Unwin.

Robinson, W. Peter (1979) "Speech markers and social class." In Klaus R. Scherer and Howard Giles (eds.), 1979. pp. 211–249.

Romo, Ricardo and Raymund Paredes (eds.) (1978) *New directions in Chicano scholarship.* San Diego: University of California Press.

Ruberu, Ranjit (1962) *Education in colonial Ceylon.* Kandy: Kandy Printers.

Samarin, William J. (ed.) (1976) *Language in religious practice.* Rowley, MA: Newbury House.

Samonte, Aurora L. (1981) "Teaching English for international and intranational purposes: the Philippine context." In Larry E. Smith (ed.), 1981. pp. 74–82.

Sanchez, Rosaura (1983) *Chicano discourse: socio-historical perspective.* Rowley, MA: Newbury House.

Sarma, Gobinda Prasad (1978) *Nationalism in Indo-Anglian fiction.* Delhi: Sterling Publishers.

Savignon, Sandra and Margie S. Berns (eds.). (1984). *Initiatives in Communicative Language Teaching: A Book of Readings.* Reading, MA: Addison-Wesley.

Saville-Troike, Muriel (ed.) (1977) *Georgetown University Round Table on Languages and Linguistics 1977.* Washington D.C: Georgetown University Press.

Saville-Troike, Muriel (1981) *Ethnography of communication: an introduction.* London: Basil Blackwell.

Scherer, Klaus R. and Howard Giles (eds.) (1979) *Social markers in speech.* London: Cambridge University Press.

Schuchardt, Hugo (1981) "Das Indo-Englische." *Englische Studien* **15**. pp. 286–305. [English translation in Glenn Gilbert (ed. and trans.), 1980. pp. 38–64.]

Scollon, Ronald (1979) "Variable data and linguistic convergence." *Language in Society* **8**:223–242.

Scott, T. (ed.) (1907) *The prose works of Jonathan Swift, Vol. XI. Literary essay.* London: Bell.

Scotton, Carol (1976) "Strategies of neutrality." *Language* **52**:919–941.

Sebeok, Thomas A. (ed.) (1969) *Current trends in linguistics.* Vol. 5. The Hague: Mouton.

Serjeantson, Mary S. (1935) *A history of foreign words in English.* London: K. Paul, Trench, Trubner. [Reprinted, New York: Barnes and Noble, 1961.]

Seung, T. K. (1982) *Semiotics and thematics in hermeneutics.* New York: Columbia University Press.

Sey, K. A. (1973) *Ghanaian English: an exploratory survey.* London: Macmillan and Co.

Shah, Amritlal B. (ed.) (1968) *The great debate: language controversy and higher education.* Bombay: Lalvani.

Sharma, P. Gopal (1968) "Problems of Hindi terminology." In Braj B. Kachru and Yamuna Kachru (eds.), 1968. pp. 116 133.

Sharp, Henry (ed.) (1920). *Selections from educational records.* Calcutta: Bureau of Education, Government of India.

Sharrad, Paul (1982) "Culture learning through literature." *East-West Culture Learning Institute Reporter* **8**(1):1–11.

Shaw, Willard (1981) "Asian student attitudes towards English." In Larry E. Smith (ed.), 1981. pp. 108–122.

Shopen, T. and J. M. Williams (eds.) (1980) *Standards and dialects in English.* Cambridge, MA: Winthrop publishers

Shuy, Roger W. (1967) *Discovering American dialects.* Champaign: National Council of Teachers of English.

Sinclair, John M. and R. M. Coulthard (1975) *Toward an analysis of discourse: the English used by teachers and pupils.* London: Oxford University Press.

Singer, Milton and Bernard S. Cohn (eds.) (1968) *Structure and change in Indian society.* Chicago: Aldine Publishing.

Singh, Amritjit, R. Verma, and I. M. Joshi (eds.) (1981) *Indian literature in English, 1827–1979: a guide to information sources.* Detroit, MI: Gale Research Company.

Singh, Bhupal (1934) *A survey of Anglo-Indian fiction.* London: Oxford University Press.

Sledd, James and Wilma R. Ebbit (1962) *Dictionaries and that dictionary.* Chicago: Scott, Foresman.

Smith, Larry E. (ed.) (1981) *English for cross-cultural communication.* London: Macmillan and Co.

Smith, Larry E. (ed.) (1983) *Readings in English as an international language:* Oxford,: Pergamon Press.

Smith, Larry E. and Khalilullah Rafiqzad (1979) "English for cross-cultural communication: the question of intelligibility." *TESOL Quarterly* **13**(13):371–380.

Smith, Philip M. (1979) "Sex markers in speech." In Klaus R. Scherer and Howard Giles (eds.), 1979. pp. 109–146.

Spencer, John (ed.) (1963) *Language in Africa.* London: Cambridge University Press.
Spencer, John (ed.) (1971) *The English language in Africa.* London: Longman.
Sridhar, Kamal K. (1979) "English in the socio-cultural context of India." *Studies in Language Learning* **2**(2):63–79.
Sridhar, Kamal K. (1982a) "English in a South Indian urban context." In Braj B. Kachru (ed.), 1982. pp. 141–153.
Sridhar, Kamal K. (1982b) "Functional distribution of Hindi vis-a-vis other languages in South India." Paper presented at the South Asian Languages Roundtable at Syracuse University, May 20–23, 1982.
Sridhar, S. N. (1978) "On the function of code-mixing in Kannada." In Braj B. Kachru and S. N. Sridhar (eds.), 1978. pp. 109–117.
Sridhar, S. N. (1982) "Non-native English literatures: context and relevance." In Braj B. Kachru (ed.), 1982. pp. 291–306.
Sridhar, S. N. (1981) "Linguistic convergence: Indo-Aryanization of Dravidian languages." *Lingua.* **53**. pp. 199–220.
Sridhar, S. N. and Kamal K. Sridhar (1980) "The syntax and psycholinguistics of bilingual code-mixing." *Canadian Journal of Psychology/Revue Canadienne de Psychologie* **34**:407–416.
Srivastava, R. N., *et al* (1978) *Evaluating communicability in village settings.* (two parts). Delhi: Department of Linguistics, University of Delhi.
Staal, J. F. (1975) *A reader in the Sanskrit grammarians.* Cambridge, MA: MIT Press.
Stanlaw, James (1982) "English in Japanese communicative strategies." In Braj B. Kachru (ed.), 1982. pp. 168–197.
Stocqueler, J. H. (Siddons, Joachim Heyward) (1848) *The Oriental interpreter and treasury of East India Knowledge: a companion to 'The handbook of British India'.* London: C. Cox.
Strevens, Peter (1977) *New orientations in the teaching of English.* London: Oxford University Press.
Strevens, Peter (1980) *Teaching English as an international language.* Oxford: Pergamon Press.
Strevens, Peter (1982) "World English and the world's English—or, whose language is it anyway"? *Journal of the Royal Society of Arts,* June, 1982, pp. 418:428.
Sukwiwat, Mayuri (1983) "Interpreting the Thai variety of English: a functional approach." In R. B. Noss (ed.), 1983. pp. 190–210.
Swift, Jonathan (1907) "A proposal for correcting, improving and ascertaining the English tongue (1712)." In T. Scott (ed.), 1907.
Taiwo, Oladele (1976) *Culture and the Nigerian novel.* New York: St. Martin's Press.
Tay, Mary W. J. and Anthea F. Gupta (1983) "Toward a description of standard Singapore English." In R. B. Noss (ed.), 1983. pp. 173–189.
Thumboo, Edwin (1976) *The second tongue: an anthology of poetry from Malaysia and Singapore.* Singapore: Heinemann Educational Books.
Timm, L. A. (1975) "Spanish-English code-switching: el porque y how-not-to." *Romance Philology* **28**:473–482.
Tiwari, Bholanath (1966) *The Hindi language* (in Hindi). Allahabad: Kitab Mahal.
Tiwari, Bholanath and M. Chaturvedi (eds.) (1973) *Technical terminology: some problems.* (mainly in Hindi). Delhi: Shabdkar.
Tongue, R. K. (1974) *The English of Singapore and Malaysia.* Singapore: Eastern Universities Press.
Tough, J. (1977) *Development of meaning: talking to some purpose with young children.* London: Allen and Unwin.
Trudgill, Peter (1974) *Sociolinguistics.* Harmondsworth: Penguin Books.
Trudgill, Peter (1976–77) "Creolization in reverse: reduction and simplification in the Albanian dialects of Greece." *Transactions of the Philological Society.* pp. 32–50.
Tsao, Fenj-Fu (1983) "Linguistics and written discourse in English and Mandarin." *Annual Review of Applied Linguistics, 1982.* pp. 99–117.

Turner, George W. (1966) *The English language in Australia and New Zealand.* London: Longman.

Turner, P. R. (ed.) (1973) *Bilingualism in the Southwest.* Tucson: University of Arizona Press.

Valdes-Fallis, Guadalupe (1978) "Code-switching among bilingual Mexican-American women: towards an understanding of sex-related language alternation." *International Journal of the Sociology of Language* 17:65–71.

Varma, Siddheshwar (1929) *Critical studies in the phonetic observations of Indian grammarians.* London: Royal Asiatic Society.

Wald, Benji (1974) "Bilingualism." *Annual Review of Antrhopology.* pp. 301–321. Palo Alto, CA: Annual Review, Inc.

Walsh, William (1971) *R. K. Narayan.* Writers and Their Work No. 224. London: Longman.

Ward, Ida C. (1929) *The phonetics of English.* Cambridge: Heffer.

Warie, Pairat (1977) "Some aspects of code-mixing in Thai." *Studies in the Linguistic Sciences* 7(1):21–40.

Warie, Pairat (1978) "Some sociolinguistic aspects of language contact in Thailand." Unpublished doctoral dissertation, University of Illinois, Urbana.

Webster, Noah (1789) *Dissertations on the English language.* Boston: Isaiah Thomas.

Weinreich, Uriel (1953) *Languages in contact: findings and problems.* The Hague: Mouton.

Weir, Ann Lowry (1982) "Style range in new English literatures." In Braj B. Kachru (ed.), 1982. pp. 307–322.

Wentz, James (1977) "Some considerations in the development of syntactic description of code-switching." Unpublished doctoral dissertation, University of Illinois, Urbana.

Whitworth, George C. (1907) *Indian English: an examination of the errors of idioms made by Indians in writing English.* Letchworth, Herts: Garden City Press. [Later edition, Lahore, 1932.]

Widdowson, H. G. (1978) *Teaching language as communication.* London: Oxford University Press.

Widdowson, H. G. (1979) "Pidgin and babu." In *Explorations in applied linguistics.* London: Oxford University Press. pp. 202–211.

Wilkins, D. A. (1978) *Notional syllabuses.* London: Oxford University Press.

Williamson, Juanita V. and V. M. Burke (eds.) (1971) *A various language: perspectives on American dialects.* New York: Holt, Rinehart and Winston.

Wilson, Horace Hayman (1855) *A glossary of judicial and revenue terms, and of useful words occurring in official documents relating to the administration of the government of British India.* [Reprint 1940: Calcutta: Eastern Law House.]

Wolfram, W. and Ralph W. Fasold (1974) *The study of social dialects in American English.* Englewood Cliffs, NJ: Prentice-Hall.

Wong, Irene F. H. (1981) "English in Malaysia." In Larry E. Smith (ed.), 1981. pp. 94–107.

Wong, Irene F. H. (1983) "Simplification features in the structure of colloquial Malaysian English." In R. B. Noss (ed.), 1983. pp. 125–149.

Yule, Henry and A. C. Burnell. (1886) *Hobson-Jobson: a glossary of colloquial Anglo-Indian words and phrases and of kindred terms, etymological, historical, geographical, and discursive.* London: J. Murray. [Reprint: New York: Humanities Press, 1968.]

Zentella, Ana Celia (1978) "Code-switching and interactions among Puerto Rican children." *Sociolinguistic working paper no. 50.* Austin, TX: Southwest Educational Development Laboratory.

Zentella, Ana Celia (1981) "Language variety among Puerto Ricans." In Charles A. Ferguson and Shirley B. Heath (Eds.), 1981. pp. 218–238.

Zgusta, Ladislav (ed.) (1980) *Theory and method in lexicography: Western and non-Western perspectives.* Columbia, SC: Hornbeam Press.

Zuengler, Jane E. (1982) "Kenyan English." In Braj B. Kachru (ed.), 1982. pp. 112:124.

Index